NATURE'S STEWARD

A History of the Conservancy of Southwest Florida

Nicholas G. Penniman IV

Pineapple Press, Inc.

Sarasota, Florida

For Linda

Inquiries should be addressed to:
Pineapple Press, Inc.
P.O. Box 3889
Sarasota, Florida 34230
www.pineapplepress.com

Library of Congress Cataloging-in-Publication Data

Penniman, Nicholas G., 1938–
    Nature's steward : a history of the Conservancy of Southwest Florida / Nicholas G. Penniman IV.
        pages   cm
    Summary: "The Conservancy of Southwest Florida will celebrate its 50th anniversary in 2014. The book will document how the organization grew land acquisition into regional advocacy and education, and how it adapted its structure, strategy, and tactics to the changing environmental climate in Tallahassee and Washington. A chronicle of the efforts of men and women committed to protecting and preserving sensitive ecosystems during one of the greatest land and building booms in American history"—Provided by publisher.
    Summary: "A well-researched history of the Conservancy of Southwest Florida, an advocacy and educational group in the forefront of environmental protection and land acquisition since its founding in 1964. This book chronicles the efforts of the people dedicated to protecting and preserving some of the most sensitive ecosystems in the United States"—Provided by publisher.
    Includes bibliographical references.
    ISBN 978-1-56164-684-5 (hardback)
    1. Conservancy of Southwest Florida—History. 2. Nature conservation—Florida—History. 3. Environmental protection—Florida—History. 4. Public lands—Florida—History. 5. Landscape protection—Florida—History. 6. Real estate development—Environmental aspects—Florida—History. 7. Florida—Environmental conditions. I. Title.

    QH76.5.F6P46 2014
    333.95'41609759—dc23
                                                    2013031938

First Edition
10 9 8 7 6 5 4 3 2 1

Maps by John G. Beriault
Printed in the United States of America

ACKNOWLEDGMENTS

*T*his book came about as a result of finding a large number of file boxes spread around the Conservancy's policy offices. About to be hauled off to storage, they became the basis for the story. I am eternally grateful to Kathy Adams for her help in locating and saving those files.

My original intent was to reconstruct 50 years of Conservancy history using smaller, human-interest stories to hold the narrative together. It soon became clear that the Conservancy was part of a larger story, a microcosm of the battles being fought and won in Tallahassee and Washington to overcome excesses and unintended consequences created by America's great industrial expansion during and after World War II. The Conservancy's coming into its fullness at the peak of the environmental revolution of the 1970s became the heart of the story.

This book would not be possible without Beth Smith, who ably assisted with more than 100 hours of interviews. Her ability to draw people out was amazing. Jennifer Hecker, Nicole Johnson, Dave Addison, and Andrew McElwaine at the Conservancy were bottomless resources for clarification and chronology. Computer whiz and cartographer John Beriault is responsible for the maps; no one knows more about the archaeological history of south Florida than John. Dennis Goodman went out into the Big Cypress at sunset following a summer storm to shoot the marvelous photo on the cover.

Meredith Morris-Babb and Sonia Dickey at the University Press of Florida, as well as peer reviewers Tom Swihart and Andy McLeod, helped me focus on the broader context surrounding the Conservancy's growth and success. June and Dave Cussen at Pineapple Press picked the book up immediately. Kris Rowland was a thorough and responsive copy editor; Shé Hicks did a superb job with the layout and graphics.

Writing a book is not easy, and the advice of my academician friends Art Ritas and Jean Baker was essential. Art retired as a writing coach at Macomb Community College in Michigan; Jean is working on her sixth book while teaching history at Goucher College in Baltimore.

The following people, in no particular order, provided oral comments and e-mail responses to questions, additional documentation, and invaluable assistance in getting the facts right: Gary Schmelz, Nancy Seeley, Gary Davis, Nathaniel Reed, Kathy Prosser-Bovard, Mike Sole, Laurie MacDonald, Dick Grant, Ellie Krier, Brad Cornell, Kathy Worley, Bob Pritt, Tom Missimer, Ellin Goetz, Lal Gaynor, Judy Hushon, and Paul Gray.

My two literate children, Rebecca and Nick, offered pointed comments that led to a more forceful narrative. And finally, the long hours of research and writing to do this project were always given the emotional support of my beloved wife, Linda, to whom this book is dedicated.

TABLE OF CONTENTS

Water

INTRODUCTION

As evening approaches, the fifty-foot pontoon *Good Fortune II* slips its moorings and heads out into Rookery Bay. Forty people on board are quietly chatting, eagerly anticipating presentations from two Florida master naturalists as they motor toward the Gulf of Mexico with dolphins surfing in the boat's wake. Within the hour, thousands of birds will come home for the night. Some mangrove islands will be white with great egrets and ibis, others brown with pelicans bending the limbs and noisily sharing the day's experience with others of their species.

A lone kayaker puts in at the south end of Clam Bay, preparing to paddle through the mangrove-fringed estuary. The top floors of an occasional high-rise peer over the treetops, but the estuary is otherwise void of urban distractions. The only sounds are those of mullet jumping, pelicans plunging headlong after one more meal, and an electric tram ferrying passengers across a bridge to the beach to enjoy another vibrant sunset. The kayaker, pausing briefly to watch a carnivorous nudibranch gradually pulse its way across the channel, will eventually end up on the beach too. She will be watching the golden orb sink slowly to the horizon, hoping to see the fabled "green flash" at the moment it passes from view.

Further inland, a small group emerges from the tea-colored water, carefully prodding the bottom with six-foot-long plastic pipes to avoid alligator holes. They are tired and wet but pleased with the day's swamp walk. They are in the Fakahatchee Strand, up to their waists all afternoon, having found fifteen different species of orchids including the ghost orchid, a leafless epiphyte of the *Angraechoid* family, dependent upon a solitary species of moth for pollination. They have passed through the "Cathedral," a corridor of fifty-foot-high cypress trees bending inward as gothic arches—soaring and delicate—amidst a riot of bromeliads. Now

1

they know why the Fakahatchee has been called "America's Amazon."

All of these experiences and encounters with exotic flora and fauna came about as a result of the efforts of a single organization—the modern-day Conservancy of Southwest Florida. For fifty years, working at times alone and other times in partnership with like-minded organizations, enlightened landowners, government officials, and committed individuals, the Conservancy was involved in preservation of more than 300,000 acres of natural beauty throughout southwest Florida.

The story about to unfold is set against the larger backdrop of a rising environmental conscience in both the United States and the State of Florida. Three themes form the backbone of the book: land acquisition, planning for growth, and water. They will be covered using a series of selected case studies. The narrative advances chronologically. Each case is covered from beginning to end, so many overlap, requiring a certain amount of time-shifting by the reader. Each case shows how the desire for growth and profit collides with irreplaceable natural resources, how Florida's environmental priorities have evolved over the past 50 years, and how cooperation created workable partnerships resulting in good outcomes.

Setting the Stage

For thousands of years, much of southwest Florida was an inhospitable landscape. As years went by, machines allowed newcomers nearly total dominion, not only over the few surviving natives but over the land as well.[1] Transportation engineers gave Floridians access to remote corners of the state by running parallel ribbons of steel down the two coasts of the peninsula; taming its interior with ditches, dikes, and drainage canals; tearing out cypress forests; and laying miles of concrete and macadam. Nature existed for man's benefit, a philosophy as old as the Western intellectual tradition itself, beginning with Socrates and Aristotle. Not all societies have embraced that worldview, but Floridians did from the day of declared statehood into the immediate present with one vainglorious corollary: Dry land was good land; wet land was useless. That was carried forward as a banner over the next hundred years by legions of large and small farmers, speculators, and developers who manipulated the landscape, unconstrained by any concern about serious, long-term consequences. But there were consequences, and the first and best way to deal with those was to simply buy land into public ownership.

Land Acquisition

The first effort of the Conservancy and the first major theme of this book—purchase of sensitive natural areas for public benefit—was achieved in the early years by commitments of private money and donations of land. It was done tediously—parcel by parcel and acre by acre. In the 1960s and early 1970s, land acquisition in southwest Florida was made possible primarily by money raised locally and administered nationally through organizations with the ability to front-end sufficient dollars to purchase large tracts of land in Rookery Bay and the Ten Thousand Islands. The local Conservancy was able to stop an infamous "road to nowhere" but struggled to muster enough capital to make large purchases even with the backing of national organizations when needed. Financial contributions came primarily from Northern transplants, people who had made their money elsewhere and wanted to preserve the beauty of their adopted state. They looked at land not as a means of earning a living but rather as something to be enjoyed in its unaltered condition. But as the price of coastal frontage began to rise, it became painfully obvious that privately raised funds were inadequate for preserving large chunks of land. Government participation became increasingly important.

The state was growing rapidly in the 1970s, with pressure-cooker boiler rooms operating seven days a week, selling developments like Cape Coral and southern Golden Gate Estates. The price of land in southwest Florida was skyrocketing. A turning point came in 1972 when Richard Nixon, carried away by the politics of the moment, proposed to buy a gigantic swamp in south Florida. The state hurriedly matched his offer by passing the Big Cypress Conservation Act of 1973, followed closely by purchase of the Fakahatchee Strand. Private donor interest began to wane as federal and state governments moved into land acquisition, and, starting with these two stunning purchases, the emphasis of local environmental organizations began to shift from raising private money toward advocating for public ownership. Land acquisition on a scale of magnitude sufficient to maintain contiguous species habitat and preserve natural systems by private funding would have simply been impossible. The state had the rarely used power of eminent domain, more effective as threat than reality, which gave it the ability to move things along quickly with a stick as well as a carrot. State and local initiatives, combined with federal inholdings such as Everglades National Park, have preserved nearly four million acres of Florida's heritage lands, amounting to 30% of the state's total land mass. The Florida electorate's support for land preservation was expressly demonstrated many times over the years as voters approved a series of acquisition programs at the local level to supplement major purchases by the State of Florida. Today more than a third of Florida's counties have funded preservation programs in place resulting from local ballot measures, such as Conservation Collier and Lee 20/20 in southwest Florida. Both passed with large pluralities. Similar programs statewide have saved another 375,000 acres.[2]

Planning for Growth

While the Conservancy's efforts were being gradually supplanted by public dollars, the second major theme of this book, Florida's landmark growth management legislation, would come into play in the early 1970s. There was no coherent land-use planning at the state level until a series of crises in the late 1960s brought the issue to a head.[3] Rising concern in Washington brought about laws seeking cleaner water, cleaner air, preservation of species, and greater regulation of coastal development. In Tallahassee, the governor and legislature embarked on a statewide planning effort. Those statutes, brought about by concern over a rapidly growing population, were designed to cluster development and direct it away from sensitive natural resource areas. In concept, it was innovative and elegant. In execution, it was flawed and sporadic. Some horizontal interdepartmental cooperation existed, but vertically—between tiers of government such as localities, counties, and the state—coordinated planning was virtually non-existent. In 1972 Governor Reubin Askew, realizing this disjunction was an impediment, convinced the legislature to pass a package of four bills initiating a comprehensive structure of organizations and processes for managing growth.[4] However, it soon became apparent to both the governor and legislature that planning in isolation at the state level was doomed to failure. This resulted in a 1975 act requiring local governments to create their own plans and adhere to them.[5] While well intended, there was no point at which local plans could be authoritatively reviewed for consistency with the state plan—because there was no state plan. There was another impediment to implementation at the local level: No money was made available by the state to hire additional staff and the whole effort died of its own weight.

Despite its halting beginnings, this new direction had a profound effect on how business was conducted in Florida. Environmental organizations needed to adapt to the reality of increasing influence of government in local growth management planning. This shift was in stark contrast to the way controversy was handled previously: face to face. At times of their own volition, and other times forced into settlement discussions, people on both sides managed to work out satisfactory solutions to controversial issues during private meetings. The introduction of citizen participation, intended to create support for orderly development, necessarily replaced a web of personal alliances carefully constructed over the years, much of the time in the shadows. In the following pages, we will meet some of these fascinating personalities and recount how their alliances functioned.

Bill Merrihue of the Conservancy and Ross Obley of Westinghouse, both trusting in the science of Bernie Yokel, were able to preserve large mangrove-fringed estuary called Clam Bay. Lawyers Ned Putzell (Merrihue's successor) and George Vega were able to negotiate a workable compromise that allowed Lely Estates, Inc., to develop parts of Barefoot Beach based heavily upon a shared concern for preserving southwest Florida's ecosystems. Cannon Island was saved by the same spirit of cooperation, as Vega, trustee Michael Miceli, and planning consultant Bill Vines each stepped into the situation at a critical point to ensure that owners of the island were being treated fairly. Later, Conservancy president David Guggenheim and Jeffrey Birr of Collier Enterprises sparred for years over the Villages of Sabal Bay and Hamilton Harbor, yet Guggenheim's notes indicated there was always an element of goodwill that allowed full and frank discussion of all issues on the table despite the influence of parties outside the negotiations. But these kinds of meetings, conducted in secrecy and without public scrutiny, had to come to an end. Henceforward, it became a colloquy of organizations. Personal relationships waned in importance as the scope of development grew larger, as permitting issues shifted from local landscapes to the ecosystem level, as regulations proliferated in both statutory form and judicial interpretation, and as decisions became more widely dispersed among multiple agencies of government.

By 1985 the legislature, under Governor Bob Graham's leadership, essentially solved the thorny problem of soft implementation that thwarted the 1972 and 1975 acts.[6] Conservancy staff were deeply involved in the citizen's side of the planning effort to meet mandates set forth in the 1985 act as it became apparent that elected officials at all levels, until they could develop adequate staff expertise, were coming to rely more heavily on recommendations from outside consultants, many of whom represented special interests, with the time to study issues in depth. Eventually some of those outsiders became insiders, part of the process of revising and amending growth management plans and land development codes, portending a shift in political tectonics for local interest groups and forcing environmental organizations to adapt their organizational structure and staff to the new realities.

By 1992 all counties and cities in southwest Florida had comprehensive plans in place. The Conservancy had recruited and developed a generation of leaders selected for their ability to function in the rough-and-tumble world of politics. The new paradigm of community-based planning required greater patience and flexibility as the rules of the game shifted to include more public participation and discussion. The state had strengthened the hand of the Department of Community Affairs, allowing it to definitively approve local plans[7] rather than simply "review and comment" on them. More teeth were added to the process when the state assumed the power to amerce non-compliant counties and municipalities and gave citizens standing to challenge local plans with remedies including injunctive relief. The Conservancy and other organizations used this expanded standing to visit the courts more frequently, as we will see in the case of the Cocohatchee Slough.

The state's commitment to environmental protection began to recede in the 1990s. Riding the crest of a real estate boom, which created jobs and a growing source of ad valorem tax revenue to local governments, permitting had become heavily layered and widely dispersed among agencies. After coastal areas were built out, developers began to move inland. State and local environmental reviewers, overwhelmed in the rush to build roads, schools, shopping centers, and waste treatment systems to handle the rapid growth, adopted a simple mathematical model facilitating wetlands destruction that the Conservancy contests to this day, a topic we will cover in the chapter titled "Water Wars." The organization was doing its best to deal with the frenetic pace of development, but its efforts, and those of its partners, met with increasing resistance from local government offices and Tallahassee. At the same time, an ingrained distrust of centralized planning and government regulation was rising, and advocates were making their presence felt in the legislature and local polities over an issue central to the value structure of many Floridians: private property rights.

The Issue of Property Rights and Role of the Courts
Beginning in the mid-1970s, it became clear that canalization, particularly in Golden Gate Estates, was wreaking havoc on the recharge of surficial and deeper layer aquifers where the city of Naples and Collier County were drawing potable water. The problem, created by a lack of ecosystem analysis or simply a lack of knowledge, showed how hard it would be to unscramble the egg and brought into focus the overarching question in Florida politics and law: Where do private property rights end when they negatively impact the public welfare? This conflict would appear again and again as the state moved into long-range land-use planning.

However, another way emerged to preserve land without running headlong into the property rights issue: a cooperative undertaking among private landholders, local governments, and citizens. In its first iteration, the rural lands stewardship program adopted in Collier County was a model of participation and collaboration. It was overseen by a citizen's committee that broadly represented diverse community interests and large property owners willing and able to direct incompatible uses away from critical watersheds and sensitive habitat. In return, landowners received increases in density allotments for clustered housing and a degree of certainty as to the rules under which development could take place. Within a context of growth management, we will examine this groundbreaking program, which allowed interested parties to sit down together and hammer out a coherent plan for nearly 200,000 acres of eastern Collier County.

Private property rights were always subject to interpretation when Florida courts recognized local land-use decisions as legislative acts. This gave the Conservancy standing in court to challenge what it viewed as inconsistent application of zoning and building codes in the case of Villages of Sabal Bay and later Hamilton Harbor. Looking back, that bitter and protracted battle might never have taken place without the citizens' ability to litigate being expanded in the 1985 act. As it turned out, the time spent in court delayed decisions until a new city council took office to deny the rezone. However, the effect of moving some land-use decisions from local hands into the judiciary had its risks because it opened the door for inconsistent application of development standards depending upon the outcome of each individual case and increased the possibility that the public process would be truncated and frustrated.[7]

Judicial intervention was nothing new in environmental law, with footings established in the spate of 1972 Congressional initiatives, including the Clean Air Act, National Environmental Policy Act, Endangered Species Act, and Clean Water Act, which President Nixon vetoed only to be overridden by Congress. These four pieces of legislation gave environmental groups an arsenal of potent weapons before federal courts. In the case of the Cocohatchee Slough, appointed guardians of clean water and listed species, the U.S. Army Corps of Engineers and the U.S. Fish and Wildlife Service, ended up as defendants.

As decisions began piling up, statutes became more nuanced by interpretation, creating a forest of rulings sometimes in conflict. To help sort through this and to increase citizen involvement, local city and county advisory committees were established throughout the state, populated by volunteers selected for their special expertise, many of whom had been involved in the comprehensive planning process. Their job was to review development and zoning variance applications for internal inconsistencies not caught by county staff. It was impossible to pay for such specialized knowledge at the staff level so the advisory boards filled a useful niche. Recommendations were generally regarded when an advisory board reached a unanimous vote; issues decided by split votes tended to be ignored. But the role of citizen advisory boards was useful only up to the point where politics took over. On balance, the system served a useful purpose, although the boards would occasionally take flak from interest groups that felt appointments (and appointees) were stacked against them.

Another element essential to coordinated planning was regional oversight for the evaluation of development impacts on larger multicounty ecosystems. The legislature, in creating Regional Planning Councils (RPCs) in 1972, also mandated that the councils consider "development of regional impact" statements for large projects. But the concept of regional oversight sputtered over the years. Given little real authority, the RPCs operated more as mediating bodies. Neither the state legislature nor county commissions were willing to grant substantial decision-making power to a group composed of appointees they couldn't always control, although the state did exactly that when it created five water management districts in the same year, accompanied by ad valorem taxing powers, the right to issue "consumptive use" permits, and oversight of long-range water supply planning and flood control despite the fact that water district board members were appointed by the governor, not elected. The most important outcome was that the districts, defined by watersheds and not by politics, had the effect of separating regional planning for water from other elements such as land use. Florida's counties, in effect, ceded water management decisions to five independent agencies over which they exercised virtually no control.[8]

Water

The quantity, quality, and distribution of fresh water comprise the third and final theme of this book. Water diversion schemes of the past 130 years, combined with rapid population growth on both coasts, have led us to the brink of an uncertain future and to the first step toward improving a deteriorating situation: The state recognized the value of managing within watershed boundaries with the Florida Water Resources Act of 1972. But the quality of Florida's heritage springs, lakes, and rivers continued to noticeably deteriorate. Non–point-source pollution running untreated off farmlands, parking lots, and subdivision lawns seriously compromised southwest Florida's coastal estuaries. Little was done to slow the decline. How the availability of water reached the point of crisis in a part of the world that receives an average of fifty-five inches of rain each year will be examined in detail in the final chapters of this book.

The consequences of continuing along the path of procrastination, inaction, bureaucratic malaise, and outright resistance from special interests that caused the problem in the first place are clear. With support from its science and policy departments, the Conservancy has become deeply involved in water issues and, as part of litigation by a consortium of environmental groups headed by Earthjustice, is determined to bring the issue to a conclusion. A solution is likely because a federal court retains jurisdiction, and the judge has made it abundantly clear he will not tolerate further dillydallying on the part of the state or the Environmental Protection Agency (EPA). The State of Florida can no longer push the solution to another year or to another generation. If the state can't come to an agreement with the EPA, both may end up again in federal court with a judicially administered solution. We will chronicle this effort from its beginnings up to the present day in the chapter titled "By the Numbers."

Science

While three themes underlie the construct of this book, there are two reasons for the Conservancy's success in advancing its environmental agenda. The first is applied science. The challenge of matching science with public policy is always a tricky business because scientists and law-makers look at the world differently and rarely speak the same language.

Scientists tend to take a long view of life, seeing it as it is and not as someone wants it to be. Conservancy scientists, while studying the environmental value of estuaries and mangrove fringe forests for years, knew that an economic argument was necessary in the political arena to give the public and legislators a basis on which to make decisions when choosing between growth and environmental preservation are mutually exclusive. In the next section, we will cover in detail how these arguments affected preservation of Rookery Bay and the Ten Thousand Islands. That said, science was never the handmaiden of other causes. Throughout the fifty years covered in this book, scientists at the Conservancy were free to explore human effects on the natural world regardless of policy positions. However, many ongoing studies conducted over decades for scientific purposes created baseline data against which the degradation of ecosystems and loss of species could be measured.[9] The first Rookery Bay Area Study Project of 1968 and the Naples Bay Study of 1979 were examples of carefully documented analyses. The first, financed by a University of Miami grant, ended up setting in motion a debate on the role of estuaries in southwest Florida. The second, undertaken purely for research purposes, became a central element in the thirteen-year controversy between environmentalists and Collier Enterprises' Villages of Sabal Bay. A similar project in wood stork research took place in Audubon's Corkscrew Swamp Sanctuary. It ended up being used in court to argue against further compromise of the Cocohatchee Slough, the main foraging habitat for Corkscrew's birds. The Conservancy's long-term sea turtle nesting project ended up being a source of advice as to the timing of beach re-nourishment as well as the characteristics of sand applied to area beaches. These were all instances where pure science became applied to issues of the moment.

Education

The second enabling mechanism is education, bringing the environmental message to the public's attention. Over the years, the Conservancy's leadership became convinced that informed citizens, appreciative of the need to preserve land and natural processes, were the single most important element in the political arena and could save more land than any amount of private funding. The biological cornucopia of southwest Florida was an ideal venue to develop an ethic based upon preservation and restoration of natural processes for a sustainable future. Southwest Florida's environmental movement made the assumption that what has an impact on people is what their children and grandchildren learn. The Big Cypress Nature Center and later the Conservancy created programs to capture the attention and interest of young people beginning at the ripe old age of four. Nature study involved touching and feeling the creatures and plants of south Florida to give children a sense of familiarity and introduce a level of comfort. The curriculum was non-ideological and taught that appreciation of the natural world could be accomplished through respect for the needs of both human beings and nature. But there was another deeper purpose. By introducing nature firsthand to children, parents might begin to think about what kind of future they wanted to leave to succeeding generations.

In Summary

What follows is the story of how a small organization established to save a backwater estuary grew to become a powerful regional voice for environmental prudence. The Conservancy's growth in size and influence was not linear and smooth—interrupted periodically by staff changes and missteps—but over time the organization adapted to shifting internal and external realities by holding to a consistent view of its mission. We will examine the effects of those transitional periods on policy issues and how they changed outcomes in the chapters titled "Changing of the Guard" and "Ebb Tide."

While this is a story written through a single lens, there are many other environmental organizations that partnered with the Conservancy in litigation, public meetings, formulation of policy positions, education, and advocacy whose absence from these pages should not diminish either their role or importance. They are part of this story too, because the natural world so important to all environmental organizations is close by, right outside southwest Florida's back door. Part of it is 110,000 acres of coastal waters and shoreline called Rookery Bay National Estuarine Research Reserve. This is where the *Good Fortune II* is headed with its forty passengers, and what follows in the next chapter is the fascinating tale of how this large part of coastal southwest Florida came to be saved for the benefit and enjoyment of its people.

SAVING ROOKERY BAY AND
THE TEN THOUSAND ISLANDS

*I*n order to tell the story of land preservation in southwest Florida, we need to start with the founding family of Collier County. Their substantial influence is felt throughout this book. Many of their undertakings were subjected to intense scrutiny as the county developed, and many of their projects were modified as a result of negotiations with the Conservancy and other environmental groups. Throughout the years, the family remained financially sound and continued to live where they worked: southwest Florida.

Barron Gift Collier was born in Memphis, Tennessee, in 1873. After bouncing around in the public school system, he started working in small business ventures at sixteen. Looking at the passengers riding electric trolley cars in his hometown, he believed that strategically placed placards—above the hat racks in each car—would capture the attention of an otherwise bored audience. His idea was eagerly accepted by local merchants, and he went on to expand the franchise throughout the South. By the turn of the century he was in New York City, owner of the Consolidated Street Railway Advertising Company and on his way to becoming one of the wealthiest businessmen in the country.

Visiting Useppa Island in Charlotte Harbor in 1911, Collier purchased the property with one house and a small hotel from his host, John Roach, president of the Chicago Street Railway Company.[1] Returning each winter, he became fascinated with the development potential of southwest Florida and in May 1923 approached the state with an offer to purchase more than one million acres in southern Lee County. His venture was enabled by the Swamp and Overflowed Lands Act of 1850,

giving the young State of Florida the right to claim land unfit for agriculture. After gaining dominion of nearly twenty-one million acres by 1855,
the state legislature created the Internal Improvement Fund—to be overseen by the governor and four Cabinet members—to control how the
newly found asset could be put to best use. In pre–Civil War days, it was
the means by which the state could legally deed over land to railroads in
exchange for running tracks throughout the state.

The fund trustees eagerly accepted Collier's offer. They even agreed
to name the new county after Collier in exchange for his commitment
to complete a partially built highway from the west to east coast of the
state: the Tamiami Trail. Lee County had failed to provide funds for the
project since 1919; the state saw in Collier a successful businessman who
would get the job done. And they were right. Centering operations in
the new county seat in Everglades City, Collier hired Graham Copeland,
an experienced engineer who took over the road project, blasting and
dredging his way across the state. By April 1928, the road was completed, thereby bisecting and draining the Big Cypress Swamp and central
Everglades. The Atlantic Coastline railroad, with its "Orange Blossom
Special," steamed into Everglades City that year, providing tourist access
to one of America's most beautiful yet inhospitable ecosystems.[2]

Collier expanded business operations in the next decade by starting
publication of the *Everglades News,* predecessor of the daily newspaper
in Naples,[3] and drilling test wells for oil in the Big Cypress Swamp, but
the Great Depression began to take its toll. While the value of his assets
always exceeded liabilities, his cash flow was being stretched as advertising revenue from the streetcar signs dried up. In order to meet his
obligations, Collier began to sell land. He died in New York City in 1939
and left his vast holdings in the hands of three sons: Miles, Barron Jr.,
and Samuel Carnes. A daughter, Isabel, would marry and continue as an
investor in various enterprises. Sam Collier died in a racing car accident
at Watkins Glen in 1950, and Miles died of a viral infection four years
later, leaving Barron Jr. to run the family's operations. It's at this point in
the family's history that the story of the Conservancy begins.

Dredge-and-Fill in Southwest Florida

In the late 1950s, Naples was beginning to boom. J. Glen Sample, an advertising executive and cofounder of Dancer, Fitzgerald and Sample, had retired to Naples in 1948 and acquired nearly two square miles of mangrove-fringed swampland at the southern end of the city. Separated from Keewaydin Island by Gordon Pass and the pockmarked remains of a worked-out shell pit, the development would be called Port Royal. He began to sell and build out his project seven years later. At the same time, another Naples resident, Forrest Walker, was busy creating Aqualane Shores northeast of Port Royal, while a Boston development company was ripping up mangrove forests to create Royal Harbor opening onto Naples Bay.

All three developments had two things in common. First, they were tearing out mangrove coastline to create additional miles of waterfront building lots with fingerlike canals. Second, they were using a construction technique called dredge-and-fill. Dredge-and-fill off coastal Florida could be done in two ways. The first used a dragline to scoop layered sediment from coastal waters, tidal inlets, and estuaries, mounding the sediment on bedrock to form a single finger of elevated land. The dragline was a large single bucket mounted on a standard crane. Fill was used as a platform for the machine to move on and then compacted over a period of time, the result being to both lower the bottom and raise the filled surface by an equal amount. A good dragline operator could cover 80 to 100 feet a day, creating a deep canal and a single spoil finger ideally suited to deepening channels adjacent to existing land masses and building roads. Most famous of all was the "walking dredge." In reality a corpulent dragline weighing twenty tons, it straddled both sides of a canal. Scooping up one cubic yard of muck with each dip, it was used to build the Tamiami Trail.

But south Florida developers who wanted to maximize waterfront exposure used a different machine: the Rodes dredge. Invented in the 1920s by Miami native Charles Green Rodes, this floating behemoth featured chain-mounted buckets circulating on a movable and submersible proboscis, scooping up muck and sediment from mangrove forests, forcing slurry into two pipes, and spewing mud out on each side of the dredge to create two fingers of land simultaneously. If the channel was going to be wide, one pipe could be shut off and muck directed toward a single finger with a slurry pipeline as long as 1,500 feet. Because of its size and complexity, the dredge was generally capable of covering only 10 to 15 feet a day, but it could cut through coral reefs and hard bottom. The final step in creating residential lots for sale was seawall construction, allowing fill material in the fingers to compact and settle. With his dredge, Charles Rodes had built Fort Lauderdale.

While creating miles of waterfront property commanding premium prices, dredge-and-fill was wreaking havoc on the intertidal zones of Florida's west coast. Mangrove fringe forests, dominating the coast south of Cedar Key, serve multiple purposes. The red and black varieties are highly tolerant of intertidal salinity changes and mitigate alterations in tidal volumes. During Florida's wet season, heavy rain runoff is buffered by the mangrove system, allowing the fresh water to dissipate in winding channels through root systems. Slow flushing brings sedimentary nutrients into the estuaries, feeding colonies of phytoplankton and zooplankton. Dramatic changes in salinity can shock shellfish, mollusks, and fingerlings; the palliative effect of the mangrove buffer reduces salinity variation. Mangroves still serve an additional purpose by providing physical protection and nourishment for small invertebrates, crustaceans, and juvenile fish. While much of their value is under water, mangrove islands of southwest Florida also serve as nesting and breeding grounds for egrets, pelicans, white-crowned pigeons, herons, and numerous smaller species, as well the raptorial eagle and osprey. All of these birds are dependent upon the availability of prey to feed and raise their families. In the nesting areas, bird droppings add nutrients to the aquatic mangrove stew, critical to the formation and growth of bacteria, algae, and fungi. Finally, one of the most important roles of mangrove forests is to moderate the effects of hurricanes on coastal communities. The soil-creating capacity of mangrove detritus (such as leaves, limbs, and roots) extends and stabilizes landmasses seaward to dampen the effect of waves and storm surges associated with hurricanes coming in from the Gulf.

The Florida legislature, realizing the possible benefits of these adaptive and valuable plants, took a first step in controlling environmental damage wrought by dredge-and-fill operations by repealing the Butler Act of 1921. The original act allowed upland riparian zone owners to obtain and maintain title to submerged lands contiguous to existing property on the proviso that the owners create a bulkhead or similar improvement to maintain a navigable channel of water flowing past the site. The new law, called the Bulkhead Act of 1957, allowed local governments to issue permits only after the state established a "bulkhead line," outside of which dredging was not permitted. (This so infuriated some local jurisdictions that one county, Pasco, attempted to set its bulkhead line two miles out into the Gulf of Mexico.) Most importantly, the act vested title to submerged lands below the high-water mark (except those grandfathered) to the Board of Trustees of the Internal Improvement Fund in Tallahassee. This last provision, as we shall see later, would provoke a major confrontation over ongoing destruction of wetlands and mangrove fringe forests in southwest Florida.

The "Road to Nowhere"

Transportation planning was the main way of directing the course of development in the 1950s. Roads went in first, and rooftops followed. Rooftops meant ad valorem tax dollars. So, as the dredges were puffing away in Royal Harbor and Port Royal, developers and their captive politicians had a golden opportunity to move from Naples southward along the coastal barrier islands, with high-rises all the way to Marco Island. It would be Miami Beach all over again, enabled by one individual (name unknown) who offered Collier County title to fifty acres on Holloway Island, forming the western barrier to Rookery Bay. The county fell all over itself, making plans to create a park from the prospective donation. A road that was almost ten miles long would begin at the end of Kelly (now Bayshore) Drive, run across and down the western edge of Keewaydin Island, cross a series of bridges and causeways and upland ridges on Holloway, Cannon, and Johnson Islands, and finally come back to the mainland, tying into County Road 952 (now Isles of Capri Drive). All of the affected islands combined to form the coastal barrier to Rookery Bay (see Map 1). The new park could easily be accessed by boat, but by using Key Island, with a bridge across the Inland Waterway at channel marker 46, Holloway would become accessible by automobile—with the road paid for by the state's road fund.

A park had been in the county's sights since 1959. A large piece of Holloway Island, known locally as Government Lands, was owned at the time by the federal Bureau of Land Management. The remainder was in the hands of the donor who had started the ball rolling. According to Harmon Turner, county engineer, "the county is planning for a future State Road to serve this area, which will also cause the land values to increase, making it more difficult to obtain land for public use. . . ."[4] This was the infamous "road to nowhere. " Turner was a major player. The "county's top nonelected official since 1946,"[5] he went to work for the Collier company in the mid-1930s and remained on its payroll during his tenure as county engineer. The county paid him a dollar a year and billed Collier for the time he spent on county business. This arrangement continued until 1960 but was never publicly criticized as an embedded conflict of interest.

The county commission, controlled by developers at the time, was salivating over the project. Massive development of a ten-mile strip between Naples and Marco Island would bring untold riches in the form of property taxes, the fillip that drove almost all decisions in Florida at the time. Looking at the projected path of the road, one might think that engineering would be daunting, but taming the southwest Florida wilderness would not be a problem for the road builders; Barron Collier had already demonstrated that the Tamiami Trail could cut through every conceivable obstacle. The county transportation department had first recommended an extension farther inland for only 5.5 miles to Shell Island Road, but the longer Key Island to Isles of Capri route held greater development potential because of its beachfront exposure. The Collier County Planning Commission had already voted to include the road on its priority list, and commissioners were scheduled to routinely approve the project on March 17, 1964. Then George Vega stepped into the picture.

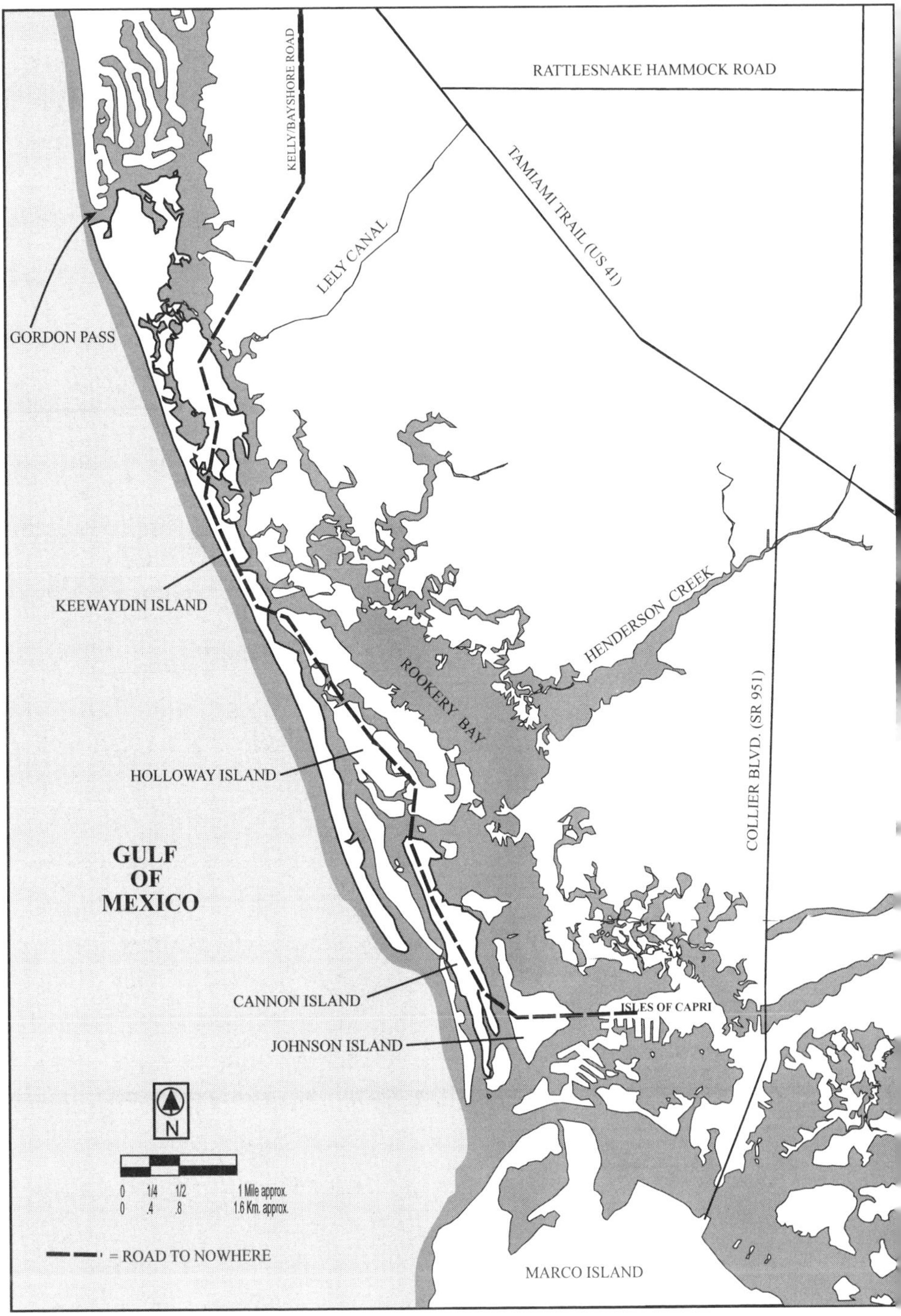

RATTLESNAKE HAMMOCK ROAD

KELLY BAYSHORE ROAD

TAMIAMI TRAIL (US 41)

LELY CANAL

GORDON PASS

KEEWAYDIN ISLAND

HENDERSON CREEK

COLLIER BLVD. (SR 951)

HOLLOWAY ISLAND

ROOKERY BAY

GULF
OF
MEXICO

CANNON ISLAND

JOHNSON ISLAND

ISLES OF CAPRI

N

| 0 | 1/4 | 1/2 | 1 Mile approx. |
| 0 | .4 | .8 | 1.6 Km. approx. |

= ROAD TO NOWHERE

MARCO ISLAND

Map 1: Road to Nowhere.

Vega, a young Naples attorney, was retained by Lester and Dellora Norris, the largest landowners on Keewaydin Island and owners of the private Keewaydin Club. The clubhouse, located on the north end of the island, overlooking Gordon Pass, could be accessed only by boat. But the new road and causeway would open the island to vehicular traffic and destroy the pristine nature of the Norrises' land. Vega wrote county commissioners requesting that they hold a special meeting to reconsider the plan. His argument was simple: "We believe it would destroy the character of this unspoiled area, which serves the City of Naples and all the surrounding areas as a major boating, fishing, and recreational area. It is believed that the road is financially unfeasible, and that it would obviously destroy natural resources and is a road that goes out of its way to lead to nowhere."[6] Besides, it would be an extraordinarily costly way to access fifty acres of parkland in the middle of a mangrove forest. However, this second argument was entirely off point. The road had nothing to do with park access and everything to do with a small group of powerful property owners wanting to develop high-rises between Naples and Marco Island.

Vega realized he had to make a dramatic impact at the commission meeting. To do that he enlisted the aid of two of Naples' young leaders at the time: Joel Kuperberg and Tom Provenzano. Kuperberg was born in Miami in 1927. After obtaining a master's degree in botany, he moved to Naples to become manager of Caribbean Gardens, then a botanical garden possessing the second largest collection of waterfowl in North America. He began and remained on a fast track in Naples, elected as president of the Naples Jaycees in 1957 and to a seat on the city council in 1960, where he would serve for eight years. In addition to his boundless energy, Kuperberg had a gift: He could explain complex scientific concepts in layman's language. Provenzano was tied to the fishing industry in Collier County and believed that construction of a causeway would degrade the environmental value of Rookery Bay as a nursery for small fish. Their job: obtain hundreds of signatures on a petition against the road.

At the March meeting, Vega introduced Kuperberg, who gave a detailed explanation of mangrove ecology in Rookery Bay, citing pioneering hydrological research conducted by Durbin Tabb of the University of

Miami. In his loquacious but engaging way, Kuperberg worked through his scientific arguments, leaving Vega an opening to unroll the petitions, which he had taped together down the center aisle of the room and up onto the commissioner's table some forty feet away. Vega pointed out that more than 2,000 registered voters were against the road and asked the question: "These are the people opposed to that road. Now where are the people who want it?"[7] No one stood up.

Lester Norris watched the proceedings from the back of room, where he was most comfortable. After the commission voted to table the road, Kuperberg approached Norris to thank him for his support, commenting that the victory was only one battle in a long war against development of Rookery Bay and the barrier islands. Kuperberg knew that a permanent solution was needed; so did Lester Norris. The makings of that long-term solution were not far away in either time or place, but the idea of a county park, which had given birth to the "road to nowhere," stayed on a slow boil. It would return.

Founding of the Conservancy

Three weeks after the commission's dispatch of the road, Kuperberg attended a gathering of the Nature Conservancy's Florida chapter at the Koreshan settlement in Estero. One of the speakers was Richard H. Pough, a leading proponent of land conservation in the United States. Pough was described as "a bloodhound. He sniffed out opportunities and ways of preserving our natural landscape."[8] Born in Brooklyn in 1904, he had a bachelor's degree in biology from MIT and an M.A. in fine arts from Harvard. After a few months working as a night shift engineer at a sulfuric acid plant in Port Arthur, Texas, he went to work for the National Audubon Society and later joined the Ecologists Union, which became the Nature Conservancy in 1950. A tall and garrulous man, Pough could charm a bird out of a tree, particularly when the bird happened to hold title in fee simple to some environmentally sensitive land that Pough had his eye on.

The topic of his speech to the assembled chapter members was estuaries and the fabric of nature. Kuperberg, struck by the "inconceivable coincidence" of the moment, gathered Pough, president of the national Nature Conservancy Dr. Walter Boardman, and chairman of the department of biology at the University of Miami Dr. Taylor Alexander for a late dinner, during which he recounted the story of the road through Rookery Bay and asked the group how to save the estuary from the dredge-and-fill mania of the time. To Boardman, the answer was obvious: Buy adjacent buffer lands to cut off access to the coastal islands. He and Pough offered to come to Naples to meet with Lester and Dellora Norris. Kuperberg was elated.

The meeting took place at the Keewaydin Club on April 5, 1964. Pough reiterated the substance of his estuaries speech, and Boardman described the mission of the Nature Conservancy in detail, offering assistance in forming a local chapter to acquire land in Rookery Bay. Lester and Dellora Norris were interested but realized a broader base of support would be required and asked John Slater and Julius Fleischmann to meet with Pough and Kuperberg. Fleischmann was important to the effort. An avid yachtsman, he was the prime mover in the Third Street South shopping district in Naples. In 1951 he bought overgrown land near the Gordon River in Naples, along with the house of botanist Dr. Henry Nehling, and in 1952 established Caribbean Gardens (where Kuperberg was executive director). Slater was a wealthy philanthropist known to be interested in land preservation. Both men were willing to support the effort financially, but neither wished to take a public role.

Pough suggested that the four become an organizing committee to charter a chapter of the Nature Conservancy. However, the group ended up being much larger. Minutes of the meeting show in attendance Lester and Dellora Norris, Joel Kuperberg, Charles Draper, Herman Teetor, Nelson Sanford, W.C. Hutchinson, John Slater, Richard Pough, Mr. and Mrs. Ben Parks, Fred Winter, a Mrs. and Mrs. Brown from Port Royal, and the lawyer George Vega, convening on Keewaydin Island on Saturday, April 11, 1964. After lunch, Kuperberg recounted the events leading up to the vote to rescind the "road to nowhere" and introduced Pough as an "engineer, ecologist, and conservationist of national note."[9]

Pough's talk was rambling and confusing: "The fabric of nature—

two billion years to develop—represents equilibria that have taken thousands of years to develop. Africa could yield more by harvesting the highly specialized ungulates (plant eaters) than by slaughtering and replacing them with cattle. Nowhere else has nature developed treetop feeders (giraffe) and swamp feeders (hippo). . . ."[10] The gathering was wondering what they were getting into, but Pough eventually got around to the main point: While a generalized body of research on estuarine habitat was available, more site-specific work on Rookery Bay was needed to establish its ecological significance and boundaries. He had talked to people in Tallahassee at the Florida State Board of Conservation who might be willing to assist, but expenses would be involved.

After an hour's discussion, it was agreed that "the Collier County Conservancy be organized as an adjunct to the Nature Conservancy, its first project to be conducted as a committee of the whole, such committee to be named the Rookery Bay Committee."[11] The use of the word "adjunct" is interesting. The original idea was to become a chapter of the Nature Conservancy, but the group was not willing to go that far, with implications that would become important two years later. Charles Draper was chosen as chairman; Lester Norris, Herman Teetor, and Nelson Sanford as vice-chairmen; Joel Kuperberg, Dellora Norris, W.C. Hutchinson, Mr. and Mrs. Parks, and Fred Winter as directors. George Vega was elected executive director, and Kuperberg secretary.

The first item of business was to set priorities: Determine ownership of all islands between Port Royal and Chokoloskee (south of Marco Island); oppose any further development in Rookery Bay; have the charming and loquacious Pough contact Barron Collier Jr. regarding a gift of property adjacent to Rookery Bay; and develop the bulkhead line south of Naples Bay down to Carnestown. While the first three steps were obvious, the last needed further examination. The bulkhead line was the border where laws and regulations governing dry land and wet land met, and in Florida this was critical because with recently passed Bulkhead Act amendments, the state assumed ownership of all lands below the mean high-water mark. As noted earlier, some counties in Florida, eager to control their own destinies (and serve the interests of developers), had established bulkhead lines well beyond logical boundaries in order to issue dredge-and-fill permits out to the coast. But Collier and Lee Counties had made no attempt (yet) to redo the line.

The last item of business was in reality the most important: money. Draper, a committed fisherman, anted up $1,000, which was matched by Norris, and Teetor wrote a check for $500. All three contributions were delivered into the custody of Joel Kuperberg and identified as "tax deductible contributions." Since the Conservancy had not yet applied for status as a 501(c)3, it is likely that the checks were made payable to the Nature Conservancy as the established parent organization rather than to its "adjunct."

Draper was a retired Air Force colonel, a tall, lean man with a serious demeanor and the ability to direct work. It was said he did not "suffer fools lightly" and was a man of few words. His first act, picking up on Pough's recommendation, was to hire Kenneth Woodburn, a marine biologist with the Board of Conservation. Woodburn, born in Pennsylvania in 1926, had moved to Florida with his family when he was fifteen years old. With an academic background in tropical and subtropical biology, his entire career had been spent working on water-quality issues. He was an ideal choice to investigate the Rookery Bay ecosystem. The Conservancy also hired Durbin Tabb, whose work had been cited by Vega at the meeting that scotched the "road to nowhere," to create a second opinion as to the land areas most critical in protecting Rookery Bay. The first study from Woodburn and Tabb, with a boundary map, was presented to the Conservancy in June 1964. The size of the project was breathtaking. It would be expensive, but Woodburn and Tabb were less committed to expediency than to the highest and best solution.

Many of the board members retired to their summer homes up north and returned in the fall to hear the bad news. In order to preserve Rookery Bay at the boundaries suggested by the scientists, it was essential to acquire Collier land, but Pough's legendary persuasiveness had failed to move Barron Collier Jr. He made it abundantly clear that the company's land in and adjoining Rookery Bay would not be donated; it would have to be purchased. While this was the initial position of the

Collier family, they would eventually become highly supportive of the project and instrumental in the acquisition of small inholdings throughout the Ten Thousand Islands. They would also donate large tracts of land. Despite this initial setback, the Conservancy decided to proceed by proposing a new bulkhead line that would chill any development in Rookery Bay. Kuperberg and Vega, the duo who had stopped the "road to nowhere," made a presentation at a commission meeting with the bulkhead line on the agenda. Vega argued for "bringing the greatest good to the greatest number," and Kuperberg explained that the proposed new line would run seventy miles from Naples southward into the Ten Thousand Islands, inside the chain of outer islands (except for Marco), to "provide a barrier for uncontrolled digging of canals and other structures which can threaten the safety of fresh water supplies of the people of the county."[12] The new line was approved but success was ephemeral; three months later, at the urging of developers, a portion of the line was moved back east to the Tamiami Trail, opening up Henderson Creek, one of the main feeder streams into Rookery Bay, for development. *Two steps forward and one step back,* thought Vega.

Money to Save Rookery Bay

In November 1964, a breakthrough occurred when Herbert Mills, an officer of the National Audubon Society, learned that Caribbean Gardens in Naples had one of the finest collections of living waterfowl in the world. He paid a visit and was escorted around the property by Kuperberg, who could not resist mentioning the Rookery Bay project. Mills was interested because the Audubon Society had a large endowment fund dedicated exclusively to wetlands acquisition. After examining Woodburn and Tabb's map, Mills offered to match dollar for dollar the Conservancy's funds for its first land purchases on the condition that Rookery Bay be designated a National Audubon Sanctuary. Sixteen hundred acres of Collier land were targeted for purchase; the asking price was $500,000. While the Collier family was not willing to donate, they were not going to hold out for top dollar. The family had methodically begun to divide holdings into a series of alphabet corporations, including two owning the mainland margins of Rookery Bay: Jibb and Melaluca. Negotiations were conducted by Gene Parker on behalf of the Collier interests, but he and Kuperberg, after weeks of back and forth, were unable to agree on what Kuperberg felt was a dollar figure commensurate with the Conservancy's ability to raise funds. Then Lester Norris entered the picture.

Norris, while remaining in the background in many matters, was a former board chairman of Texaco. He knew that many deals were made at the point of exhaustion, so he invited Parker to join him at the Keewaydin Club, from which Parker could not escape except on Norris's ferry. Negotiations began in the morning over coffee and continued throughout the day. Parker declared an impasse a number of times and got up to leave, but Norris would not give in. He kept looking for common ground, and after seven hours found it by agreeing to purchase a parcel of Collier land contiguous to his own family's property. The 1,600 acres would go to the Conservancy for $300,000, with $30,000 down in 30 days and the balance paid within two and a half years.

Even with Norris's backing, raising money locally would be a problem. Kuperberg sought to assess the level of support from other community leaders in Naples, and the conversations were not going well. It was clear that finding even the initial $30,000 was going to be a stretch, so Kuperberg called the Nature Conservancy to learn that Walter Boardman had rather abruptly retired but that his successor, Huey Johnson, was willing to listen. Kuperberg flew to Washington to describe the work of the Rookery Bay Committee and recounted the matching funds agreement with Herbert Mills and the Audubon Society. Johnson, a man committed to land preservation, wrote a check for the full amount. Savior of the day, he would later carve out a career as a giant in the environmental movement, going on to become California Resources Secretary and a founder of the Trust for Public Land. His instantaneous support of the Rookery Bay purchase gave the infant Conservancy the confidence—and the money—to proceed with its ambitious program. Without Johnson's help, Rookery Bay would likely have become Biscayne Bay West.

There was one other source of money at the time. The state legislature had recognized for years that private development on both coasts could eventually crowd out public beaches and recreational opportunities for visitors and that uncontrolled development of natural areas in the interior would reduce land available for hunting and fishing. Purchases were made at the behest of individual legislators who inserted budget line items for very specific parcels. Realizing that this method was creating a hodgepodge of isolated and unrelated parcels that were hard to manage, the legislature dipped its toes into the water in 1963 by creating the Land Acquisition Trust Fund (LATF). With a little more than $1 million being collected each year from a 5% tax on recreational equipment and clothing, the fund was used to purchase land for state parks chosen by the Department of Natural Resources. The program was hampered by a pay-as-you-go policy, however, restricting the purchase of lands to smaller, less expensive parcels. The impact was minor, but an important principle was established: Users of recreational lands should pay for their acquisition.

The Conservancy had little contact with Tallahassee during its early years, believing it could raise enough money locally to pay its mounting bills. The board chair, Charles Draper, realized that his strength was in organizing, not in fund-raising, so he recruited Lester Norris, Joel Kuperberg, and Nelson Sanford, a garrulous and charming man, to act as solicitors. Norris preferred to operate in the background and offer guidance only when he felt it necessary. He agreed to be part of the effort because he knew his leadership gifts would set an example. Sanford and Kuperberg were natural fund-raisers, and the group successfully raised money from a few wealthy citizens, mainly Northern transplants and vacationers in Port Royal. But the narrowness of his financial base got Draper thinking about a public campaign and broadening community support, a matter that would plague Conservancy leaders over the next decade.

Dallas Reach Finds the Message

At the recommendation of Glen Sample, the Conservancy asked Dallas Reach, a transplanted New Yorker who had just bought a home in

Sample's Port Royal development, to join the board and take on advertising and public relations. This was common practice in the early years. With no staff and no offices, Conservancy directors took up issues on an as-needed basis and were responsible for seeing each project through to the end. Reach's first effort featured directors and officers giving their thoughts on the future of Collier County. Local media were encouraged to run stories on the biological diversity of the Ten Thousand Islands, and Kuperberg offered to assist reporters in researching articles. Reach felt that support from the local press was essential despite the fact that the major daily newspaper in Naples was owned by the Collier family.

The first print ad was a full page in black and white with the headline slogan "Save Rookery Bay." The second lead in the ad was "How to Eat Your (fish) Cake—and Have it Too," done at the request of fishermen on the board of directors. The ad went on to explain the function of an estuary and to ask for donations to save Rookery Bay. However, there was no suggestion as to the total amount needed—and for good reason. The effort was now to save 2,600 acres—well over the initial purchase of 1,600—because another 1,000 had been added. Leadership of the Conservancy, emboldened by their success in attracting Nature Conservancy and National Audubon Society dollars, had made an offer to another of the Collier companies for extra acreage encompassing the lower bays and mouth of Henderson Creek. It had the potential to chill development inside the county's newly revised bulkhead line. The price was $150,000 with 10% down, and the Conservancy was now faced with raising more than $450,000.

After seeing the first "Save Rookery Bay" ad, local developers realized their plans for Rookery Bay were in jeopardy. They formed an organization called Group of Tax Conscious Naples Citizens, backed by their own full-page ad:

> Reflect a little. . . . Instead of an inaccessible, mangrove-lined, mosquito-infested shoreline, beautiful Naples-type shoreline could appear. Flowers bursting with exotic colors, green lawns, and graceful palm

trees could replace present mangrove and scrub jungle growth. But, if you support the Conservancy, this land will remain, for the most part, an impenetrable mangrove swamp largely inaccessible and useless. The eventual development of this land is vital to the growth and future of Naples and its economy.

The Conservancy's somnolent "Fish Cake" campaign was no match for bucolic images. The ads were not working and the soliciting team was discouraged, so Reach yanked the campaign from newspapers and switched to radio—with the same desultory result because the science of estuaries was complex and hard to explain to a radio audience. Donations fell even further. Reach was convinced the message was adaptable to the airwaves but didn't know how to adjust it. Then one afternoon, after sailing in the Gulf of Mexico, he tacked into Gordon Pass and heard an enormous dredge ripping out the mangroves. The noise was deafening. Reach docked his boat, hurried to his typewriter, and wrote the following spot:

(Sound effect) Roar of a dredge at work and clangor of a bulldozer tearing up trees.

(Fade sound and emphatic voice-over) When you hear the roar of the dredge and the harsh, jarring sounds of the bulldozer, you know our priceless environment is being destroyed for real estate development. All of us know Naples must grow, but we also know we must *control growth.* The Collier County Conservancy was established to protect the *character* of our community and the *lifestyle* we enjoy.

Within seven months, the revitalized campaign raised $400,000. Contributions came from more than 1,400 citizens and 20 business and civic organizations. The Sinclair Oil Company placed a full-page color ad in national publications, congratulating the Conservancy on its success in saving a part of Rookery Bay from the ministrations of the dredge. Despite this success, Draper was convinced the Conservancy needed to shift its focus to the federal government and wrote Secretary of the Interior Morris Udall suggesting a study be undertaken to designate the area as wilderness. Udall's reply pointed out that only federally owned lands were eligible for inclusion in the national wilderness preservation system, but he suggested that Draper contact Ney Landrum at the Land and Water Conservation Fund in Tallahassee. Undaunted, Draper made a second attempt to involve the federal government that November by hosting the U.S. Fish and Wildlife Service's regional staff to show them the significance of the Ten Thousand Islands. While nothing came of either contact, the Conservancy's leadership had expanded its thinking beyond the borders of Collier County, convinced that a comprehensive federal analysis might pose a compelling argument to protect the entire ecosystem.

Three unintended benefits came from these seemingly failed efforts. First, the Conservancy was introduced to Ney Landrum, who would become one of the great champions of saving the Ten Thousand Islands and would go on to a remarkable career as head of Florida's state parks. Second, because of the unwillingness of federal agencies to undertake a baseline study of Rookery Bay, the Conservancy was forced to internalize that function, resulting in the creation of a science division that would eventually move it toward a broad platform of advocacy on a variety of issues. Had the government agreed to a study of Rookery Bay, the Conservancy might have kept its focus on land acquisition to the exclusion of science and the much broader environmental agenda that would ultimately bring it to regional prominence. Finally, in March 1966, three weeks before formal designation of the Rookery Bay Audubon Wildlife Sanctuary, George Vega filed papers incorporating the Collier County Conservancy with the chartered purpose to "maintain a widespread series of nature preserves and wildlife sanctuaries." Upon incorporation,

the Conservancy severed its two-year relationship with its parent organization, the Nature Conservancy, taking another step toward a more
robust platform beyond land preservation.

"Road to Nowhere" Reappears

With 2,600 acres in hand, the Conservancy carefully began to catalog
and value all parcels within the Rookery Bay boundaries located by
Woodburn and Tabb, entering into private and confidential discussions
with numerous owners. Records from this period are skimpy because
much of the work was carried on in personal conversations. But storm
clouds loomed on the horizon. The Collier County Planning Commission (CCPC), with four of its five members either land developers or
in the real estate business, was expected to hold a routine meeting in
April 1967. The Conservancy got word that for $15,000 the CCPC had
hired Adley & Associates of Tampa to draw a map of the Ten Thousand
Islands, showing the most likely corridors for development. On that map
was a dotted line running from Marco Island twenty miles south toward
Carnestown, representing a scenic drive cutting through the heart of
coastal mangrove forests and snaking down a series of small barrier islands. The planning commission, meeting immediately prior to the Collier County Commission, was prepared to urge adoption of the map as
part of the county's comprehensive plan. While the scheme was initially
presented as an amenity for visitors, county planners added offhandedly
that two-thirds of the periphery of the highway would be set aside for
development, a formula common throughout Florida at the time. Roads
were built without regard to hydrology, wetlands, animal corridors, mi-
gratory patterns, and functionality of ecosystems as many government
officials clung tenaciously to the proven paradigm: Build a road and development will follow.

Leaders of the Conservancy were incensed. Draper first called Al-
len Wysor at Adley & Associates, asking him to explain the map. Wysor
was circumspect, telling Draper that it was only a map and not a proper
amendment to the county's comprehensive plan. But in a moment of
candor, Wysor offered his opinion that coastal development would in-

evitably depredate the entire ecosystem south of Marco Island. He suggested Draper attend the commission meeting but eschew "bird-watcher" arguments.

After talking to Wysor, Draper assembled an expert witness team.[13] Their presentation amounted to a plea for further study, taking environmental considerations into account. The main argument came from Ken Woodburn, who explained in layman's terms what was at stake: "Naples and fishing, like love and marriage, go together. It is possible to have one without the other, but it is better with both. Fishing brings forty percent of the people here. Many of them to catch snook, next to pompano the most delicate Florida fish."[14] Draper warned commission members "there is a widespread and mistaken notion that the Ten Thousand Islands lie within Everglades National Park. The fact that Collier County is considering the possibility of two-thirds of these islands being classified for urban development would result in unpleasant national publicity."[15] Planning board member James Bell moved that the hearing be closed and the dotted line removed from the map, subject to further study. The county commission met that same day and accepted the recommendation with little discussion; no one from the development community spoke in opposition.

But as with the "road to nowhere," the Conservancy's ability to suppress a road from Marco Island to Carnestown was only a temporary respite. Draper knew that arguments about how fish tasted wasn't going to be persuasive in the long run and turned his full attention again to exploring ways to interest the federal government in the Ten Thousand Islands. Based on his experience in fighting the road to Carnestown, he began by contacting leaders of the Florida's commercial and sportfishing industries to gather support. With their help—and after weeks of concerted pressure, with back-channel assistance in Washington, from Charles Foster of the Nature Conservancy—Draper wheedled the county commissioners into applying to the U.S. Bureau of Sport Fisheries and Wildlife for a study of the economics of southwest Florida's fishing industry. Draper knew that studies took time and did not always shake loose dollars needed to purchase vast lands, so he enlisted his old friend Walter Boardman's support in his search for funds. Boardman had moved to Volusia County and had been testifying before Congress, where he met Raymond Dasmann, who at the time was working as an ecologist in the nation's capital and writing one of the classic books on Florida ecosystems.[16] Dasmann, in turn, contacted Russell Train, then head of the Conservation Foundation, explaining the situation in Collier County and asking if the foundation could help. Train—a graduate of Princeton and Columbia Law School, founder of the World Wildlife Fund in 1961, and head of the U.S. Environmental Protection Agency under Presidents Nixon and Ford—was interested.

Dasmann also went to work on the National Park Service—through a friend in the Atlanta office, E.T. Heinen—to include the Ten Thousand Islands as part of the American Island Study team's work identifying islands throughout the United States and its territories for federal protection and perhaps purchase. Most of the islands under consideration were geologically stable and permanent; the Ten Thousand Islands would be unique, being dominated by constantly reshaped barrier islands. Kuperberg received one letter stating, "Mr. Heinen had been keeping me advised of your activities and interest in the Ten Thousand Islands area. I was most pleased to see that you share our enthusiasm for getting a project started in that area,"[17] which he took as an indication that the government might be interested. But Draper could not share in that "enthusiasm" because he passed away that November at his summer home in Kennebunkport, Maine. His obituary in the *Naples Star* read in part: "Each time a child or any human being visits the Rookery Bay Sanctuary in future years and wonders at its serenity and natural beauty, its birds, fish and wildlife—which dwell there in safety, now protected in living tribute, an eternal monument to his dedicated efforts to keep this natural beauty undisturbed."[18]

Draper's death had little to do with the hard reality that all contacts with the federal government would be buried in feasibility studies and endless analyses when the real need was for money to quickly stem the tide of development along the coast. Studies took time, and Florida was beginning to boom.

Draper's Passing Presages Changes

The year 1967 marked a turning point in the history of the Conservancy. Draper was gone, but a superb fund-raiser stepped into the breach: his good friend Nelson Sanford, who had spent most of his working life in the timber business. He claimed his conservation ethic came from an understanding that natural resources, whether trees or estuaries, were not inexhaustible. Walking with a cane as a result of a logging injury, Sanford had an aristocratic demeanor but a magical touch when it came to motivating people, whether to donate to the cause or to volunteer on behalf of the Conservancy. He was inclined to delegate and rely upon teamwork, an entirely different approach from Draper's more direct, hierarchical management style. Sanford also felt that the Conservancy's efforts suffered from a seasonal (summer) lull, and memos from that era indicate his main concern was how to extend fund-raising beyond the winter months by going deeper into the Naples community, beyond Port Royal. The organization was not successful in doing this until much later, but Sanford laid the groundwork for one of the major events in Conservancy history: a merger with the Big Cypress Nature Center in 1974.

A celebratory moment took place at Naples High School on January 21, 1968, when management of the Henderson Creek preserved area was turned over to the National Audubon Society. Rookery Bay was now a 2,600-acre sanctuary; the State of Florida had added 1,400 acres of jurisdictional wetlands. Dignitaries were in attendance, including Tom Richards, president of the Nature Conservancy, but not present was the man who had made it all happen: Charles Draper.

The moment would be enjoyed only briefly, though, because word was on the street that Alico Land Development Company had property in the Ten Thousand Islands for sale. And indeed it did. Alico owned more than 187,000 acres to the west of Everglades National Park, beginning at Fakahatchee Bay and running southwest out to the Gulf through Fakahatchee Pass. Kuperberg, intent on leaving no stone unturned, convinced George Cooley, noted philanthropist and vice chairman of the Nature Conservancy board, to pledge $25,000 of his own money toward an effort to buy as much of Alico's land as possible. This was a fortunate turn of events because that July all of the federal agencies Draper had been pursuing backed off. Private money had to do the job, and Kuperberg went right back to the deepest pockets of all: Tom Richards and the Nature Conservancy. The response was immediate: "it should not be difficult to raise approximately $200,000 to knock off some of the Alico holdings." [19] A little less difficult with $25,000 already in hand from Cooley.

In September 1968, another shoe dropped. *The Daily News* carried a front-page story that a Dutch firm headed by Christiaan Duvekot had spent several million dollars to purchase 656 acres of mangrove forest and uplands around the western periphery of Dollar Bay, the first major bay south of Gordon Pass and the northern entrance to Rookery Bay on the inland waterway. The firm owned Lely Estates, eponymously named for the chairman of the corporation, and had a number of large parcels of developable land between Naples and Marco Island. Duvekot was exuberant: "I have traveled all over the United States, through California, Texas . . . and other states, and I have found in Naples a charm which is not evident in any other section. We have [spent], and will continue to spend, millions there. . . ." [20] His plan was to create a second Port Royal once the county commissioners agreed to extend Kelly Road. But this was a battle that had already been fought, and Conservancy directors needed to dampen Duvekot's enthusiasm.

Their strategy was to press for more land to isolate Duvekot, and the first break came when Jack Spratt, president of Alico, sent the Conservancy a letter indicating his willingness to negotiate over certain Rookery Bay parcels. He included a map showing the land he had in mind: two infill parcels immediately adjacent to Everglades National Park, totaling 1,735 acres. This was not near Lely's purchase, but Kuperberg needed to establish credibility with Alico. Working with Spratt throughout the fall, he eventually negotiated a purchase option for $175,000. Then he had to find the money, even with Tom Richards' cautiously worded commitment in his back pocket.

Enter Bill Merrihue
Kuperberg and Nelson Sanford had to open the fund-raising throttle, but

Sanford wanted to retire as chairman. He felt the job carried too much responsibility, so he created an executive committee to weigh in on major decisions: Stuart Smith, Lester Norris, Thor Johnson, John Burnham, and John Blair. He created a paid position of executive director and appointed Kuperberg to that post. His choice as chairman Bill Merrihue, who had taken over the Collier County Audubon Society in 1965, when the membership was a mere 290 souls. By 1969 it was the second largest local Audubon chapter in the United States with 2,600 members, more than 10% of the population of Collier County. Merrihue was diminutive of stature, full of energy, imbued with boundless self-confidence, and brimming with ideas. He was ubiquitous in Naples and a fixture at the Port Royal Club, where it was reported he and his wife, Gay, danced the night away at every opportunity.

With Merrihue in the chairman's job, Kuperberg put all of his energy into finding money for the Alico property. He thought he had an ace in the hole in Ney Landrum, who had by then become director of the Florida Outdoor Recreation Council. Enlisting the assistance of Tom Richards, Frank Craighead, Ed Carlson, and a young man named Nathaniel Reed in Governor Claude Kirk's office, Kuperberg went after state money by asking Craighead to send off his presentation made to the county planning commission against the Marco-to-Carnestown scenic road in 1967. Craighead did so, and Landrum responded after making contact with the Nature Conservancy's regional office. "Mr. Richards has given me a copy of your letter to him and it would appear that you are doing quite a lot to stir things up down there."[21] The stirring did some good because in April 1969 the Nature Conservancy sent a $10,000 check to Spratt as a down payment on Alico's two parcels. It was most likely a pass-through donation from St. Charles Charities of St. Charles, Illinois—the summer home of Dellora and Lester Norris—but in any case the deal was on. It included Cooley's $25,000 to be paid sixty days after approval of the abstract, which was a matter of some concern because boundaries for Everglades National Park were never clearly established and no government survey was available at the time. Nonetheless, the abstract was received and certified by Thomas Brown of Carroll,

Vega, Brown and Nichols in early June. Payment was due over the next thirty months. Exhausted, Kuperberg left for an extended vacation.

While Kuperberg was recharging his batteries, Ney Landrum was working his magic in Tallahassee. He knew the Internal Improvement Fund (IIF), composed of elected Cabinet members and the governor, was scheduled to meet in October to consider establishing sixteen aquatic preserves in the State of Florida. Landrum was able to get Rookery Bay on the list. Final ratification was up to the legislature, but this delighted the conservation community because dredge-and-fill operations in state aquatic preserves would be permitted only for "authorized public navigation projects." [22] More important, the likelihood of state acquisition was looming larger because the Conservancy's newly formed Rookery Bay Committee would be responsible for sketching the boundaries of the preserve's ecosystem, and the work was already done by Walter Boardman and Durbin Tabb, both of whom were well known in Tallahassee.

The pace of activity picked up in the fall. To keep the heat on public officials, the Conservancy chartered a flight over the Ten Thousand Islands in an airplane loaded with the press and government dignitaries. President Richard Nixon gave the effort a boost in a letter to Bill Merrihue, congratulating the organization on being an example to other groups interested in conserving America's natural resources. However, there were mixed signals from Tallahassee when Landrum wrote on Department of Natural Resources stationery "the only feasible way to ensure protection of the area is through outright acquisition of all private landholdings" but then admitted the state did not have the resources necessary to close the deal.[23] The legislature adjourned without ratifying the selection of Rookery Bay, and the matter lay dormant in Tallahassee for five years.

However, other small pieces were falling into place. One of Charles Draper's forays unexpectedly paid off when the Ten Thousand Islands were targeted as the first parcel for acquisition in the southeastern United States by the American Islands Study. While no funds were appropriated, the action gave Kuperberg and Merrihue confidence that there was some interest in Washington. But purchase by any agency required a full legal description of the preserve area, not just ecosystem boundaries, and that was going to be an ongoing problem despite the abstract issued for purchase of the Alico properties. Then in early 1968, C.J. Copley offered the Conservancy his homestead on forty-four acres at the end of Shell Island Road in Rookery Bay. Kuperberg expressed interest but was overwhelmed at the time with the Alico transaction. Copley had been offered nearly $200,000 by a motor home park operator but was determined to sell his land to the Conservancy. He was willing to be patient. In 1969 the Conservancy purchased the property for $100,000 and established the first private estuarine research station in Rookery Bay, Norris Marine Research Laboratory, named for the family that had once again funded a major acquisition. The organization now had a laboratory to gather and analyze baseline data of ecosystem functionality in both Rookery Bay and the Ten Thousand Islands—useful data to add to the push for government ownership. Then, either Merrihue or Kuperberg (the record is unclear) was able to convince the Collier-Read Company to donate approximately 390 acres of undevelopable wetlands guarding the southwest approach to the newly acquired area, an act of beneficence that presaged the purchase of an additional 20,000 acres by the state from the Collier family in 1975.

Much of the activity during this period was aimed at identifying the Ten Thousand Islands as an ecological wonder, setting it apart enough to make public acquisition attractive. The initial thrust—to purchase shoreline and stable high ground surrounding Rookery Bay where development was most likely to occur—was done piecemeal, relying heavily upon cooperation from the two major landholders in the estuary, the Collier family and Alico Land Holdings. Both were willing to sell their land at a fair price while giving the Conservancy sufficient time to raise money. And the Conservancy had been wise in choosing recognized, credible scientists like Frank Craighead and Ken Woodburn to argue its case. The lesson was simple: Good science would drive good decisions. This was not lost on Bill Merrihue.

During the post–World War II boom, science was thought be a subject for the lab and the university, but when Rachel Carson's *Silent Spring* pointed out the effects of human intervention (mainly with pesticides) on the balance of nature, applied scientific research took on new importance. In early 1970, the federal government, through the Office of Water Resources Research, made a $78,000 grant to the University of Miami to study water quality in Henderson Creek and Rookery Bay. The Norris Marine Research Laboratory was selected as the site, and the university placed Bernie Yokel in charge of designing the study. Yokel's appointment coincided with heightened awareness, in both Washington and Tallahassee, that mangrove-fringed estuaries played a central role in the reproductive cycle of many aquatic species. The attention resulted in a raft of legislation restricting dredge-and-fill activities in coastal Florida and sponsored creation of federal estuarine research reserves, of which Rookery Bay would soon become a member.

Yokel would stay in Naples and become an integral part of the Conservancy. He testified as an expert witness in a number of proceedings and became the scientific conscience of southwest Florida environmentalism in the 1970s and 1980s, particularly in the Deltona controversy (covered in a later chapter). Immediately following his appointment, a burst of publicity accompanied activities at the laboratory, and the Conservancy was able to acquire a large landmass adjacent to the facility, called Shell Point, for $180,000. But progress did not stop there, for the Conservancy was on the verge of a small acquisition in the heart of Rookery Bay that would unlock an era of cooperation with the Collier interests.

Fakahatchee Island

The story began in 1966 at an appellate court hearing, during which Phleany Daniels sought to establish adverse possession of Fakahatchee Island, a remote piece of land between 130 and 140 acres owned by the Ben Hill Griffin family's Alico Land Development Company. Daniels claimed to have a 1918 title to the island from a man named McCloud and was represented in the appeals hearing by Clark Nichols, who happened to be George Vega's law partner. The township in which the island was located had never been surveyed due to the inherent difficulties of traversing mangrove forests. The island, on the north side of Fakahatchee Bay, had about fifty acres of shell ridges from prehistoric occupation.

The Daniels family, who occupied only a corner of the island, claimed that they had effectively settled the entire island through farming activities and therefore owned the property by "color of title." The appeals panel upheld the original ruling against the family but permitted them to retain title to a house and family cemetery.

The local Conservancy was working on the Daniels' inholding. In early May 1969, Kuperberg (perhaps at the urging of George Vega) made a phone call to George Huntoon, who at the time was running part of the Collier-Read Company. Huntoon was a former race car driver for Jaguar when he met Sam Collier on the circuit in the late 1940s. The two struck up a friendship, and Huntoon eventually was hired by the Collier family. Kuperberg knew the Colliers owned no part of Fakahatchee Island but was also aware that Huntoon was favorably disposed toward public ownership of the Ten Thousand Islands. During the phone call, Kuperberg asked Huntoon how to approach Alico, despite the fact that he had been working with company officials on two small parcels in Rookery Bay. The deeper motive may have been to engage Huntoon in conversation to assess the Collier family's position on public ownership in the Ten Thousand Islands. It worked because four days later, Alico's attorney wrote George Vega, inquiring if the Conservancy might want to buy it out. Then, one month later to the day, a letter arrived on Kuperberg's desk from Gabe Luff, a real estate agent representing the Daniels family, offering to sell their property for $1,000 per acre, meaning the entire island was available. And in late December, Lester Norris stepped in to support purchase of the Daniels' inholding at $500 per acre and offered to help find funds to buy out Alico.

Emboldened by Norris's generosity, Kuperberg turned his attention back to the Collier family. His personal notes at the time, titled "re Collier gift in Rookery Bay," read in part:

> The Ten Thousand Islands came up in
> the discussions. Doyle Connor and Hux
> Coulter (Chief Forester of Florida) spoke
> to Huntoon and Herren at the IIF board
> meeting in Tally yesterday re the Collier

holdings in the Ten Thousand Islands, indicating that someone had suggested that the Colliers might be ready to give the Islands to a preserve use. The Collier reps dispelled that thought and Huntoon inquired as to its possible origins. JK explained that the negotiations with Ney Landrum re State acquisition of the Alico holdings, pending Federal legislation and disposition to acquire the entire 10,000 islands through *purchase* after negotiations with the Colliers (per the many conversations twixt Huntoon, Herren, the BOR and Fish and Wildlife people, and JK). This seemed to satisfy Huntoon. JK and Huntoon agreed to an early meeting to review the matter as both feel the idea is beginning to take shape and should be worked out more fully, before the Colliers hear of the idea through the back door, as it were.[24]

While it was only one small piece, the Fakahatchee Island acquisition, in a way, opened the door to the entire Ten Thousand Islands. The Conservancy and its conservation partners knew that 100% acquisition of the Ten Thousand Islands would never happen unless both the Collier family and Alico agreed to sell their holdings. Kuperberg believed from past dealings that both would act responsibly. He was particularly impressed by Collier's relinquishing undevelopable acreage to protect the entrance to the Norris Marine Research Center on Shell Island Road.

Over the ensuing years, Huntoon became a valued adviser to the Conservancy. Operating behind the scenes, he facilitated the purchase of the 116-acre Adams properties on Periwinkle Island to the east of Little Marco Pass in 1971 and the 40-acre Allsop property north of Henderson Creek a few years later. The Allsops received $40,000 for their land; in a typical move, Merrihue sold them a $5,000 lifetime Conservancy membership to be taken out of the proceeds.

Arthur Godfrey to the Rescue

By now the Conservancy was deeply in debt, but Bill Merrihue had an idea. He knew, after nearly six years of continuous fund-raising, that both his solicitors and major donors were weary. Support from the Nature Conservancy and Conservation Fund was shrinking because competing applications were taking a toll. So on February 10, 1971, with fanfare and great publicity, Merrihue held a fund-raiser featuring Arthur Godfrey, who agreed to come to Naples through the good offices of Tom Richards at the Nature Conservancy. Godfrey, America's most popular television personality and entertainer of the 1950s, was on the downside of his career, but Merrihue knew that his guests, many of whom were of that generation, had fond memories of the "old redhead." The event was held at Naples High School auditorium, the only venue in Naples at the time capable of seating 300 diners. Merrihue presented a slide show of islands saved from the Rodes dredge by the Conservancy. Godfrey, inspired by the moment, pledged $50,000 for naming rights to an open area at the mouth of Henderson Creek. It was to be named Nature Conservancy Bay, and a small island to the east appeared briefly on maps as Arthur Godfrey Island.[25]

Godfrey's largesse became a launching pad for Merrihue. At dinner immediately following the talk, he made sure wine was freely poured and convinced Lester Norris to respond when asked if anyone would buy an island. Norris, always supportive, stood up on cue and bid $15,000 to have naming rights to an island. The Benedum family from Pittsburgh immediately bought another island. Merrihue then picked up the pace, offering bays, peninsulas, fishing holes, and even oyster bars to the delighted and well-lubricated, guests. The evening's tally exceeded $200,000. The Conservancy's fund-raising teams were energized and, led by David Lasier, John Dearholt, and Gene Bewkes, raised an additional $400,000 in the next four months, allowing the Conservancy to pay off its debt to local banks with a balance left over to purchase additional threatened lands. In 1971 the Conservancy raised more than $740,000 from individuals and local businesses.

The following year, the idea of a county park, which had originally spawned the "road to nowhere" in 1964, arose again. County engineer Harmon Turner, still burning over the defeat of the Kelly Road extension, had his eye on the area known as the Government Lands as a "boat-accessible" amenity for county residents and visitors. The Conservancy, against it because of the rampant destruction of mangroves to build docks, was convinced it was little more than a "wedge to get a road built to that area and eventually to Keewaydin. Others (notably Harmon Turner et. al.) see it as a direct slap at the Conservancy and support it with a vengeance just to reassert their dominance."[26] The county planned to apply for transfer of title to the property, but as soon as the Conservancy learned about it, it filed an application with the federal Bureau of Land Management requesting that title, along with an additional 200 adjacent acres, be turned over to Rookery Bay rather than to the county. And the Conservancy had an ace in the hole in Washington: Nathaniel Reed, formerly Claude Kirk's environmental adviser, who had recently been named Assistant Secretary of the Interior for Fish and Wildlife and Parks. But both petitions got sidetracked by a federal court case brought by a man named Barney Colson seeking title to the Government Lands based upon Indian scrip, the highest form of claim under existing law. The district court in Jacksonville eventually booted Colson's claim, opening the path for Turner. "This being public land, it does appear that the logical recipient would be the county."[27] Then, in May 1974, under great public pressure, commissioners voted unanimously to vacate their application. Turner had to back down again based on the reality that road access to the property, his real motive, would be politically impossible. But he would not give up without extracting from Merrihue a promise, in front of commissioners, that the Conservancy would exert best efforts to help locate a county park somewhere in the East Naples area.

State of Florida Becomes a Player

While the Government Lands were being pursued by Turner, Joel Kuperberg left to accept Governor Reubin Askew's appointment to be executive director of the Florida Internal Improvement Fund.[28] Always wanting to keep moving parts well oiled, he wrote Patrick Noonan at the Nature Conservancy to suggest that Rookery Bay lands acquired and under management by Audubon should be transferred, in the near future, to the State of Florida based upon the state's desire and ability to protect the entire estuary. "I believe that I am in a position to prevail upon the Trustees (of the Internal Improvement Fund) to make this acquisition of all the lands within some 60,000 acres of land and water in the area north and west of the holding which the Collier County Conservancy acquired in 1968. Conveyance of this parcel at this time would provide the necessary incentive to see the balance of the 10,000 Islands come into public ownership."[29] A delighted Noonan wrote Merrihue that the Nature Conservancy would deed title to its parcels, including Fakahatchee Island, to the Collier County Conservancy for later transfer to the state. Merrihue was elated; the deal closed in May 1973.

But purchase of the additional 60,000 acres stalled in Tallahassee, so the Conservancy never relinquished its holdings. Kuperberg, frustrated with the capital's politics and its practitioners, resigned after his brief stint at the Internal Improvement Fund. That left Merrihue to acquaint the new director, Joseph Landers, with the long history of the Rookery Bay project. He reiterated the Conservancy's willingness to fulfill its end of the bargain and requested a meeting in Governor Askew's office to include Landers, Ney Landrum, and Kuperberg. Being new to the job, Landers suggested that Merrihue call Askew personally to ask for the meeting. The governor was noncommittal, so Merrihue went to work with characteristic energy assembling a letter signed by Collier County Audubon Society (of which he had been president), the Isaak Walton League, the Naples Woman's Club, and the Naples Garden Club, reminding the governor how many registered voters those organizations represented. The reaction came back quickly over the signature of the Conservancy's old friend, Ken Woodburn, who had moved into the governor's office from the Florida Fresh Fish and Game Commission at the sugges-tion of Nathaniel Reed. Having performed the first study on Rookery Bay in 1964, Woodburn was familiar with the situation and was able to restart negotiations. Talks continued throughout the winter of 1974.

A break came in late January 1975, when the state purchased 396 acres at Cape Romano, on the coast south of Marco Island, for $408,000. The following week, the Collier family announced it might consider sell-ing 20,000 acres of its holdings between Marco Island and Everglades National Park. Norman Herren, the new operating head of the Collier Company in charge of the negotiations, was quoted in the local press: "He (Landers) came down to investigate our holdings to see what they were like. He wanted to know our attitude—if we would sell and at what price. I told him we will have a board meeting in March to discuss the matter."[30] And by then, word was getting out in the local press, controlled by the Collier family, that the Internal Improvement Fund had "cast its eye" on the Ten Thousand Islands and was preparing to commence negotiations.

Then in May the deal got blown to kingdom come in Tallahassee. The state had sufficient funds to buy only 12,300 acres (from when Ku-perberg was executive director). As a first step, the legislature had to accredit Rookery Bay as a state aquatic preserve but, despite the Conser-vancy's best efforts, adjourned after taking no action. Merrihue was furi-ous, but Landers had warned him that some south Florida developers with coastal property were becoming uncomfortable with the Conser-vancy's plans for the Ten Thousand Islands and that the legislature was paying attention to them. However, in 1975 Merrihue totaled up the tab: more than 5,000 acres purchased for $1.4 million; 450 acres gifted by the Collier, Mackle, and Timken families; and 1,400 acres owned by the State of Florida had been turned over to Audubon to manage as a sanctuary.[31] But development pressure in the area was growing, and Merrihue knew he had to quickly gather support from other powerful environmental organizations within the state get the job done. While the Conservancy was willing to act as a pass-through for Nature Conservancy lands, it was unwilling to pass title on until Rookery Bay was legislatively mandated as either a state park or an aquatic reserve.

The impasse in the state capital continued for years, described in a letter from Senator Philip Lewis of Palm Beach County to a landowner whose holdings had been in Merrihue's inbox: "My investigation of the proposed acquisition of lands around Rookery Bay for a sanctuary has revealed that this is almost a dead issue. Problems encountered in seeking appropriate management for such a sanctuary have apparently been too difficult to surmount. It is my understanding that an agreement between the Collier County Conservancy and the state on management could not be reached."[32]

Difficulties in designating Rookery Bay as an aquatic reserve created uncertainty in the minds of Conservancy leaders. The main sticking point wasn't management, which was in Audubon's hands, it was the Conservancy's insistence that it retain title to the lands and the state's insistence that title pass to it prior to designation as a reserve. The fear was that, without adequate protection, the state might turn around and either sell or lease the land, as it had done in earlier years to encourage Henry Flagler and others to bring rail service the length of the state.

Finally, with urging from Governor Reubin Askew, the legislature designated 58,000 acres of Rookery Bay as a state aquatic preserve in August 1977. But it came too late. The Conservancy, sick and tired of the dithering in Tallahassee, had already approached Audubon's national office in Washington with another idea: to seek designation of Rookery Bay as a National Estuarine Research Reserve. Those efforts by Audubon's staff in the nation's capital paid off, and in 1978 more than 110,000 acres were identified to be set aside. The research reserve program, established under the Coastal Zone Management Act of 1972, was a cooperative state and federal effort to preserve estuarine resources throughout the United States. Rookery Bay was the third accepted into the system. A number of initiatives based on scientific analysis and education would be funded over the years through different agencies, with the National Oceanic and Atmospheric Administration (NOAA) as the lead administrator. Today there are twenty-eight such bioregions designated.

With this assurance, transfer of title to the acquired lands passed to the State of Florida and on January 29, 1980, a ceremony dedicating the

Rookery Bay National Estuarine Sanctuary was held, honoring the work of Governors Askew and Graham and recently appointed Executive Director of the Department of Natural Resources Elton Gissendanner. The sanctuary would be governed by a three-member board, including representatives from the Conservancy, the National Audubon Society, and the Department of Natural Resources. Bill Merrihue, acting as master of ceremonies, was beaming throughout. It was another step toward saving Rookery Bay.

With both state and federal designation, future development within Rookery Bay was limited and the Ten Thousand Islands would continue on the path to preservation throughout the 1980s, as parcels fell into place one by one with the cooperation of large landowners willing to donate or sell sensitive lands, and elected officials who worked tirelessly to appropriate funds for purchases. In order to understand how that remarkable commitment to purchasing massive tracts of land for public benefit came about, we now need to shift attention back to Tallahassee to explore briefly the work of three governors and the state legislature in funding land acquisition.

ACQUIRING LAND

CHAPTER 1

LAND FOR FUTURE GENERATIONS

*I*n the 1960s, land acquisition in southwest Florida was made possible primarily by money raised locally and administered through organizations such as the national Nature Conservancy and the Conservation Fund, which had the ability to front sufficient capital to purchase large tracts of land in Rookery Bay and the Ten Thousand Islands. Without this capability and the tax deductibility of donated land, it is unlikely Rookery Bay would have been preserved before the dredges and bulldozers had their way with primary and secondary barrier islands along the coast. The local Conservancy was able to stop the infamous "road to nowhere" but struggled to make large purchases. Then, the state stepped into the picture.

In 1966 Claude Kirk was elected Florida's first Republican governor since Reconstruction. He sponsored the Air and Water Pollution Control Act of 1967, a needed update of the Bulkhead Act (covered later in the chapter on Deltona), and, more importantly, appointed a young man named Nathaniel Reed as his special advisor on environmental affairs. Reed, whose family had developed Jupiter Island, was able to convince Kirk that Florida's abundant natural resources were being rapaciously exploited and something needed to be done quickly. However, innate suspicion of Kirk in the Democrat-controlled legislature led to little progress, with one exception: In 1968 lawmakers created indebtedness of $20 million of recreation bonds for land purchases, funded by a documentary stamp tax on real estate transactions to replace a 1963 program funded by outdoor equipment and clothing (known as the "bathing suit tax"). With that, payment shifted from users to the main cause of open space loss, and from smaller to larger transactions, stemming the tide somewhat.[1] The legislature was beginning to understand that the state's natural resources were being plundered by development, resulting in the loss of nearly 170,000 acres of coastal mangrove fringe forests since the 1950s. As a stopgap measure, legislators passed a law in 1970 giving the Internal Improvement Commission (at that time) review and veto power over all dredge-and-fill permit applications.[2]

When the legislative session convened in 1972, Democrat Reubin Askew was in the governor's chair, encouraging the state legislature to pass a slew of powerful environmental laws. Many were related to growth management (dealt with in a later chapter), but one was notable for land acquisition: the Land Conservation Act, which created a bonded fund of $240 million, $200 million of which was earmarked for the Environmentally Endangered Lands program (EEL) to purchase sensitive lands dedicated to natural resource protection for public purposes, with the $40 million balance for recreation. Voter approval was required; the measure passed in November by a two-thirds majority. The EEL program differed from the earlier LATF in that it allowed individual citizens, groups, and local governments to nominate lands for purchase by the state. After undergoing staff review and public hearings, properties were given priority rankings for the head of the Department of Natural Resources (DNR) to have appraised and negotiate a price with the owner. The Internal Improvement Fund then approved the final purchase. This program would become critical in purchasing land on Marco Island from Deltona (covered in a later chapter). With overwhelming approval by Florida voters, it became obvious that land acquisition was a legislative objective enjoying broad bipartisan support.

Another piece of legislation affecting land acquisition was the Environmental Land and Water Management Act of 1972, which created "areas of critical state concern," (ACSC) allowing state and local governments joint oversight of those areas so designated for their historical, natural, and environmental value and placing final power of designation in the hands of Internal Improvement Fund trustees: the governor and elected Cabinet members. The IIF had its origins in 1851 when the legislature created the Internal Improvement Board to manage state lands, generally as a way of attracting railroads to the state. In 1885 the modern IIF was created. Its powers have been altered over the years, but it has always been, and remains today, the single most influential group in the state for land acquisition. In passing the Environmental Land and Water Management Act, the legislature grandfathered existing development rights and allowed no more than 5% of the state's remaining undeveloped lands to be on the ACSC list at any moment in time. This last provision was a significant departure from the legislature's normal grasping for either approval or review of nearly everything that went on in the state. The bill, along with three others passed in later years, eventually grew into one of the largest public investment vehicles in the United States. While not specifically either appropriating or directing funds for land purchase, the act set the stage for the purchase of critically important lands and taking by condemnation, provided funds were immediately available to compensate the property owner. The bill was, in fact, a hybrid of land acquisition with a growth management component, the first formal introduction of land-use planning in the state. At the federal level, the Coastal Zone Management Act so critical to Rookery Bay was also passed in 1972, leading to greater emphasis on the importance of coastal areas, which Florida possessed in abundance.

Bob Graham was elected governor in 1980. In the prior year's session, the legislature had decided to rework and expand the successful EEL program with the landmark Conservation and Recreation Lands Act (CARL). A trust fund was established to receive revenues from a tax on mineral extraction within the state, and funding was expanded to include documentary stamp taxes from real estate closings. But the most significant change was in the process by which land was ranked and chosen for purchase by the state. The legislature created a review committee of six department heads within state government who would meet regularly to review and vote on the prioritization of lands to be placed into state ownership. The list would go to the IIF to authorize purchase depending upon available funds. The governor and Cabinet had the power to remove individual projects but could not change priorities set by the review group. Finally, in response to a scandal involving the head of DNR, the legislature set forth an exhaustive list of procedures for appraising and negotiating land deals in hopes of creating a higher level of transparency. The CARL program would last for three decades in various incarnations and became the means for a massive state investment in public lands. How this all functioned in the real world will be examined in later chapters on the acquisition of Big Cypress Swamp, the Fakahatchee Strand, and Cannon Island.

Graham, with great support in the legislature, expanded the state's capacity to purchase coastal land in 1981 with the Save Our Coast Act (SOC). Concerned that the LATF was beginning to deal with only small parcels after being dwarfed by the massive CARL program, the act added bonded indebtedness to the LATF and enabled the purchase of $275 million of coastal acreage and beach access for the state parks system. It played heavily into the history of southwest Florida and the story of the chain of barrier islands and beaches from Barefoot Beach and Little Hickory Bay all the way down to Key Island and Rookery Bay (covered in a later chapter.) Without the SOC, southwest Florida's coast might well look like Miami Beach.

A final piece of 1981 legislation created the Save Our Rivers Act (SOR). Funds collected from the documentary stamp tax, a popular source of revenue, would be distributed to the state's five water management districts and title to lands purchased would remain in the district's name.

The year 1986 marked the inauguration of Republican Bob Martinez, a strong environmental advocate, who supported the largest land acquisition program in Florida's history, Preservation 2000. Martinez appointed a citizen's study committee charged with creating a prospective on the state's environmental challenges and opportunities. The committee pointed out that despite the availability of funds and broad political support, acquisition of sensitive lands was lagging behind due to rapidly accelerating land values. The CARL list by 1988 was populated with hundreds projects, all worthwhile and all supported by insistent and persistent constituents. One committee staff estimate set the price of lands on the priority list at $5 billion.³ The solution: immediate issuance of a massive bond issue, backed by the creditworthiness of the State of Florida. With a deft series of compromises, Martinez convinced lawmakers to pass Preservation 2000 with a $3 billion price tag. Bonds would be issued over ten years, with half the proceeds to the CARL program, 30% to the Save Our Rivers program (administered by water management districts), 10% to communities throughout the state,⁴ and the balance to other departments including parks, fish and wildlife, and forestry. Preservation 2000 and (later) Florida Forever ended up being the largest state-funded land acquisition program in America.

While these programs were being enacted—each larger than its predecessor—Florida was moving toward Republican political dominance. Growth management rules and regulations were being pared back, but the legislature's commitment to land preservation was barely touched by shifting politics within the state. Land acquisition programs were still well regarded by an increasingly conservative Republican electorate, who believed that natural resource preservation was the best means to ensure native species survival, recreational opportunities, and the wonderment and beauty of Florida. Beginning with the LATF in 1963 and ending with Preservation 2000, the state's efforts had been supported by governors from both political parties. The laws described here changed the way money flowed. Acquisition on a scale of magnitude sufficient to maintain contiguous species habitat and preserve natural systems at their highest level of functionality through private means was becoming prohibitively expensive. With bonding capacity, large sums of money were made available immediately. Voters in Florida always understood the value of preserving land for public benefit, demonstrated many times at the county level with the approval of a series of local initiatives to supplement purchases by the State of Florida. Today more than one-third of Florida's counties have funded preservation programs in place, resulting from local ballot measures such as Conservation Collier and

Lee 20/20, both of which passed with large pluralities. These programs have saved an additional 375,000 acres. With state and local initiatives, combined with federal inholdings such as Everglades National Park and lands managed for conservation, Floridians have preserved nearly ten million acres of heritage.

In the next three chapters, we will examine how state and federal land acquisition programs played out in southwest Florida. In the case of the Big Cypress, federal intervention was critical and opportune. Purchase of the Fakahatchee Strand and Golden Gate Estates, with numerous small lot owners and inholdings, presented more complicated circumstances, requiring lengthy negotiations and infinite patience. The final stories, about Keewaydin and Cannon Islands, will complete the case histories of buying land for public benefit and use.

CHAPTER 2

BIG CYPRESS SWAMP AND THE FAKAHATCHEE STRAND

T o the west of one of the world's most unique eco-systems, America's Everglades, lay the Big Cypress Swamp. It was also a national treasure: an enormous wet landscape stretching nearly to the coast, draining south into the Ten Thousand Islands. Some six million years ago, a vast, shallow sea blanketed the area with sedimentary deposits of calcific invertebrates, forming a base of porous and permeable limestone. The ecosystem that evolved over the eons on the surface was a curious combination of "uplands, hydric hammocks, poorly drained pine flatwoods, bay swamps, shrub bogs, and cypress swamps . . ."[1] intermingled with trees more than 100 feet tall and 400 years old, a profusion of bromeliads and orchids, and a thriving small prey animal and deer population to support the iconic, endangered Florida panther. Its watershed was also the site of rampant land speculation in a huge development called southern Golden Gate Estates (see Map 2).

An integral part of the landscape was the Fakahatchee Strand, lying immediately to the west of the Big Cypress. It formed a part of the larger swamp but was geologically and ecologically unique. A twenty-five-mile-long shallow valley running north to south, the Fakahatchee had always been critical to the hydrology of southwest Florida. The swamp is fed on the northeast by the Okaloacoochee Slough. Groundwater runs down

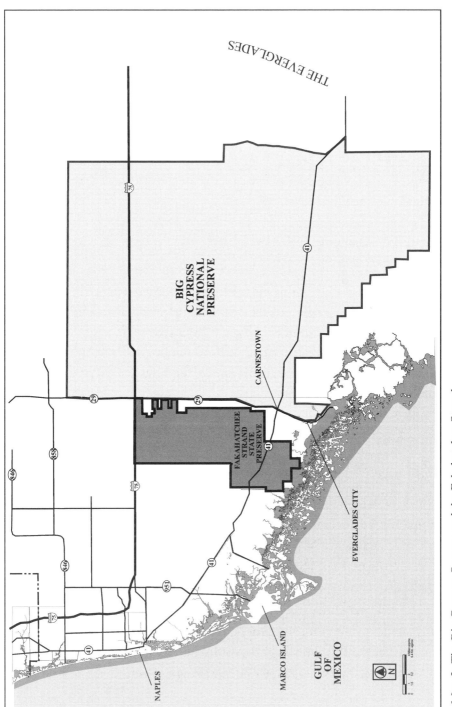

Map 2: The Big Cypress Swamp and the Fakahatchee Strand.

the inner edges of the gradient—only a few miles wide—until it reaches the central strand. There, the water seeps southward beneath a majestic overstory of cypress trees, cathedral-like in their appearance, offering a silent backdrop to the riot of epiphytic bromeliads, ferns, lichen, mosses, and orchids growing among bald cypress knees and lettuce lakes in the understory of a classic strand. But the Tamiami Trail changed that. In the early 1940s, enabled by dragline technology, timber magnates moved into the strand, crisscrossing it with railroad tracks laid on cypress ties and laying waste to the wilderness by clear-cutting the forest, despite a plea from the superintendent of Everglades National Park to his superiors in Washington in 1948, asking them to declare the Fakahatchee a national monument.

Gulf American Corporation

Gulf American Corporation was chartered in 1957 by Baltimoreans Leonard and Julius Rosen for the purpose of selling land in Florida by the bucket to be paid for by the month. Their first development was Cape Coral in Lee County, originally a mangrove forest between the Caloosahatchee River and coastal Pine Island, where the Rosens built model homes around community centers with churches, recreation facilities, and a yacht club—all designed to promote the image of a prosperous and thriving community.

The Rosens, flush with success at Cape Coral, looked south in the early 1960s. Gulf American purchased 112,000 acres north of the Tamiami Trail from the Collier family, to be called Golden Gate Estates. Much of the family's holdings in the eastern and southern parts of the county were areas that were wet and unsuitable for either farming or grazing.

By 1967 Gulf American was the fourth largest publicly traded company in Florida. It owned or controlled more than half a million acres of land but had hit a little bump in the road in Lee County after ripping out mangroves and filling in beyond the bulkhead line to build Cape Coral. The process was delicately phrased "over-dredging" and affected 170 acres. The Internal Improvement Fund in Tallahassee got wind of the matter, and Gulf American, to head off any adverse publicity, offered to swap mangrove fringe it owned at Matlacha Pass as a form of compensation for over-dredging. Damages had been assessed at $765,000, an amount some members of the fund thought inadequate at the time, but the principle of trading land as an offset or mitigation for financial damages held some appeal for the fund's trustees. The Conservancy's old friend, Ney Landrum (at the Division of Recreation and Parks in Tallahassee at the time) held a number of negotiating sessions on behalf of the fund, but Gulf American never offered more than the Matlacha property to atone for its disreputable behavior. Little ever came of the discussions.

Gulf American's over-dredging was, in reality, the least of its problems. By 1968 the company was using photos of Cape Coral in its advertisements for Golden Gate Estates to sell unimproved land to unsuspecting buyers who might assume they were getting all of the amenities shown in the company's elegant and colorful brochures. Backing up the ads were high-pressure boiler rooms, filled with telephone salesmen unloading raw land as fast as they could.

Troubles continued to mount. Three lawsuits were filed against the company, alleging misrepresentation by failing to provide buyers with the exact location of lots they had purchased. Wolves were circling, earnings began to decline, and the American Stock Exchange suspended trading in the company's stock. A fast, prepackaged bankruptcy ensued, and Gulf American sold out to a large national corporation, General Acceptance Corporation of Philadelphia, which formed a new subsidiary called GAC Properties, Inc., to receive the assets.[2]

When Gulf American became GAC, the pace of settlement discussions for over-dredging violations picked up. Conversations held with the Division of Recreation and Parks took on new urgency as GAC sought to clean up the public relations mess left by Gulf American, and it was reported that Landrum had suggested over-dredging fines might go away in exchange for the Fakahatchee Strand. Landrum admitted this had been alluded to from time to time but denied it was part of an overall settlement package. Maybe not, but rumors were flying in the local press that a trade for the Fakahatchee was under way. While mitigation discussions were going on in Tallahassee, GAC voluntarily ceased drainage operations in Golden Gate Estates. Company officials were concerned that the strand, which they were now attempting to trade or sell to the state as a natural area, was being compromised by drainage ditches on the north and west perimeters. As a further attempt to burnish its environmental credentials and move away from the Gulf American mess, the company proposed to fund a new institution called the Fakahatchee Environmental Studies Center. The program would be housed at GAC's Remuda Ranch facility in southern Golden Gate Estates, just to the west of the strand. Scheduled to open in 1972, it would be run by Cedar Crest College of Allentown, Pennsylvania, with a curriculum designed to facilitate a better understanding of subtropical and marine environments, despite the fact that the Fakahatchee was well removed from any marine environments.

Conservancy records indicate that its officers were regularly in touch with Landrum during these negotiations, proposing that not only the Fakahatchee but the entire Big Cypress Swamp watershed be put on the table for acquisition by the state through the EEL program. Part of the Conservancy's reason for approaching Landrum was historical, and the story is worth telling because it introduces important players in the drama about to unfold.

The Big Cypress had been proposed as the site for a massive jetport, which the Dade County Port Authority claimed would serve tens of millions of passengers each year. The groundbreaking in 1968 was attended by the quirky but environmentally attuned Republican Governor Claude Kirk, who supported the project at the time. The first of two runways was built. The second was in trouble because Joe Browder, an Audubon officer, convinced a young man named Nathaniel Reed, recently appointed as Kirk's special advisor, to look at the impact of the project. Reed, according to some accounts, convinced Kirk that the whole thing was a Democratic boondoggle not worth supporting.[3] Kirk then called President Richard Nixon's Interior Secretary Walter Hickel in March to alert him to the situation and invite him on an overnight camping trip, during which he had a chance to look at damage already wrought by the project. Nixon, never terribly concerned about the environment but keenly attuned to politics, had a burning desire to upstage Democratic Senator Henry "Scoop" Jackson's Senate Interior Committee June hearing in Miami on the subject of uncontrolled development in the Big Cypress.

At the urging of Reed, Browder (who had moved to Washington to lobby for environmental groups), and newly appointed Interior Secretary Rogers C.B. Morton, Nixon stunned everyone by asking Congress to appropriate $156 million to acquire the huge swamp in southwest Florida. The Democrat-led Congress got bogged down when Representative Claude Pepper of Florida introduced a competing measure asking for more money to buy more acreage. Nixon swallowed hard and decided to ask Democratic Governor Reubin Askew, newly elected in 1970, to share the cost. Askew, riding a wave of popularity, easily convinced the state legislature to pass the Big Cypress Conservation Act of 1973 to designate the swamp as an "area of critical state concern" and then convinced IIF trustees to put the item on its agenda at its next meeting.

Bernie Yokel appeared before fund trustees to make the case. "It has become abundantly clear in recent years that the limiting factor in maintaining south Florida as a viable environment for people and our wildlife is water."[4] He went on to describe southwest Florida as a unique ecosystem dependent upon clean water flowing slowly into its estuaries, supporting commercial fishing activities with an economic value to Collier County alone of nearly $2 million annually. And one of the main sources of that clean water was the Big Cypress drainage system. While the delicate issue of water quality had always been a key element in the Conservancy's presentations favoring land acquisition, Yokel's economic argument helped because trustees voted to set aside $40 million toward purchase of the swamp. But to seal the deal, the state had to conduct a public hearing.

Opposition arose immediately. Land speculators, including the Rosen brothers, had been selling lots as hunting camps in the Big Cypress for years and were not about to let the state play in their backyard. Conservancy vice president William Oberhelman took detractors to task in July 1973, saying he would not be the least bit sorry if speculators lost value in an area of critical state concern, allowing that purchase of almost any real estate in south Florida was tantamount to gambling. On the other side, Ellis Chism from Miami wrote Askew in December 1973, stating that by buying land in the Big Cypress the state would be committing a "crime." He claimed to be appointed by Dr. Jack M. Weidersheim of the East Collier Landowners' Improvement Committee, an organization numbering 400 but claiming to speak for 35,000 people who owned property north and west of Everglades National Park. Chism claimed that on one occasion, he had traveled "for hours" and seen nothing but upland pine forests and not a single cypress tree. In his opinion, land values in the swamp were comparable to prices of lots on Florida's Gold Coast.

Askew, as the final "area of critical state concern" hearing drew near, decided to personally preside over the two-day meeting in the Naples High School auditorium since the Big Cypress case was the first major test of the Environmental Land and Water Act of 1972 and its provision to set aside important natural areas for conservation. On November 12, 150 people signed up to speak, and more than 800 people attended with signs like "Join the Audubon Society and help make people extinct." Speaking for the Conservancy, Bill Merrihue praised the designation, saying it would be a model for other states. Forty-nine other people spoke, including the Reverend Babb Adams, who said "the issue is clear; it's individual rights."[5] Another speaker argued it was all a communist plot. Despite the uproar, Askew kept control of the meeting. One week later, the Cabinet voted the Big Cypress—but not the Fakahatchee Strand—an "area of critical state concern."

Despite the state's commitment of $40 million, federal funding again languished in Congress as competing bills were introduced and tabled. After Nixon's resignation and some behind-the-scenes maneuvering by Reed and President Gerald Ford, a bill for purchase of a "national preserve" for $117 million passed and was signed on October 11, 1974. Severance damages from the construction of I-75 would provide $45 million, and a swap with the Collier family for federal land in Arizona would provide 83,000 acres. The "national preserve" was a new designation that allowed some flexibility as to oil and mineral exploration rights (retained by the Collier family on the swapped land), development, hunting, fishing, and timbering within the boundaries of public lands. A press release cited three reasons for the purchase: protection of the endangered Florida panther, the economics of tourism, and preservation of south Florida's fresh water supply. The last two arguments were right out of Yokel's playbook. Appropriation quickly followed and on July 9, 1975, Vernon and Loi Duckett of Maryland sold 420 acres, the first sale of an individual holding. By November more than forty people were working on federal and state acquisition of small parcels, a sustained effort that took years to complete.[6]

It was, at the time, the largest expenditure in American history for an addition to public lands, but the job was not complete. The first bill covered a little less than half the acreage; the remainder was purchased by the federal government in 1988, expanding it to nearly 730,000 acres[7] extending from north of highway US 41 down along highway SR 29 to the mangrove forests of the Ten Thousand Islands bordering Everglades National Park.

The Collier family maintained mineral rights after leasing 260,000 acres to the Humble Oil Company, which brought in a well. The family entered into negotiations with Washington in 2002 to buy out those rights, but Congress failed to appropriate the funds. Today, Collier Resources and Breitburn LLC (which now leases the land) are preparing to do a 3-D seismic survey to determine the extent of a possible oil field in the Noble's Grade area of I-75. Another company, Dan A. Hughes of Texas, has decided to lease acreage for test wells to explore for oil and gas outside the western edge of the Florida Panther National Wildlife Refuge.[8]

Saving the Fakahatchee

Saving the Fakahatchee was the lifelong dream of Mel Finn, an attorney and founder of the Florida Nature Conservancy. Along with Captain Franklin Adams, who would later become active in the Florida Wildlife Federation, Finn attempted to have the strand declared a National Monument in 1966. The effort failed, and Gulf American started building hotels on both sides of the highway US 41 junction where it crosses the Faka Union Canal (now known as Port of the Islands).

But Finn never quit. Eight years later, backed by an array of environmental organizations, he convinced the State of Florida to appropriate funds to purchase 24,500 acres in the Fakahatchee Strand from GAC for $4.4 million. The land lay west of highway SR 29, south of Alligator Alley, and north of the Tamiami Trail. The entire parcel was appraised at $9.2 million, and a first right of refusal for the state to purchase remaining lands at the 1974 appraised price was written into the agreement negotiated by Ney Landrum. As part of the deal, GAC agreed to trade lots they had sold in the Fakahatchee for other parcels in Cape Coral and Golden Gate Estates to reduce private inholdings. In 1975 the company deeded an additional 350 acres to the state in lieu of a fine for over-dredging. The following year, Florida purchased another 8,800 acres, and the Conservancy turned over title to 2,000 acres. There were still more than 6,000 lots in private hands within the boundaries of the park. If owners decided not to trade out, they could retain title, and by 1989 very few of those lots had been acquired by the state. But the strand was so inhospitable to permanent human occupation that it had few dwellings and even fewer people who wanted to build a retirement home there.

The Fakahatchee was essentially saved, but it was plagued throughout the ensuing years by poaching and orchid thievery, which led to Susan Orlean's book *The Orchid Thief* and a later movie titled *Adaptation* starring Meryl Streep and Nicholas Cage. The logging road down the spine of the strand would become Jane's Scenic Drive, bisecting the Fakahatchee beginning at SR 29, from which the wondrous cypress forest and numerous small lakes could be seen and enjoyed by thousands of visitors each year. Private inholdings presented few problems, and successive governors have continued to press for land acquisition on a parcel-by-parcel basis.

Saving the Big Cypress Swamp was a straightforward deal enabled by massive amounts of federal money appropriated for a specific purchase. The fact that most of the land was owned by the Collier family was beneficial because negotiations could be conducted with a sophisticated seller. The next case presented a different challenge. There was another

112,000 acres of soggy land in southern Collier County up for development with platted lots, roads, and drainage. The ownership situation was similar to the Fakahatchee with deeds in fee simple sprinkled among numerous small owners and investors. It became the most protracted and difficult land purchase in southwest Florida's history. We now turn to the second chapter in the history of Gulf American Corporation and its successors and the saga of southern Golden Gate Estates.

CHAPTER 3

SOUTHERN GOLDEN GATE ESTATES

*T*he history of Golden Gate Estates brought into focus an overarching question that will arise repeatedly throughout the cases presented in this book:
Where do private property rights end when they negatively impact the
public welfare? This conflict between the common good and property
rights was debated for years in Tallahassee and the courts. The fact that
landowners were compensated assuaged some opponents, but others
saw a more nefarious purpose behind a government agency's attempt to
impose its will on private owners. This was the central issue in the story
about to unfold.

Lying to the west and north of the Fakahatchee Strand and bisected
by Alligator Alley—at the time a two-lane thoroughfare between Naples
and Fort Lauderdale—were two separate Golden Gate Estates. North of
the Alley, Gulf American owned some 70,000 acres, mainly upland forest
with soil that would percolate for septic systems. Another 42,000 acres
in the southern section were virtually uninhabitable, a vast landscape
covered with saw palmetto, cabbage palm hammocks, grassy marshes,
and invasive plant species (see Map 3).

Gulf American believed it could leave northern Golden Gate Estates
in "as is" condition by draining vast areas to the south. Prospects were
encouraged to buy five acres at a time for later subdivision at great profit.

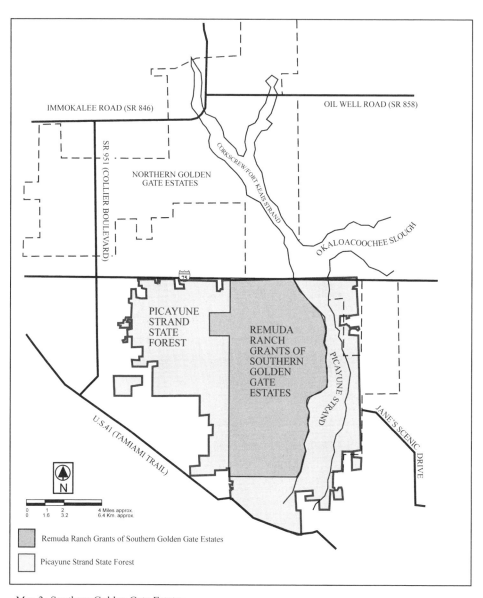

Map 3: Southern Golden Gate Estates.

"Buy it by the acre and sell it by the lot" was the sales pitch that worked best, sucking in many buyers who had no intention of living there but hoped to make a quick buck on resale. Visitors were invited to spend a few days in paradise, flown in from major cities in the eastern half of the country on Gulf American DC-3s to be wined, dined, wined again, and flown over a verdant, saturated landscape.

In addition to 112,000 acres, the Rosen brothers doubled down with a second purchase, including 28,000 acres in the Fakahatchee from the J.C. Turner Lumber Company, parent of Lee-Tidewater Cypress Company, which had also purchased the land from the Collier family for timbering.

The company added part of that land, immediately to the east of southern Golden Gate Estates, to its marketing portfolio by offering parcels in the strand as recreational property for hunting camps with the proviso that it would remain a swamp and never be built out. An area along the edge of the Fakahatchee was marketed as the Remuda Ranch Grants. Lots were sold for as much as $1,000 an acre, which included membership in a skeet-shooting range and the right to hunt in the strand.

By 1973 between 30,000 and 40,000 lots on both sides of the Alley were in the hands of private owners; as time passed, the two sections would go separate ways.

When Gulf American's assets were sold in 1968 by the bankruptcy court (covered in the previous chapter), one of the conditions required the buyer to upgrade infrastructure in the Estates by dredging more than 180 miles of new canals and building hundreds of miles of new roads. By 1974 hydrology in both the northern and southern sections was significantly altered. Former wetlands were dry year-round, and wild fires were breaking out with greater frequency. The canals were carrying a five-fold increase in nitrogen and ammonia and ten times more phosphorous into receiving estuaries.[1] The Faka Union system alone was draining up to 400 million gallons a day during the wet season, disgorging runoff directly into Fakahatchee Bay in the Ten Thousand Islands rather than allowing nature's palliative filtering to process the nutrients. But the more important long-term effect was that salinity was beginning to intrude inland without the constant hydrologic resistance of slowly oozing water.

Nature's drainage system is the most important recharge mechanism for potable water in southwest Florida. Collier County is a contoured landscape, its elevation sloping from forty-two feet at the Immokalee Rise to a little more than three feet at Everglades City. Rainfall drains slowly southward toward the coast; runoff, when allowed to seek nature's water courses, recharges the shallow non-artesian surficial aquifer to provide groundwater for individual homeowners' shallow wells throughout Collier County. Some is lost to evapotranspiration, and some filters through the surficial aquifer and down through porous limestone.[2] Pumping of the intermediate aquifer by the City of Naples and Collier County was creating a hydrologic vacuum, allowing salt water from the coast to insinuate into the system. This problem would increase as population of the city and county grew.

While the City of Naples was concerned about its wells, Collier County was dealing with the escalating expense of constantly fighting fires on dried-out land where no one lived, prompting the county commission to convene a special workshop in the spring of 1975. The Conservancy's Bernie Yokel, invited to speak about downstream effects, blamed the canals for posing a long-term threat to coastal waters by pouring large concentrations of nutrients into nature's nurseries. Taking a page from his presentation to IIF trustees on the Big Cypress, he reiterated that 90% of the species taken in the Gulf of Mexico had begun their lives in an estuary, and that the value of commercial fishing to Collier County was nearly $2 million annually, not including 40,000 sportfishing days a year by tourists and visitors.

Yokel was only one of a long list of speakers at the meeting. The thorny subject of property rights arose again and again, prompting commissioners to "kick the can down the road" by appointing a study committee, which they hoped would keep deliberating through the next election cycle. But the committee was led by Norman Bacon, a man intimately familiar with property rights issues from his time on the Coastal

Area Planning Commission. He brought in Dean Frank Maloney of the University of Florida College of Law as an independent expert to offer advice on how to apply property rights law to essentially undevelopable land in the southern Estates.[3] Maloney was well known throughout the state and highly respected. He had been researching Florida water law for more than ten years and was convinced that, based upon precedent in both federal and state court decisions, landowners could be required to relinquish title to prevent further irreversible damage to the well fields. Bacon was in agreement: "Full-scale development of Golden Gate Estates would be the absolute destruction of southwest Florida. You may not live to see it, but I can guarantee you our children will. Further development is wrong. And it was wrong in 1964."[4]

During the early months of the Bacon committee's work, GAC Properties agreed to suspend road building and canal construction in the most sensitive section of the Fakahatchee drainage system. However, the rich stew of cooperation turned to thin gruel as the matter dragged on. The county, which had once approved GAC's massive development, was having second thoughts about restoring natural flows to rehydrate the area and suppress fire dangers. To add to the concern, parts of the canal system were becoming choked with weeds, making drainage unpredictable and ineffective. The state was putting pressure on the county to assume responsibility for the canal system since the northern Estates was becoming more populated. GAC, seeing this as a chance to unload a problem, threatened a lawsuit if the county failed to take over maintenance of the northern canals. But the company had problems of its own. It was being squeezed by the Federal Trade Commission (FTC) to make good on promises to deliver habitable, well-drained land to almost 40,000 buyers, many of whom were demanding that the situation be addressed quickly since much of the southern Estates had only a thin cover of topsoil, which would not allow for percolation of septic systems.

A sense of urgency was added in the spring of 1976 when Mel Lehman, a hydrologist hired by the county, released a study on water withdrawals from aquifers in southwest Florida. His conclusion: "The stage is set for the evolution of Collier County from a green area into a desert."[5] Lehman estimated that 100 billion gallons of salt water had intruded into the aquifer system beneath the county since southern Golden Gate Estates was canalized. He also pointed out that if you ran a finger around a high school globe at twenty-six degrees north latitude, your finger would pass over the Sahara and other deserts in Saudi Arabia, India, and Mexico. If drainage continued, despite weeds choking the canals, the southern Estates might become another desert in the middle of a prehistoric swamp.[6] Even the esteemed Dr. Frank Craighead could not resist piling on. In a speech delivered to the Collier County Historical Society about man's impact on south Florida, he opined that should the southern Estates be built out, residents would be visited by "clouds of fine quartz sand drifting through every crevice during the winds in winter and by smoke from constant forest fires, while in summer mosquito control would be needed for the intermittently flooded ponds."[7]

Lehman's report led to a series of preposterous ideas, including one that all owners within the 175 square miles of the Estates trade their land for apartments in high-rise condominiums to be built in the Estates,[8] but then a novel proposal emerged. County planning staff, gaining new energy after passage of the Local Comprehensive Planning Act of 1975, suggested subdividing the Estates into three areas based upon suitability for development. Most of the southern Estates would fall into Type III lands, designated as unsuitable. Only 20% north of the interstate fell into that category. The idea, separation of the Estates into northern and southern halves, was not adopted but was prescient in setting the parameters for an important decision leading to hydrologic restoration of southern portion and the Picayune Strand thirty years later.

In September 1977, the State of Florida entered the picture by requesting the Corps of Engineers design a water management system to rehydrate the Estates. The state was fed up with inaction by local study committees whose recommendations kept getting shuffled aside, but its request ended up low on the list of Corps priorities. Bill Merrihue was equally frustrated. "Laid out in the 1960s in a refrigerator-tray design to sell lots sight unseen to buyers all over the world, this vast, desolate, 173-square-mile planners' nightmare, located east of Naples, is criss-crossed with 813 miles of substandard, deteriorating roads and 183 miles of man-made canals, which suck out fresh water into the Gulf at the rate of 162 billion gallons per year. If allowed to develop as now designed, it could accommodate 500,000 people and bankrupt the county to provide support facilities and services."[9] His comments fell on deaf ears.

Then the ground shifted in two places. First, the FTC forced GAC into bankruptcy court for fraudulent sales practices. (GAC later re-emerged as Avatar Holdings, Inc., eventually becoming a successful and respected developer of residential, commercial, and industrial properties.) As a part of the court's orders, the burden of safety and road maintenance in the refrigerator tray was thrown onto property-owning taxpayers of Collier County. The second shift was more subtle: a framing of the long-term ecological consequences carefully documenting the downstream impact of draining the northern Estates. It was called the Naples Bay Study.

The Naples Bay Study

In 1976, under Bernie Yokel's leadership, the Conservancy began work on its signal scientific achievement of the era. Taking more than three years to complete and issued in 1979, it represented the organization's second comprehensive scientific exploration of one of Collier County's two major coastal ecosystems (the other being Rookery Bay).[10] The document represented a quantum leap forward as the Conservancy moved out from beneath the familiar umbrella of land acquisition and into the glare of applied science absent the credibility of a large, established national partner. The board recognized this and made every attempt to assure the public that the study was conducted in an unequivocally independent manner: "The Collier County Conservancy has no constituency to support, no peers to satisfy or to compromise, no fears as to disagreement by people who insist on control due to financial support. The investigative team was free to completely point out the plain, unvarnished facts and to suggest the remedies."[11]

The study was led by Bruce Simpson, who in 1975 had become director of research for the Conservancy and would become a major player during the Golden Gate Estates battles. Born in Chicago and admitted to the Illinois bar in 1937, he became a registered mechanical engineer after being elected CEO of the National Engineering Company of Chicago. Simpson's eclectic background resonates throughout the study. Most chapters on hydrology, water quality and public health, biology, and jurisdictional control over the bay and its tributaries were written by a team of experts in each field, including the redoubtable Bernie Yokel, but the first fifty pages were written by Simpson and were aimed squarely at informing the lay public of a disaster aborning.[12]

The study set out to determine hydrological and chemical characteristics of water in the bay at all depths and on the submerged biota of the bay, with particular emphasis on human health consequences. Geographic scope of the study began six miles from the Golden Gate inflow point and ended at Gordon Pass. Hydrological problems fell into two categories: (1) the effect of flushing fresh water into the main channels of the bay during the wet season from May to November; (2) the sedimentation in and stagnation of water in canals of Port Royal, Aqualane Shores, Royal Harbor, Rock Creek, and the upper reaches of the Gordon River.

Naples Bay was fed by more than 100 separate canals and water sources, each of which had a separate effect on both nutrients and salinity levels in the upper parts of the bay, with the salinity gradient being highest at Gordon Pass and lowest at the headwaters. Average salinity varied from 20 to 35 parts per thousand (ppt) during the year, which prevented a healthy population of filter feeders (such as oysters and clams) from establishing permanent colonies in the bay. Freshwater inflows from small creeks combined for an average input level of 100 cubic feet per second (cfs). However, the Golden Gate Canal during May through November discharged up to 1,500 cfs into the headwaters of the bay. High flows created a stratified freshwater wedge at the top of the bay that prevented the mixing of oxygen and organic materials.[13] This stratification, a lateral divide between salt and freshwater, meant that the heavier salt water would gather on the bottom, killing beneficial sea grass and turtle grass beds in the benthic habitat that relied upon gradual mixing to dilute salinity.

Submerged aquatic vegetation is one of the most important indicators of inland bay health in southwest Florida. It is the proverbial canary in the coal mine. The Golden Gate Canal, draining more than 100 square miles, commenced operations at full capacity without giving plant life and bottom-dwelling creatures of the bay sufficient time to either adapt or move. Dissolved oxygen levels also varied widely, creating profound mortality rates on species unable to survive extreme short-term stress.

A second hydrographic problem revealed by the study was uneven bottoms in the canals dredged to build Port Royal, Aqualane Shores, and Royal Harbor. Dragline operators, knowing they had to fill fingers of land to a given elevation, would simply scoop as much detritus as needed and then move on. The effect of this was to create a series of holes into which heavier and sometimes toxic substances would gather and settle. In addition, many canal entrances had been constructed at a ninety-degree angle to Naples Bay, so when tidal changes occurred there was no directed flushing mechanism in place. The water simply bypassed the canals, sometimes scouring the bottom of the entrance, other times filling in with sediment.

The study's findings on the bay's chemistry were equally startling. Dead-end canals all suffered from extremely low dissolved oxygen levels. The City of Naples' sewage treatment plant, its capacity outstripped by population growth, was the principal point source for phosphorous loading. Urban runoff from parking lots, rooftops, and lawns was the main non–point-source for inorganic nitrogen. An excess of nutrients created massive, suspended, surficial algae blooms in the Gordon River and the upper reaches of the bay. Bacterial contamination was epidemic and especially dangerous to human health in Rock and Haldeman Creeks, where the county had approved "package" septic treatment plants that simply weren't functioning as designed.[14] The two creeks showed unacceptably high levels—exceeding state and federal standards—of vibrious cholera, staphylococcus, salmonella, and *clostridium welchii* (which can cause gangrene in open wounds). The study was blunt in its conclusion: "The County's sanitation system is beyond fixing or being tolerated. It is an outright menace to the citizens of Naples."[15] A planned addition to the city's sewage treatment plant would not, in the study team's estimation, adequately process all effluents. During peak storm events, overflow would continue to be discharged into public waters to prevent the system from being overwhelmed. The authors deemed this totally unacceptable.

In a curtsy to county politics, the study specifically disavowed northern Golden Gate Estates as the source of high nitrogen levels but cited flow variability during the rainy season as the main cause for smothering benthic habitat in the upper bay. The recommended solution was to limit freshwater coming down the canal to twenty to thirty million gallons per day (mgd) through a series of retention ponds and runoff barriers called plugs. Bulldozed into place, they would raise the overall water level to overrun the plugs during summer rains throughout the 100 square miles being drained with a series of control elevations. In addition to regulating inflow to Naples Bay, the system would impound freshwater in upland areas for recharge into the surficial aquifer as a way of renourishing drinking water for the growing multitude of homeowners' shallow wells within the county.

The study set forth a number of other recommendations, each exhaustively researched from both a scientific and legal perspective. One idea, quickly abandoned, was that homeowners' discharge pipes from swimming pools, tennis courts, lakes, and roof runoff be directed into the sanitary sewer system. This was totally impractical at the time because the sewer system was at or over capacity.

Another recommendation was a detailed plan to deal with eutrophication of canals abutting the bay, mainly Port Royal and Aqualane Shores, by dredging them to uniform depths, followed by periodic inspection and maintenance. This would be financed by a single, independent taxing authority to assume management of the entire system from the Estates to Naples Bay. Water flowed with no regard for political boundaries, and creation of a district based upon an ecosystem was innovative and threatening. In the case of the Naples Bay watershed, jurisdictions included private landowners, the City of Naples, Collier County, the South Florida Water Management District, the Big Cypress Basin Board,[16] the Florida Department of Environmental Regulation, the Florida Department of Natural Resources, the Environmental Protection Agency, the U.S. Army Corps of Engineers, and a host of subsets of each. Many of the agencies had been created in the distant past to deal with entirely different problems. The authors acknowledged that existing government bodies would never relinquish turf without a battle and suggested that each agency first agree that the *status quo* was unacceptable and then contribute to the creation of alternatives, emphasizing voluntary cooperation rather than mandated solutions.

The science of the study was never contested, but other than modifications to the East Naples sewage treatment plant and passage of ordinances involving seawall and dock safety equipment, few recommendations were seriously considered, much less implemented. Most were politely ignored, with one notable exception. That is where we now turn.

Enter the Kruses

With unwanted maintenance on its shoulders, the county commission had come to regard the southern Estates as the county's "biggest single problem" and, with encouragement from Bernie Yokel, voted to ask for federal intervention, that is, the Corps of Engineers.[17] When Yokel's name appeared in the newspaper, it provoked two Estates residents, Paul and Mary-Frances Kruse, into ginning up a mimeographed newsletter warning: "There is a growing uneasiness among Golden Gate Estates people regarding the long-term and potentially unhealthy interest shown by the Collier County Conservancy in the Estates area."[18] Rhetoric was notched up in each successive issue. Initially regarded as irrelevant to the debate, the newsletter began to be taken more seriously in November 1980 after Mary-Frances Kruse was elected to the Collier County Commission and her husband announced publication of a broadsheet newspaper, the *Golden Gate Eagle*, to replace mimeographed mailings.

Then a new player, the Big Cypress Basin Board, entered the game, covering the Big Cypress Swamp basin in Collier County and tied in to the larger South Florida Water Management District. Citing the Naples Bay Study, the board petitioned the state to purchase fifty square miles of land in the southern Estates abutting the Fakahatchee. Mary-Frances Kruse, with her newfound megaphone as a county commissioner, weighed in: "It's that encroaching green mass again," she said in reference to state purchases in Everglades National Park, Rookery Bay, and the Big Cypress.[19] Despite denials to the contrary, the Kruses had decided the Conservancy and Corps of Engineers were conspiring to plug the Golden Gate Canal. Claiming to represent anywhere from 60,000 to 90,000 homeowners, they started firing away, complaining at a February 1981 seminar put on by the local Audubon chapter:

> A combination of bureaucratic stupidity and a full-scale propaganda effort by the special interests deluged the scientifically naïve public with misquotes, twisted data, and outright fabrications. It is axiomatic in the field of propaganda that if you make a lie big enough and repeat it often enough, it will be accepted as the truth. Perhaps the two most blatant efforts were the heavily biased Phase I, Golden Gate Estates Redevelopment Study, paid for primarily by the Collier County Conservancy, and the hastily drawn Naples Bay Study published by the Collier County Conservancy, a private and originally a land acquisition company.[20]

Bruce Simpson, who authored the executive summary of the Naples Bay Study and been recently elected president of the Southern Waterways Society, wrote the *Naples Daily News* to intone, "Mr. Kruse is a nobody in our field. He is not a marine biologist and does not hold any credentials in the field. He has spent his life as a photographer and currently works for Collier County as a restaurant inspector."[21] Undaunted by the criticism, the "nobody" founded the Land and Water Management Council of Collier County, Inc., appointing himself as executive director. Membership in the organization was $10 per year; one could become a trustee for $1,000. Interestingly, one of the other founders listed was the president of Lely Estates, Inc., Christiaan Duvekot, who in 1976 had attempted to cut a deal with the Conservancy for the purchase of Barefoot Beach in an attempt to turn a quick buck (covered in a later chapter titled "Pelican Bay and Barefoot Beach").

Charges and countercharges were being aired publicly, but three realities were becoming clear to almost everyone. First, southern Golden Gate Estates was virtually uninhabitable. The area was being used as a drop point for South American drugs being flown in by DC-3s. Second, the 71,000 acres north of Alligator Alley, with their water table dropped by six feet courtesy of the Golden Gate Canal, contained nearly 22,000 already. It would be patently unfair to inundate the subdivision during the rainy season. Finally, the Collier County government had no stomach and little money to rebuild the Golden Gate Canal into a meandering flow way with a series of controlled elevation barriers and retention ponds to cleanse freshwater flowing into Naples Bay.

In early spring 1981, the Southwest Florida Regional Planning Council awarded the Conservancy a $65,600 contract to extend its study of the chemical characteristics of storm water runoff into Naples Bay. The Kruses went ballistic. Mary-Frances Kruse opposed the contract from her commissioner's perch because she believed the first Naples Bay Study was full of inaccuracies.[22] Paul Kruse's organization, now called Golden Gate Estates Residents and Supporters, promised to launch a letter-writing campaign in which 60,000 property owners would write President Ronald Reagan and Governor Bob Graham, expressing their displeasure with the contract. While it gathered banner headlines in the *Miami Herald* and *Naples Daily News*, the letter-writing campaign failed, partly because the letter-reader in Tallahassee was one of the great proponents of wetland restoration in south Florida.

By April 1981, Merrihue, exasperated by lassitude on the part of state and local officials, wrote Senator Lawton Chiles, characterizing the situation in Golden Gate Estates as "a problem far beyond our capabilities to solve without Federal help—and (to) let you decide if it is worthy of receiving your help."[23] He went on to explain that the Corps' belated study on drainage, planned for 1982, might be the sword to cut the Gordian knot. After appearing before the Senate Appropriations Subcommittee on Energy and Water Resources, Chiles replied that members were sympathetic. Finally, with continuing support from Chiles, the Corps study was funded for 1982 and 1983.[24]

Later that year, Fred Vidzes of the Big Cypress Basin Board, who had first proposed state purchase of fifty square miles in the southern Estates, was at it again. Having been deeply involved with the IIF in the late 1960s and early 1970s as head of the Land Management Division and instrumental in getting Rookery Bay designated as a state aquatic reserve, he based his argument on a conservation agreement negotiated when GAC came out of bankruptcy, suggesting that landowners south of Alligator Alley be offered two choices: File claims against the company or trade for land in the northern section of the Estates. Mary-Frances Kruse jumped all over the proposal, arguing that the issue of land ownership was not settled by the bankruptcy court. "It would just add more players to the game," she said.[25] Vidzes' proposal came to naught, but the subject of dividing the Estates into northern and southern sections, originally the idea of county planning commission staff in 1977, was back on the table. The main reason Vidzes' idea failed was that the state was running out of money. But the next year, Dan Crabb, a land purchase specialist at the Department of Natural Resources, wrote Merrihue: "It has come to our attention that Collier County has been auctioning a number of the Remuda Ranch lots for delinquent taxes. This disturbs me because the state will eventually have to buy these same lots back at market value (possibly more in the case of condemnation)."[26] Crabb went on to suggest that the Conservancy might short-circuit rampant land speculation in the southern Estates by purchasing lots on the courthouse steps and selling them back to the state at cost. Merrihue was intrigued for two reasons. First, the plan made sense to him. Second, the Conservancy was in a full-court press to get Crabb's department to buy Cannon Island (covered in the next chapter). But the idea never gained traction because Conservancy leadership, already stretched thin, had its hands full with other matters.

Changes in the Wind: The State Intervenes

By 1986 the annual maintenance cost to taxpayers of maintaining roads and canals in the northern Estates was $1.8 million. Hardly any work was being performed on the 290 miles of roads in the southern Estates, but the cost of fighting fires was running more than $1 million a year. The *Golden Gate Eagle*, started by Paul Kruse, was now in the hands of Jerry Drake as a sixteen-page broadsheet with an editorial focus on the northern Estates. The federal government had decided to upgrade Alligator Alley into an interstate highway, which would require fencing and complex interchanges, limiting access to both northern and southern Estates. The upgrade had bipartisan support in Congress, provided landowners received proper compensation. Finally, the Corps issued its long-awaited report recommending that the two easternmost canals in the Faka Union drainage system be decommissioned and that a series of water-control structures (weirs) be built to re-create sheet flow to diminish seasonal freshwater inundations of Fakahatchee Bay and the Ten Thousand Islands.

In May 1986, the *Miami Herald* ran a story under a banner headline that began "The Conservancy won tentative approval Thursday of its request to add nearly 55,000 acres of low-lying land in southern Golden Gate Estates to the Save Our Rivers list."[27] Created by Bob Graham when he was governor, it was technically known as the River Resources Act of 1981 and would eventually save 1.7 million acres throughout the state. The program allowed water-management districts to purchase sensitive lands and lease them for suitable uses.[28] The Save Our Rivers designation by the water district was critical because the CARL program was underfunded at the time and the southern Estates were ranked low on the priority list. A Save Our Rivers designation was the best hope; the South Florida Water Management District (SFWMD) had $40 million available from a documentary stamp tax, generating $4.5 million a year.

By August the persistent Fred Vidzes was heading a study committee established by the (then) Department of Environmental Regulation and backed by the Corps to "prepare a plan of action for the protection and restoration of southern Golden Gate Estates."[29] Called the Committee on the Restoration of Golden Gates Estates, one of its members was Toivo Tammerk, new president of the Conservancy. The committee had two overriding concerns: Plugging the southern canals must not cause flooding in the northern Estates, and property owners must be fairly and fully compensated. At its mid-October meeting, the group floated a recommendation that the southern Estates be designated an "area of critical state concern" to help fast-track acquisition. Two weeks later, in an attempt to gain public support, Vidzes' group met at the Golden Gate Community Center before an unsympathetic gathering of landowners who alleged, among other things, that the state was trying to flood out the northern Estates to gain mineral rights to the entire area. It was not going to be easy.

Finally, at a November 1986 public meeting on the Conservancy campus, Vidzes' committee issued its recommendations: expand the Big Cypress "area of critical state concern" to southern Golden Gate Estates; move it up on the state's CARL list and complete acquisition within five years; accept the Corps' proposal after review by the water management district; establish a land acquisition office in Collier County; place a moratorium on permitting in the southern Estates; and undertake a massive program of public education about the pending buyout. With support from the governor's office and the Department of Environmental Regulation, the county did not have to take the considerable heat. It was delighted to be able to sit this one out.

Buyout Begins

The buyout proceeded slowly, mainly due to a lack of staff to locate more than 17,000 owners throughout the world holding title to 41,000 acres. After the first five years, the state office in Tallahassee had managed to purchase only 1,300 acres. The Conservancy took over much of the clerical work, having interns and volunteers comb through county records and prepare contracts for sale before sending them to Tallahassee to forward to landowners. The effort paid off. After two years of slogging through thousands of deeds recorded with Collier County, the Conservancy had managed to contact nearly all property owners. Forty percent of them—mostly small-lot holders—accepted either the first or second offer from the state.

While the buyout proceeded, legal battles continued. A suit was brought by landowners in 1988, alleging that the state's offers were too low. Reappraisal resulted and land sales resumed, but by 1996 only 18,000 acres had been purchased. A number of larger landowners and speculators remained unwilling to sell, and the state refused to start plugging canals and removing roads until all parcels had been purchased. Avatar, successor to GAC, was making matters even more difficult by continuing to sell lots to buyers in Miami.[30]

The Conservancy's interest languished during the late 1980s but was reinvigorated when David Guggenheim became its new president. Concerned about sporadic funding from Tallahassee, he plunged in by encouraging Collier County, which had been contentedly sitting on the bench, to proceed on its own path independent of the state's efforts. In September 1996, with formation of the Keep Collier Paradise committee, county commissioners were pressed into voting a green space tax—a half-cent sales tax increase—on the November ballot to generate $80 million over four years. The initiative went down in defeat, an unusual loss in southwest Florida brought about by a lack of enthusiasm from bench-sitting commissioners and an effective anti-tax campaign.

The chain of events reached an even lower point when the county commission voted in late 1996 to eliminate any support for further buyout by deleting a section of the county's comprehensive plan supporting acquisition of the southern Estates, replacing it with a vaguely worded nostrum pledging protection of natural resources. The timing could not have been worse because southwest Florida's Washington delegation had lined up matching funds from two sources: the Farm Bill and the Water Resources Development Act (WRDA). Both pieces of legislation were known as "Christmas trees" decorated with earmarks. The Farm Bill had a history of financing a multitude of local projects favored by individual members of Congress; WRDA mainly covered federal projects related to the waters of the United States, including wetlands.

With money waiting to be appropriated in Washington, local support was critical in shaking loose state funds as part of a fifty-fifty match. The situation brought the Conservancy and other environmental groups to a raucous commission meeting on April 22, 1997, where they won a reversal of the initial decision to delete that part of the comp plan pulling back from supporting a buyout of the southern Estates. Part of the deal with the county was a commitment by the Conservancy and partner groups to keep pressure on the Department of Environmental Protection to complete reappraisal of the land as soon as possible. Finally, in June, Vice President Al Gore announced that $25 million from the Farm Bill would go toward the purchase of land in Collier County, to be matched by the state's Preservation 2000 program. The two together would enable the purchase of an estimated 62,000 acres. Maybe.

In a somewhat perverse development, the 1988 and 1992 lawsuits filed by landowners began to work in favor of the state. By November 1997, settlement agreements mailed out to plaintiffs were coming in faster than expected. The economy was booming, and many speculators were looking at better investments than mosquito-infested swampland in interior south Florida. To move things along, the Conservancy repeated its earlier effort by assigning a full-time staff member to keep track of property owners' responses, and by June 1998 the $25 million promised from the federal Farm Bill was deposited in Tallahassee.

A major breakthrough occurred in September, when Avatar Holdings, after eighteen months of negotiation, agreed to part with 8,500 acres of its land. This gave the state additional momentum. Then, as the dot.com stock market bubble burst in 2000, many investors and specu-lators were pressed for liquidity. By 2005 all parcels except two were in state ownership. The first parcel, owned by the Miccosukee tribe, was condemned by the state. It became the subject of a lawsuit filed by a tribal lawyer and ended up in settlement. The other parcel was owned by Jesse Hardy, a tough, old Cracker and former employee of GAC who claimed to farm and mine 160 acres. The state wheedled and cajoled to no avail and in April 2005 received court approval to condemn Hardy's land. For a short time, he became a local hero to the horde of property-rights proponents in southwest Florida, until finally relenting and selling his property to the state for $4.95 million.

With the last two parcels in hand, the SFWMD and Corps began to methodically plug canals, fill in ditches, and reintroduce sheet flow. A series of weirs trapped water so it could percolate and allowed a series of natural wetlands to develop throughout the 60,000-plus acres compris-ing the Picayune, allowing seasonal freshwater outflows to be filtered and partially absorbed into the aquifers before reaching Fakahatchee Bay and the Ten Thousand Islands. Conservancy scientists under con-tract to the SFWMD have been carrying out a series of baseline studies to measure the rejuvenated and burgeoning biota. Birds, animals, and reptiles are returning to reclaim their natural habitat, and the ecosystem is gradually returning to its aboriginal state. The restoration project is a shining example of nature's ability to bounce back despite decades of abuse, and the result to date has been remarkable.

Lessons Learned

Experience with Big Cypress, the Fakahatchee, and Golden Gates Estates carried with it a number of lessons. The purchase of southern Golden Gate Estates demonstrated the value of Florida's Conservation and Rec-reation Lands Act of 1979 in its various iterations over the years. With-out ongoing financing through the original act and its successor, Preser-vation 2000, the southern Estates would have remained an encumbrance to the health of the Ten Thousand Islands. In 2011 an additional $50 million was appropriated for reconstruction. Support from Washington and Tallahassee was available for two reasons: The project created good jobs, and appropriations for Corps projects are made annually and, once funded, are generally carried through to completion.

Golden Gate Estates and the Fakahatchee were examples of government preemptively taking land. The southern Golden Gate Estates buyout and restoration was facilitated by federal intervention because local elected officials preferred to stay out of the interstice where private property rights and the general welfare came into conflict. They appointed committees to act as proxies on their behalf and generally stayed out of the line of fire.

The experience taught environmental groups that consistently applied pressure at the federal, state, and local levels was critical even though it might drag on for decades. Persistence became the critical denominator of success. It also called into question the prevailing wisdom, based on the Big Cypress buyout, that large chunks of land could be brought into public ownership with relatively little opposition. The problem was a misunderstanding of the motives for small inholdings—ranging from private hunting camps built with little or no expectation of municipal services to residential sites purchased with the belief that they represented a little piece of paradise. Opposition to government purchase was vigorous and sustained when it had a central focus, such as the efforts of Paul and Mary-Frances Kruse—less so when there was no rallying point.

The next two cases were quite different. Unlike southern Golden Gate Estates and the Fakahatchee, both involved large and sophisticated private owners making it easier to establish a platform for substantive negotiations. We now turn from inland to the coast, to Keewaydin and Cannon Islands and to the gateway to Rookery Bay. Bill Merrihue knew the two islands represented the best opportunity remaining in southwest Florida for a long ribbon of beachfront high-rises after fighting the "road to nowhere." Combined, they formed the outer buffer to his precious Rookery Bay, and they had to be preserved to prevent despoiling the ecosystem he worked so hard to save.

CHAPTER 4

KEEWAYDIN (KEY) AND CANNON ISLANDS

K eewaydin is the main outer island protecting
Rookery Bay. As a classic barrier island, it was
constantly changing due to the interaction of
colonizing plants, tides, wind, and weather. Beach plant communities
were limited by the low nutritional value of the growing medium, generally a combination of quartzite and calcium carbonate (highly pulver-
ized shells) forming the protective fore dunes populated by sea oats and
herbaceous scrubs. Attempts to stabilize the island's shoreline by introducing exotics such as the Australian pine[1] created a threat of dominating native plant species adapted to coastal weather. Keewaydin varied
in width from 4,000 feet at the northern end to less than 200 feet at
the southern tip, with elevation ranges from three to seven feet on the
western edge gently sloping downward toward a back bay to the east.
The island's beachfront had been periodically reshaped by wind-driven
downdrift, tropical storms, and hurricanes. The northern tip was developed in a relatively minor way with low-impact camping facilities.

Dellora and Lester Norris began accumulating land on the island in
the 1940s and by the 1960s owned the northernmost 70%. The northern
tip had five cottages, a lodge, and a school originally built as a summer
camp in the 1930s by Chester Kittridge. The school's curriculum was
based on the island's marine ecology. The facility passed through two

successive owners and, after falling upon hard times during the Second World War, was sold to the Norris family. John Pulling, a member of one of Naples' oldest families, owned the southernmost two miles.[2]

In 1960 Hurricane Donna inundated and destroyed much of Gordon Pass. The storm was a wake-up call to coastal development. With a twelve-foot surge forcing water inland almost ten miles, homes along Naples area beaches were hard hit; more than 300 were totally destroyed. Lester Norris attempted to prevent future damage from the Gulf by building a rock jetty to create a swirling deposition that would eventually use wind and tide to build a deep, sandy beach at the northwest corner of his property. But by 1977 the jetty was failing to protect the island, and strong northwest winds had moved most of the sand as far south as Little Marco Pass. Australian pines that had been uprooted by wave action were strewn about, and La-vern Gaynor, the Norrises' daughter, recalled arriving from Chicago to see that more than 100 feet of beach had washed away. "It's scary," she said, "I was shocked when I saw the beach."[3] Lester Norris asked the State of Florida to come look at the problem. Department of Natural Resources investigator Spencer Rogers, after walking the beach, declared that sand movement on barrier islands was a naturally occurring phenomenon and recommended the state take no action.

Norris finally convinced the Corps of Engineers to use the northern end of the island as a deposition site for sand dredged out of nearby navigable channels, which led to a public argument over federal funds being used to preserve private beaches, an argument Lester Norris earnestly wanted to avoid.[4] To put a good face on the controversy, he deeded acreage in the middle of the island to the State of Florida as a form of voluntary compensation. It was a good move politically, but the controversy would continue publicly, to Norris's great displeasure. He was a very private man who avoided the spotlight whenever someone wanted to shine it on him or his wife.

Dellora Norris passed away in 1979. After her death, Lester Norris brought his children into joint ownership of the island and in 1980 told the *Naples Star* that he was considering a plan to develop 375 of the 2,700 acres owned by the family: 175 acres in the City of Naples and 200 in Collier County. He sketched out two different alternatives. The first included a golf course with clubhouse amenities, the second, a passive natural park traveled only by electric carts. The announcement was met with some dismay, but Key Island, Inc., made a brilliant move by hiring the man Merrihue had worked with on Pelican Bay, John Simonds, who favored the development plan. Despite affirmation by Simonds, the Conservancy was concerned:

> At present the owners have in mind no specific proposals for either short-term or long-range developments, having an existing resort installation of unquestioned quality and approximately 900 acres total of high and developable land. It is only their reasonable intent to keep their future development options open. As any specific expansion or development proposals may be formulated they will of course be subject to all normal planning, regulations, procedures, reviews, and hearings then required.[5]

Norris went to great lengths to assure the press that his ideas were only conceptual; development was not imminent. The plan never made it off the drawing board, and with Lester Norris's passing in 1981, his daughter, Lavern, was left to spend the next seven years attempting to get the State of Florida to buy the family's holdings on the island for a state park.

There was no progress in Tallahassee—the price tag was simply too big for the Conservancy to swallow whole—but Merrihue had his heart set on preserving Keewaydin Island. The first ray of hope shone in 1983, when the Timken family of Canton, Ohio, offered to donate two slices purchased from John Pulling at the northern edge of his subdivided land—not a lot of acreage, but it marked a beginning. Appraised at $100,000, the two parcels would become the first property to be placed in a conservation easement under a new law passed by the Florida leg-islature. Sponsored by Mary Ellen Hawkins, a local legislator who had been strongly supported in Tallahassee by the Conservancy and Florida Audubon, the law allowed a property owner to sell, lease, or bequeath land restricted in perpetuity use by future owners in exchange for a 60% reduction in ad valorem taxes.[6] A soon as the bill was signed into law, Merrihue mailed letters to all property owners on the island, informing them of the new benefit. There is no record as to how many responded, but Merrihue confided in a letter to Timken that he was not sanguine and sought permission to sell the donated lots after having them des-ignated as conservation.[7] Merrihue's plan was to use Timken proceeds buy up other properties on the island, place them under easements, and resell them in a daisy-chain series of transactions. Timken consented, but the program never produced the result Merrihue hoped for.

While Merrihue was working on slices in the lower part of Kee-waydin, Lavern Norris Gaynor was doing all she could to get the state interested in the northern end. She felt she was making little progress, although one offer from the state in August 1981 had been turned down by the Key Island, Inc., board due to complexities in settling Lester Nor-ris's estate). Gaynor finally got an option agreement, which the state, at the last minute, indefinitely extended with no explanation.

In May, Senator Franklin Mann, who had been instrumental in saving Cannon Island (covered later in this chapter), introduced a bill to extend the state's jurisdiction and "quick-take" powers in Rookery Bay, including Keewaydin Island. Gaynor reached the boiling point: "I wish to state my objections to your SB 40, which will empower the State's threat of eminent domain being applied to Rookery Bay property. . . . we would not be in favor of the tendency of a morally arrogant environmental movement to give short shrift to landowners. Your SB 40 certainly supports that ten-dency, and I feel that your bill is very socialistic and unfortunate."[8]

According to Gaynor, negotiations with potential private party buy-ers began in 1984.[9] She knew Internal Improvement Fund trustees had $30 million available and could approve purchase of the entire island, but she failed to understand their reluctance. She was also concerned that some potential buyers would want unrestricted development rights so she negotiated only with those she felt would act responsibly, eventually making a deal with John Remington to purchase all 2,700 acres and build only seventy-five homes (contingent upon receiving zoning changes and permitting approvals). An option agreement was signed in January 1988 after notifying the Department of Natural Resources and the Conservancy that a deal was on the table. Any further negotiations with the state were terminated that March.[10]

Before Remington's plans for the island were formally presented to the Naples City Council, a petition was filed with the city's planning board for a non-conforming use: a new two-story parking garage and fuel station at the southern end of Gordon Drive in Port Royal to serve as a launching site for Key Island residents and visitors. A small parking area and fueling station already existed at the site, but expansion into a garage required rezoning. Residents along Gordon Drive were incensed and marched *en masse* to the June planning board meeting to blast the plan. Nancy Stroud, an attorney representing property owner Jack Donahue, founder of the Federated Funds in Pittsburgh, complained "the use is incompatible with the residential nature of Gordon Drive. It could not be more incompatible."[11] Conservancy attorney Dick Grant reiterated the organization's belief that the parking garage was little more than a prelude to full development of the island. After nearly five hours of heated testimony, the board adjourned to take the matter up again three days later.

When the meeting reconvened, acrimony ruled. Joel Kuperberg, after years of involvement with the Conservancy, had been hired by the Gaynor family partnership as a consultant. He excoriated the city for failing to press the state to buy the property from Key Island, Inc., suggesting that the city and Conservancy restart negotiations (which was unlikely because Remington's option had foreclosed that possibility until January 1989). George Gaynor accused the Conservancy of ducking the subject during the previous seven years and, until the Remington deal was announced, having no interest whatsoever in supporting public purchase of the island. Gaynor's attorney, Dudley Goodlette, who fifteen years later would become a state representative, fumed over the apparent disregard of property rights throughout the discussion. The planning board continued to take comments until exhausted; it adjourned at midnight for a week. But the next two meetings were no better and, after twenty hours of testimony, the board was at impasse. The matter was pushed to the Naples City Council with no recommendation.

Skirmishing over the garage was just the opening salvo. The full Keewaydin Island development package was scheduled for hearing at the planning board in August, and both sides were bringing in heavy artillery. When Remington's plan for the island was made public, it turned out to be a bit tumescent. In addition to seventy-five homes for members of the Keewaydin Club, it proposed construction of forty-three guest-houses, thirty staff-housing units, and forty-five boat docks. A shocked Mary Dearholt, board chair of the Conservancy, urged a letter-writing campaign to city council members, noting the irony of a situation in which Lester Norris's property on the island should be subject to such controversy. She went on to warn Remington and his investors that "there is no right or guarantee to recover anticipated or desired profits,"[12] a statement lawyer Goodlette found appalling.

The Conservancy, at the root of it, viewed development of any barrier island as an incompatible use. Arguments presented at the planning board centered on the city's comprehensive plan, which identified "vital and conservation/limited development areas" as requiring formal assessment of environmental impacts, which would potentially diminish natural resource values at the site or in surrounding areas. In the organization's opinion, Remington had not dealt with the impact on water quality, had inadequately described the extent of support activities such as mosquito spraying, and had completely ignored the long-term cumulative effect on Rookery Bay Aquatic Preserve. Nor did Remington's plan address possible development of the 200 acres he owned within Collier County's jurisdiction after the city portion was built out.[13]

Adding fuel to the fire, George Gaynor learned about pending condemnation of Cannon Island by the county to smooth the path for a $2.9 million state purchase. Gaynor thought he could see handwriting on the wall and asked the county commission to send a letter to Tallahassee indicating interest in buying the northern end of Keewaydin Island, which would automatically preempt any condemnation proceedings. The commission declined by a vote of 4–0, but Gaynor persisted after commission chair Burt Saunders admitted he intended to bring up the subject of condemnation at the next meeting. Gaynor saw this as a plot to discourage Remington from exercising his option and publicly accused Saunders of being "in bed" with an unnamed local environmental organization. The Conservancy, in turn, saw Gaynor's actions as a sneaky way to derail state purchase of Cannon Island just to the south and east of Keewaydin.

In May the planning body voted 3–2 to recommend approval of a revised plan submitted by Remington for 70 houses, expansion of the clubhouse, and construction of 40 boat docks. This followed its vote five days earlier to allow 51 parking spaces at the shore station. As a *quid pro quo*, Remington agreed to apply for city annexation of 2,270 acres currently in the county, which he believed would preempt the Conservancy's concerns about the rest of the island.[14] With its decision, the planning board completely ignored city comprehensive plan amendments adopted that January, as well as recommendations from natural resources and planning staff at city hall, and the issue was scheduled for hearing and vote by city council in June.

In a stunning reversal, the council voted 4–3 against Remington's plan but allowed him to build 42 homes at elevations to exceed federal guidelines in effect at the time.[15] The deciding vote was cast by Ned Putzell, former president and board chair of the Conservancy. While Remington's application was deficient in its failure to identify financial backers (a standard requirement in the application process), it also failed to describe a rationale for the project. Putzell based his vote upon compliance with the city's comprehensive plan despite an outcry that other factors were at work. In addition, while offering conservation easements for some tidal areas, Remington insisted on retaining ownership of the bay bottoms, which negated any public benefit, a necessary component of the application.

With approval for 42 dwellings and despite litigation still before the courts, Remington and his partners, Bolton and Lu Drackett, decided to close on the property with Key Island, Inc., which had placed the Keewaydin Clubhouse on the National Registry of Historic Places before closing on the sale. Two years later, the Drackett family bought Remington out and eventually sold about 2,600 acres to the state for $13.5 million, at which point the public owned 85% of the island. The balance remained privately held and went through a series of ownership changes until 1997, when Jack Donahue purchased the northern tip of the island for a family compound, demolished the existing cottages, and replaced them with houses built to contemporary standards for a barrier island. He relocated the clubhouse and faithfully restored it to original condition.

Keewaydin Island Beach Club

With the state owning most of the island, the story should end, but a number of lots from the John Pulling days remained in private hands in the lower part of the island. In 2007 Jack Antaramian, through Basil Street Partners, had completed a large multi-use commercial and residential complex at the head of Naples Bay and needed beach access as an amenity to attract buyers. He approached the county to grant a conditional-use permit for two of the privately held lots, which would allow him to build a beach facility of 2,925 square feet with a boat dock on the Inland Waterway for members and their guests to disembark. Power would be provided by generator, a septic system would be installed, drinking water would be brought in by shuttle, and the facility would close at dusk. Basil Street Partners advertised the beach club in both print ads and on its website, but when the county Environmental Advisory Committee heard the proposal in January 2006, it was unanimously voted down as an incompatible use.[16] The petition was pulled by the developer and put on indefinite hold until early 2007, when Basil Street Partners proposed a scaled-back version. While reduced, it still represented the first facility to apply for a conditional-use permit on Keewaydin Island under terms of the latest growth management plan. It was the proverbial "camel's nose under the tent."[17] The Conservancy opposed it based on grounds that a special overlay required any conditional use to have a public benefit. Basil Street, realizing this, had thrown in a few "public" memberships to sop up the opposition, but the idea ran aground again at the county's advisory boards.

Then politics began to sneak in. Collier County floated the idea of running a shuttle to Keewaydin Island from Bayview Park. The City of Naples, not to be outdone, proposed to annex the entire island. This last maneuver would give remaining private owners on the island a right to create a "planned development," offering more flexibility than county zoning. Jack Antaramian had done a number of developments in the city and was known to be tight with Mayor Bill Barnett, but annexation required state participation because the Department of Environmental Protection owned the Dracketts' land through Rookery Bay National Estuarine Research Reserve. Finally it came down to a matter of dollars and sense; the numbers simply didn't work. Ad valorem revenues would fall well short of covering expenses to provide city services to the island, and a staff memo to the Naples City manager ended with a cold warning: "Expenditures in this report exceed the estimated revenue by $126,763 (per annum)."[18]

Basil Street Partners finally gave up on its beach club and the county shuttle was deep-sixed by the economy, but the island remains vulnerable even today. Private inholdings in the middle of the island could be built out, albeit with highly restrictive code requirements. Owners could sell their land for commercial facilities despite the battle fought and lost by Basil Street Partners. On the positive side of the ledger, the presence of the Donahue family at the north end of the island represents a stabilizing force, and Rookery Bay staff is working hard to maintain the pristine beauty of the island—one of the premier sea turtle nesting locations in southwest Florida—while providing access for use by the public in a manner compatible with sustainable management of a barrier island. Most of the Keewaydin Island story is one of land preservation through purchase, but the beach club facility required a shift in emphasis: how to plan for the appropriate use of sensitive resources. Landowners will almost always attempt to maximize the value of their holdings, as in the case with Basil Street Partners, but a rapidly growing state like Florida needed some controls.

Cannon Island

The story of how Cannon Island came into public ownership is worth telling because it was a microcosm of the broad range of difficulties encountered in creating the massive sanctuary that is today Rookery Bay National Estuarine Research Reserve. It also tested the Conservancy's determination to preserve all of Rookery Bay by not stopping at the 10,000 acres designated a federal research reserve in 1978. It illustrates how political power and influence were used in conjunction with the Save Our Coast Act of 1981 to preserve environmentally sensitive lands. It marked a turning point for the Conservancy, away from depending heavily on private donors to subsidize purchase of individual parcels and toward working with elected officials who understood how to operate in Tallahassee. Most importantly, this last change brought to the surface the festering, tense relationship between Bill Merrihue and his successor.

Cannon is located inland of the chain of low-lying outer barrier islands between Gordon Pass and Marco Island (see Map 4). Geologically ancient, it is protected from direct exposure to the Gulf of Mexico by Little Marco and Sea Oat Islands; it covers 412 acres bisected by a central ridge built up by successive storms over the centuries. Vegetation consists of mangroves and a mature upland hammock with live oaks and a freshwater lens in the center. Orchids grow on the south end of the island. Because of its elevation, it is suitable for habitation. Two small shell mounds, remnants of Indian tribal occupation, were built on the site as well as a historic windmill. A small vacation cottage on stilts was located on the north end.

The island had gone through a series of owners. By 1982, the same year Congress passed the Coastal Barrier Resources Act restricting development of shorelines, all parcels save one had been assembled by Haxel Corporation. Its officers and majority shareholders were two Germans, Karl Haydn and Axel Schneider. They were represented locally by Bill Vines and Stanley Hole, respected consultants in Naples. Vines had a

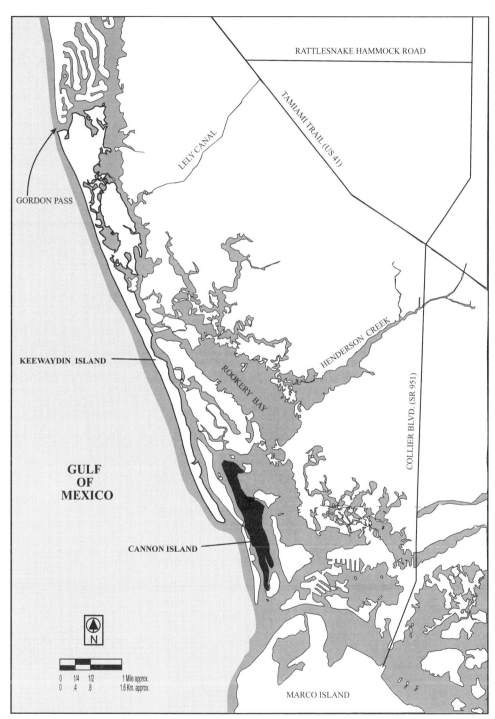

RATTLESNAKE HAMMOCK ROAD

TAMIAMI TRAIL (US 41)

LELY CANAL

GORDON PASS

HENDERSON CREEK

KEEWAYDIN ISLAND

ROOKERY BAY

COLLIER BLVD. (SR 951)

GULF
OF
MEXICO

CANNON ISLAND

N

| 0 | 1/4 | 1/2 | 1 Mile approx. |
| 0 | .4 | .8 | 1.6 Km. approx. |

MARCO ISLAND

Map 4: Keewaydin (Key) and Cannon Islands.

long history in land use, having been hired in December 1964 by Collier County as its first planner; his salary was paid by the Conservancy. The county commission, upset with some of the restrictions he recommended, declined to renew his contract. On the advice of Vines, one of the owners went out of his way to engage Ned Putzell by writing him early in the planning process to say "we would like to review the whole planning process with you and assure you that we will keep in mind the interests of the Conservancy at every step."[19] A formal request for rezone was filed with Collier County in June 1984, which started Merrihue actively working for state acquisition of the entire island. "If they develop Cannon Island, the next to fall would be Little Marco," he told the *Naples Daily News*. "We ought to be quite concerned about that."[20] Preliminary plans showed a private club, 180 dwellings, sufficient boat docks to handle both day trippers and residents, and utilities. Drinking water would be transported from the mainland. The project would have a rainfall catchment and recycling system for irrigation, large septic tanks, a small-scale gasoline-powered generator, aerial mosquito control, and an antenna for communications unless—and it was a huge unless—the "need for additional facilities are required."[21] The initial plan also included a dolphin research facility as a sop to soften environmental objections.

Putzell had talked the Conservancy's executive committee into accepting the possibility of limited development on the island, but to cover his flank he had also written to Elton Gissendanner, proposing that Cannon be made part of the larger Rookery Bay acquisition by the Conservation and Recreation Lands program.[22] Gissendanner, gatekeeper for designation of lands to be purchased, had been seeking help from the Conservancy in purchasing Remuda Ranch lots in the southern Golden Gate Estates and copied Merrihue on all correspondence, bringing him into the picture while Putzell was trying to keep him out. He urged the Conservancy to press its case for preserving Cannon by uniting all environmental groups in southwest Florida and enlisting the support of local legislators.

Merrihue, with Gissendanner coming down on the side of preservation, ignored the executive committee's position structured by Putzell and pressed for acquisition of the entire island. By the end of July, he had enlisted support from Collier County Audubon, the Izaak Walton League, the League of Women Voters of Collier County, Isles of Capri Property Owners Association, and Florida Wildlife Federation. But more importantly he had enlisted the support of Senator Franklin Mann, a Fort Myers Democrat and member of an iconic southwest Florida family whose members cared about the environment. He was a power in Tallahassee and ready to go to work.

Vines, aware of the pressure coming from Merrihue for state ownership of the entire island, attempted to slow the momentum. On behalf of his clients, he again appealed directly to Putzell, setting forth Haxel's development plans in greater detail and writing in closing, "We were disappointed in statements attributed to Willard Merrihue, and [sic] Executive Vice President of The Conservancy, by a June 26th front page Naples Daily News Story, headlined 'Sanctuary Board Fights Project North of Marco.' Merrihue's statements fail to acknowledge the position of The Conservancy Executive Committee, as documented in its May 29 minutes. Further, they contain a substantial misstatement of fact. We realize that The Conservancy was not responsible for the inaccurate remarks, but we believe the average reader will assume Merrihue was speaking for The Conservancy."[23] Vines' attempt at damage control was partially successful because Putzell was later quoted in the press as saying "we believe public ownership is indicated but if not, their program meets our environmental standards."[24]

As the dustup within the Conservancy became more public, Frank Mann was working methodically behind the scenes to move acquisition through the Southwest Florida Regional Planning Council (SFRPC), located at the time in Tampa, and on to the CARL review committee's agenda in September. Mann's committee assignments in the state senate were in business, appropriations, governmental operations, natural resources, and conservation. His *modus operandi* was smoothly engaging, and he was pleased to be supporting an organization with growing influence. "My staff tells me that the esteem and credibility that the Conservancy support of this project carries with state officials is evident with all they talked to on this project."[25] Mann's pressure brought immediate approval from the SFRPC, and he subsequently talked CARL committee chair Randall Kelley into taking up Cannon Island at the group's September meeting, where the Division of State Lands was scheduled to make a full presentation.

As the hearing date approached, Putzell was trying to keep peace with Vines by reiterating the position of his executive committee but began to edge away from support for Haxel's plans. "The Conservancy, as well as the State, has utilized acquisition as the best, and in some cases, the only method which would achieve the long term principal sanctuary goal. . . . This continues to be our position and we are pleased; in your parallel concerns for this beautiful and productive estuary, you can understand and acknowledge this stance even though it may diverge somewhat from your own."[26] After Putzell altered his position ever so slightly, he and Merrihue drew closer and began preparing together for the CARL committee hearing in Tallahassee by cranking up a letter-writing campaign.

Mindful of Gissendanner's plea to gather broad community backing for state acquisition, the Conservancy sought and received support from the South Florida Water Management District Board despite Vines' warning that "there's no way this has any impact on our petition."[27] When Collier County's Environmental Advisory Committee (EAC) heard the case, senior scientist Mark Benedict made an impassioned plea to recommend denial of the pending rezone petition, backed up by an eighty-four-page analysis. The council unanimously refused to recommend the project to the county commission; Vines reacted by saying the appointed body was being "impossible and unreasonable."[28] Then, on September 21 the state's effort hit a brick wall.

Cannon Island was in second place on the state's priority list of CARL eligible projects, but confusion over boundaries of the property and concern over available funds caused the committee to strike Cannon from its agenda. According to minutes of the meeting, while problems of boundaries and money needed to be resolved, there was a larger question on the minds of members: Where was the endpoint of the Rookery Bay acquisition program? Prior to 1984, CARL land purchases were for small, isolated parcels, the pattern by which Merrihue had acquired small islands and coastal mangrove forests in the Ten Thousand Islands with private funds. The only way out was for the Department of Natural Resources to clearly define boundaries for the sanctuary. But the job needed to be done quickly because Bill Vines, despite being turned down by the county's EAC, was doing everything within his power to gain commission approval. Mann knew this and turned his attention to preventing any state permits being issued, which he knew would postpone the county commission's vote on the rezone petition. He then insisted the Department of Natural Resources have a recommendation on Rookery Bay boundaries for presentation at the next meeting of the CARL committee.

On September 28, Trust for Public Land (TPL), a national nonprofit specializing in the purchase and conveying of land to public ownership, announced a tentative agreement with Haxel to limit development to a small portion of Cannon Island and sell the remaining acreage to the state. Vines had been working behind the scenes on this compromise, and the announcement was made by Joel Kuperberg, former executive director of the Conservancy, who had recently become the land trust's senior vice president for special projects. Kuperberg expressed his belief that limited development of sensitive areas, if environmentally compatible and carefully restricted, would encourage Haxel to sell the larger portion of its property into public ownership as an enhancement to the development.

At the CARL meeting in October, Cannon faced another formidable obstacle: The island was left off the acquisition list because a competing proposal to restart acquisition in southern Golden Gate Estates in Collier County, also pushed by Gissendanner, had higher priority. The slope was becoming steeper, and the Conservancy was more willing to consider the Trust for Public Land's proposal.[29] Bill Vines and Karl Haydn were by now touting the TPL proposal and sought the Conservancy's unqualified support—again through Ned Putzell only. Realizing that Merrihue would be opposed, Putzell organized a series of boat tours for his board of directors and staff to visit the island and see firsthand the development footprint. After the trip, the Conservancy board, reflecting deep division over the two choices and the two men, declined to take the matter up. In a file copy of a letter, Putzell penciled in this notation: "Met with Haydn for 3 hrs 22 mins in his office as he requested—told him the C [Conservancy] will do *nothing* until after the state decides whether to put the island on the CARL list."[30]

Vines and Haydn, along with their investors and bankers, were becoming more insistent on a resolution because the stock market was headed down in 1984 and prospects in southwest Florida were dimming. "Until now, we have invested 1.4 million dollars after having been assured by The Conservancy Executive Committee in the spring of 1984 that there are no objections to realize our project, if we meet all the standards as described."[31]

At the January 1985 CARL committee hearing, Dr. Leo Minasian, an environmental administrator from the Department of Natural Resources, put up a map on the wall with proposed boundaries for Rookery Bay remarkably similar to the Woodburn and Tabb map of 1964. It was immediately dubbed by the new chairman, John DeGrove, as the "Wishing Project."[32] The map was based entirely on an inventory of natural resources suitable for acquisition, preservation, and management by the state. In the audience listening to the presentation was John Orwell, representing one of south Florida's largest landowners and most prestigious families. He was shocked. "Collier Enterprises, in addition to the lands . . . described, which to our surprise fell into this new boundary, also owns land to the north of the parcel. Collier is very sensitive to and aware of the State's needs. . . . We don't know for sure how this is going to turn out, but it may well be as they develop plans for that property, litigation will be an issue."[33] There it was, another obstacle to acquisition of Rookery Bay, dropped strategically by a powerful landowner in southwest Florida. After Orwell returned to his seat, Bernie Yokel, president of Florida Audubon, rose to express his discomfort at removing Collier Enterprises' land from the sanctuary. In his matter-of-fact way, Yokel reminded the panel that by pulling out pieces, the whole would be inevitably compromised, making scientific investigation of the estuary impossible. As the hearing continued, it became obvious that Vines had been working behind the scenes; the CARL committee knew details of the revised plan were being worked out with Kuperberg and TPL. Vines kept boring in on the Conservancy's shifting support, forcing Yokel to publicly admit he knew that the Conservancy was in favor of the TPL agreement with Haxel.

The committee saw it as a Mexican standoff. Staff emphasized that the maps on the wall were limited to protection of the estuary for long-term scientific research, while private property owners like Collier and a number of small inholders complained that they not been informed of the plan. But Yokel would not be sidetracked despite the Conservancy's history of ambivalence. He made another plea to retain all areas, regardless of ownership, within the natural resource boundary despite objections. It was necessary, he argued, for sound scientific research to have the entire ecosystem available for study with minimal human impact. With that, Vines went "all in": "We've made the assumption in our Cannon Island planning that public recreation is going to happen in this area because of the nature of the natural resources. If that's dead wrong, and public recreation is going to be prohibited, our plans for Cannon Island don't make any sense at all. And you've got to buy the island."[34] The committee got ready to vote on the boundary map. With a motion to approve on the table, chairman DeGrove looked at John Orwell: "Would this give Collier heartburn . . . ?" Orwell replied: "We still have heartburn."[35] The map was approved unanimously, but acquisition of Cannon Island was tabled. The reason was succinctly expressed by Victoria Tschinkel, secretary of the Department of Environmental Regulation, who likened the various layers of analysis to peeling an onion until she fell back on the most critical point: with the final layer of the onion being availability of funds.

Throughout the spring and summer of 1985, the Conservancy worked behind the scenes with TPL to structure yet another deal for 309 acres at a price of $750,000 with an option to purchase the balance—the developable portion—for an additional $1.55 million.[36] Putzell was away for the summer, and Toivo Tammerk, the Conservancy's new president, became more deeply involved in pursuing the TPL compromise. But the indefatigable Frank Mann was off on a different tack.

The CARL program had about $300 million of projects on the approved list in 1985, including another 2,704 acres within Rookery Bay, but only $35 million to spend. Cannon was a secondary barrier island, and the legislature, urged on by Governor Bob Graham, had passed the Save Our Coast Act in 1981, and between $2 and $4 million might be immediately available. Mann pressed the Department of Natural Resources to commit the funds. After being put off, he went directly to Graham, who assigned the project to special counsel Art Harper with instructions to put the proposal at the top of his in-box. Mann told Harper he wanted to place the entire Rookery Bay ecosystem into public ownership based upon the Minasian map despite the fact that, other than approval of the conceptual boundary, CARL discussions had centered only on Cannon Island.[37]

To rally community support, a small group of citizens began a petition drive for public ownership of the entire chain of barrier islands in Rookery Bay.[38] Cannon was still sitting in the second position on the CARL list, and the Conservancy was concerned that pressure to acquire all islands would confuse the situation. Mann intervened, suggesting it was important for the Conservancy to sign the petition for presentation to the CARL committee in November. Besides, he noted, it was always his intention to work toward full buyout.

As the meeting date neared, Tammerk received an unexpected telegram from a law firm in Miami: "Unfounded reports have been circulating to the effect that Canon [sic] Island is to be sold to the Trust for Public Land. The facts are that Canon [sic] Island owners continue without change to seek state approval of a previously submitted proposal to develop a recreational complex on 10% to 15% of the island's area with the remainder to be made available to the state for a below-market price."[39] The telegram was clearly designed to quell any incipient rebellion among major players in TPL negotiations with Haxel Corporation. All parties stayed in place. Cannon Island was once again designated as second on the priority list, but the committee was informed, due to previous commitments, funds would not be available for another two years. That left the Save Our Coast Act as the only source of money.

But there was one significant change: The CARL committee voted to place *all* of Cannon Island on the list. The Conservancy and Florida Audubon always preferred to have the entire island in public lands but were frustrated by the lack of money. TPL and Kuperberg were trying to make the best of the situation by working with the landowners toward a practical solution allowing partial development. Frank Mann was determined to see the state acquire the whole island as part of the larger project, and he held sway in Tallahassee where the decisions were made. By enlisting Senator Bob Graham's support, Mann was able to keep the project front and center before the CARL committee. There is no record of this, but given the relative passivity of major environmental groups at the November hearing, it is likely that Mann, with help from Graham's office, had convinced the CARL committee to go the distance.

This surmise is supported by a letter from committee member Victoria Tschinkel to the governor in which she revealed that back-channel negotiations with the county had produced a remarkable agreement: "[Collier] county says they will not zone for development of any kind; it is currently zoned agricultural."[40] The Conservancy was not made aware of this until early December but with that knowledge could breathe a sigh of relief.

With CARL hamstrung by a lack of funds, Haydn filed a rezone petition from "agricultural" to "planned unit development" with Collier County's planning department. Apparently unaware of the county's assurance to Tschinkel, he brought in one of the Conservancy's old friends, George Vega, to press the case. "The idea is to sell nature. It would be insane to do anything else," Vega commented to a Miami newspaper, calling the latest proposal "modest."[41] Yokel of Audubon continued to be somewhat supportive, saying that he preferred full state ownership but would accept carefully restricted development as a last resort. The Conservancy's leadership, now aware that the county would not grant a rezone, pressed the island's owners by floating another idea in the local press: "The question is whether there should be development in that particular area. The Conservancy is willing to help [Haydn] implement the plan in a different location."[42] But the state would have to be involved in any swap and in January 1986 asked Haydn for a new appraisal. The possibility of a compromise was still in the wind. "If we are unable to negotiate a sale, then we would entertain a discussion with you on other possibilities such as transferring development rights to Keewaden [sic] Island and the possibility of limited development on Cannon Island."[43] The appraisal was submitted but negotiations were put on hold again; the island's ownership was undergoing reorganization.

The final chapter of the Cannon Island saga began two years later. Michael Miceli, a Bonita Springs businessman and trustee for Haxel Corporation property, signed an option for state purchase of the entire island with the exception of one small, privately owned parcel. The Conservancy had served as mediator in the negotiations. The governor and Cabinet, acting as the Internal Improvement Fund, approved the option in February 1988, setting a cap of $8,500 per upland acre, but one obstacle remained: The legislature had to pass a special act to give the Department of Natural Resources eminent domain powers to acquire the property.

With condemnation, owners of the property could sell their holdings for $2.9 million and minimize capital gains with a "threat of condemnation" tax credit. Without condemnation, the price would have to be the higher appraised value. But the legislature refused to go along, and the deal fell through once again. The state wanted yet another survey of the island to settle on the number of upland acres (at a higher price) as well as a second survey of the mean high-water profile, both on Miceli's nickel. He refused, withdrew the offer, and brought George Vega back into the picture to restart negotiations.[44]

In the meantime, Toivo Tammerk had researched comparable condemnation proceedings. With Department of Natural Resources support, he petitioned county commissioners to condemn the property. At its August 1988 meeting, the commission declined based upon opposition from Commissioner John Pistor of Marco Island, who was still smarting over a $2.5-million reimbursement shortfall promised by the state for the county's Lely Barefoot Beach purchase earlier in the year. The county's general fund had made up the difference, but Pistor wanted nothing to do with further acquisitions involving the state.

But Pistor was misguided because purchase of Cannon Island would be between the state and the island's trustee; the county was not on the hook. All the commission needed to do was agree to condemn the property. Finally, through the singular efforts of chair Burt Saunders, condemnation passed the county, a price of $2.98 million was agreed to, and the deal closed in November 1988. The state owned all but ten acres on Cannon and could turn its attention to the rest of Rookery Bay.

Reflections

The sale of Cannon Island was possible because of two critical dynamics: first, reasonable and willing sellers, Karl Haydn and Michael Miceli, who understood the centrality of the island to the entire Rookery Bay ecosystem. They represented their economic interests within the established process for state acquisition of public lands without duplicity. They neither attempted to dispute scientific assertions about the value of research in an unspoiled natural setting nor did they politicize the science, which is so prevalent in today's world. Second, public officials were deeply involved. Elton Gissendanner and Frank Mann, working the corridors in Tallahassee, Bob Graham in Washington, D.C., and county commission chairman Burt Saunders all shared a vision of preserving Rookery Bay. The Conservancy backed up their work at the local level, but public officials carried through with the heavy lifting.

While maneuvering at the CARL committee level and the county planning department was going on, an exchange of letters took place between Dave Addison, senior scientist at the Conservancy, and the Department of Community Affairs in Tallahassee. Addison, writing as a private citizen, wanted the state to buy the entire island. Darst replied, setting forth his main concern: "The program receives $40 million a year; this amount is dwarfed by the estimated cost of the acquisition properties. The CARL committee is trying to make the program more efficient by encouraging the use, where appropriate, of alternative acquisition techniques that are less expensive than the traditional fee-simple acquisition. Cannon Island seems a good place to explore such techniques."[45] This view was clearly conditioned by limited resources available at the time, and a priority list numbering in the hundreds of parcels.

Addison acknowledged the reality of Darst's argument but cited seven reasons that Cannon was not a suitable test bed. First, partial development of a coastal barrier island should occur only in proximity to an existing development with infrastructure. Second, recently passed laws, especially the federal Coastal Barrier Resources Act of 1982, discouraged development. Third, tidal flow, due to dredging of Hurricane Pass and Little Marco Pass, would push any point-source pollution from the island into the gut of Rookery Bay. Fourth, the state would be subsidizing developers by purchasing land in the middle of an aquatic preserve. Fifth, partial development of Cannon Island would set a precedent for others, namely Collier Enterprises, to follow suit. Sixth, the proposed Haxel project would have to include mosquito control measures affecting the mangrove ecosystem. And seventh, there would be loss of public recreational opportunities because private owners had a history of taking extraordinary measures to protect their beaches from public use.[46] Addison's points succinctly summarized the case for public ownership.

The stories of major coastal preservation in southwest Florida are now complete. Many had their beginnings during Bill Merrihue's time at the Conservancy. He was deeply involved in every case covered so far in this book, although he did not see each to its conclusion. His goal was always to create more public lands. His willingness to engage in discussions relating to development, rather than purchase, reflected growing awareness that the world was changing. The Conservancy's heavy investment in land acquisition had price beyond the purchase transaction—an incipient commitment to ensuring the biological vitality of its holdings. The organization was being pulled, by necessity, into land-use planning and environmental regulation, issues beginning to emerge front and center in Tallahassee in the 1970s.

MANAGING GROWTH

CHAPTER 5

FLORIDA'S GROWTH MANAGEMENT EVOLVES

One way of looking at how rapidly growing Florida adapted to a massive influx of people—all requiring essential services such as water, sewers, roads, and schools—is review a series of growth management laws passed beginning in the early 1970s. These acts served as a basis for the state to fitfully introduce a process designed to analyze land and resource use at all levels of government, and to guide development with some forethought and coherence. Without these laws, developers would be free to plat large subdivisions—southern Golden Gate Estates and Lehigh Acres, for example—with minimal essential services and few amenities like parks and green space. The scope of legislation was conceptually broad and innovative and, by being introduced gradually, partially overcame inbred resistance to government intervention among politicians and citizens. In doing so, it also created confusion between layers of government and eventually intensified the distrust of those opposing state-mandated guidance of growth. A fitful beginning was followed by gradual refinement. Controlling urban sprawl with minimal disruption to natural resources was difficult, at best, and would become more so as property rights advocates became more adamant.

The issue was forced upon the legislature after serious droughts in 1970 and 1971 caused water rationing on the Gold Coast and a one-third cut in agricultural allocations, creating an uproar from suffering suburbanites furious that their lawns might turn brown and farmers economically harmed as their harvests suffered.[1] The moaning was audible all the way to Tallahassee. Governor Reubin Askew, sworn in that January, sensed the moment was right to address longer term growth issues throughout the state and appointed a Task Force on Resource Management to devise a plan for dealing with land use and water management. He believed the two issues desperately needed attention, with the massive migration of retirees from the North seeking better weather, inexpensive housing, and lower taxes. He felt the state had to take control of growth management because local governments woefully lacked planning expertise.

The well-spoken and well-educated Askew had been elected by a majority consisting of young people, Northern transplants, and blacks when he ran against Claude Kirk on a platform of economic development tempered by environmental sensitivity. Aware that Florida legislators and local officials would balk at simply regulating development, the governor suggested to his task force a hybrid approach: Guide growth with an emphasis on planning. Askew understood that planning and land-use regulation were two innately different political approaches toward the same goal: managing for future growth. Planning in the broadest sense involved anticipation and participation, and he believed land and water use would eventually come down to instituting command and control, steps already taken by the U.S. Congress in the prior year when passing the Clean Water Act (CWA) and Endangered Species Act (ESA). Classic command and control necessitated an orderly sequence of setting goals, obtaining baseline data and outlining criteria for measurement of progress, establishing standards, and creating mechanisms for enforcement. Both federal acts were examples of the weaknesses and strengths of heavy federal regulation; they offered few incentives and set forth serious penalties while often failing to specify relevant technologies available to solve the problems. Further, the CWA addressed only the chemistry of water while failing to deal with volumes or supply. On the other hand, the two federal statutes had a dramatic effect on some of the nation's most egregious environmental violations by restoring Lake Erie to healthy condition, dramatically reducing smog in the Los Angeles basin, and bringing a number of iconic species back to thriving populations.

The governor's task force, populated by citizens from a broad range of backgrounds and interests, was aware of the awakening environmental conscience throughout the country. It recommended the state prioritize and regulate lands essential to the overall functioning of natural ecosystems by creating the designation "area of critical state concern" (ACSC) to identify areas "having a significant impact upon historical, natural, or environmental resources of regional or statewide importance." The underlying concept was to direct growth away from geographic resource areas critical to the state. Taking it a step further, in recognition of the inevitable, it suggested a second designation: "development of regional impact" (DRI) to provide a mechanism for public notification and review of any plan that would "because of its character, magnitude, or location have a substantial effect on the health, safety or welfare of citizens of more than one county."[2] Twelve types of activities were iterated, including port facilities, large shopping centers, and residential developments, all embodied in the landmark Florida Environmental Land and Water Management Act of 1972.

Taking into account local government's resentment of state intrusion into their politics, the task force attempted to blunt opposition by suggesting creation of eleven joint state-local regional planning councils (RPCs). These RPCs were intended to bring together elected officials and staff to review detailed plans for every DRI proposed for areas of environmental interest to the state and to recommend areas to be set aside for protection. Citizens and local governments could also nominate properties for review by an RPC with final approval by the Department of Community Affairs. A second restriction, one that led directly to the Big Cypress Act of 1973, was that no more than 5% of land could be designated as ACSC at any one time. The law required public hearings before the governor and Cabinet gave final approval, a step that would eventually play heavily into the state's approach to southern Golden Gate Estates. Bob Graham, later to become Florida's governor and a United States senator, was the bill's floor manager in the state senate; passage was due in large part to his ability to make necessary political adjustments.[3]

In the same year, the legislature passed the innovative Florida State Comprehensive Planning Act. As a first step toward integrated growth management planning at all levels of government in Florida, it required the governor to create a plan aimed at "long-range guidance for the orderly social, economic, and physical growth of the state" and submit it to the legislature for approval, allowing the elected body to maintain a high degree of control over the outcome if not the process.

The third important piece of legislation passed in 1972 was the Water Resources Act, which created water management districts aligned with five natural drainage basins throughout the state. The idea was to establish ecosystem-level jurisdiction to manage increasingly scarce freshwater supplies. The districts were defined by surface watersheds, not geopolitical boundaries. The South Florida Water Management District covered an area from the Kissimmee Lakes north of Lake Okeechobee all the way to Florida Bay and the Keys. Florida's counties, in effect, were forced to cede some decisions with regard to their water supply to five independent agencies over which they exercised virtually no control despite the fact that districts were supposed to coordinate with local entities.[4] Powers were invested in appointed governing boards with oversight by the Department of Natural Resources and the Florida Cabinet. Having the governor appoint board members was intended to remove politics from the selection process. In reality, it did nothing of the sort. Vested interests such as industrial agriculture, developers, businesses, and urban water systems established control over the process, with campaign contributions giving them a large say in appointments.

Growth management acts passed in 1972 (except the Water Resources Act) were innovative and daring in concept but flawed in execution because of four factors. Local authorities were able to circumvent or bypass state laws with preemptive statutes. Plans were not law, and land development codes and zoning had to be put in place. Land-use lawyers were able to squeeze their clients' proposals through thousands of loopholes created, sometimes purposefully, to get around both the spirit and intent of the original legislation. With the population of Florida increasing by almost 300,000 souls each year, legislators didn't want to get in the way of development. Finally, and perhaps most significantly, there was no approved state comprehensive plan. Without a guiding vision, local officials and regional planning councils (in their early years) tended to be parochial by advocating for projects to benefit their respective jurisdictions because of increased ad valorem revenues from development.

At the federal level, 1972 saw passage of the Coastal Zone Management Act (CZMA). For the first time, planning was aimed at preserving beaches, shoreline, estuaries, and tributaries as an ecological necessity. A federal-state partnership, the CZMA provided technical assistance to states opting to participate in exchange for rights to override certain federal permits for operations such as offshore drilling. Florida was an early participant because Askew, impressed by elements of the CZMA, wanted to show his support for oversight of coastal development.

The governor was determined to make the 1972 state laws work. So was the legislature, which authorized another citizens committee, the first Environmental Land Management Committee (ELMS I), to review efficacy of the 1972 legislation. It became obvious to ELMS I that little progress had been made in comprehensive planning at the regional and local levels for a number of reasons. First, planning at the state level was in disarray. Second, there was a lack of money to hire planning expertise at the county and local levels of government. Third, there was a lack of enforcement: The planning effort lacked teeth. After receiving ELMS I recommendations, the legislature attempted to deal with these problems with the Local Government Comprehensive Planning Act of 1975, which required local governments to create their own comprehensive plans and adhere to them by following through with land development codes that reflected the intent of the comp plan. The state's role was to be advisory, but no interface was created where local plans could be reviewed for consistency with the state plan—mainly because there was no state plan. And despite the insistence of the ELMS I committee, the legislature failed to provide financial assistance to counties and municipalities, already reluctant partners, to hire additional staff.

The 1975 act made meaningful changes. It further formalized the organizational structure of the five water management districts created by the 1972 Water Resources Act. Each of the districts was given the power to issue "consumptive use" water permits, oversee long-range water supply planning and flood control, and levy ad valorem taxes, despite the fact that governing board members were appointed, not elected. The act vested pollution control regulatory authority in a new Department of Environmental Regulation (later the Department of Environmental Protection). Finally, the legal standing of individual citizens, environmental organizations, and other interveners to challenge land-use decisions before the Florida Land and Water Adjudicatory Commission (created in 1972) was severely restricted. The legislature was willing to go just so far with the 1975 act but validated, for a second time, the concept that basin boundaries was the best way to effectively manage freshwater distribution.

During the time this spate of laws was being debated and eventually passed in Tallahassee, a series of development plans was in the works, stretched along southwest Florida's coast from Marco Island in the south up to Big Hickory Bay and Barefoot Beach above the Lee County line in the north. The emergence of growth management laws was an essential element in controlling development on the barrier islands protecting Rookery Bay, as was cooperation between Audubon Florida and the Collier County Conservancy. Assisted by an awakening environmental ethic throughout the nation, the two organizations reached out beyond land purchases and into a new field of endeavor: directing growth away from sensitive areas.

The first case we will study was in the heart of the Ten Thousand Islands, a project permitted in the late 1960s, quickly to become a test of the state's resolve to enforce newly passed laws. We now turn our attention to an examination of how the environmental community adapted tactics to limit Deltona Corporation's development to Marco Island and away from the heart of Rookery Bay.

CHAPTER 6

DELTONA AND
MARCO ISLAND

*I*n the early 1960s, the Mackle family of Miami had successfully developed a number of properties in Florida, including Key Biscayne on the east coast and Port Charlotte on the Gulf of Mexico. Always looking for new opportunities, they turned their attention to the southwest corner of the state. While flying over the Ten Thousands Islands, with the fishing villages of Goodland and Marco the only signs of human life, the Mackles were captivated by a four-mile stretch of pristine white-sand beach that soon would become the centerpiece of a massive development—and a long-standing source of controversy between environmental groups and the family's company, Deltona.

The flight was followed by on-site analysis of an area posing nearly insurmountable problems. Red mangroves dominating the coastal zone had done their job for thousands of years, creating more than 40 feet of muck in the process. Marco Island was prone to hurricane damage; Donna blew through in 1960, with storm surge up to twelve feet (as indicated by high-water marks on surviving palm trees). Freshwater had to be brought in, captured in rain barrels, or pulled from deep wells. Further inhibiting development, there was a high ridge around Barfield Bay—as high as forty feet—a place where indigenous people had lived for thousands of years. The existence of mound structures had been known to locals for years. What was not known was the extent of settlement on 243-acre Horr's Island, facing Barfield Bay to the northeast, until Michael Russo, an anthropologist from the Florida Museum of Natural History in Gainesville, performed extensive excavations of the area. Russo was aware of the settlements on the high Pleistocene sand dunes from a 1979 backhoe excavation by Alan McMichael of the University of Florida. But what Russo found, after a year's work, was a large pre-ceramic site occupied, according to radiocarbon dating, more than 4,000 years ago—well before the Calusa became the hegemonic tribe in southwest Florida. Excavation revealed middle and late Archaic occupation dating back as far as 4,800 B.P.,[1] placing it among the earliest known human settlements in the southeastern United States. A number of post holes, indicating habitation structures, were noted throughout the site. A mound was discovered with human remains; a head facing east indicated an intentional ceremonial burial. Russo's work was controversial because the prevailing archaeological paradigm for permanent human occupation of the coastal environment argued that many of southwest Florida's estuaries were not intensively exploited by large population groups until about 2,700 years ago.[2] The Mackles, of course, had no way of knowing that they were about to develop one of the most important prehistoric sites in southeastern America. Horr's Island, purchased in 1970, was destined in the master plan to be the venue for high-end, single-family homes and docks. It remains today an ongoing problem for the Conservancy. But that story must wait until later.

How Deltona came to purchase Marco Island is unclear from the records. Some reports say Barron Collier Jr. approached the Mackles; some indicate it was the other way around. In either case, the Mackles proceeded to form Marco Island Development Corporation in 1964 with Deltona Corporation in a 50% position. The remaining half was bought by an investment group, including Barron Collier Jr. and his sister, Isabel Collier Read. The corporation owned 6,700 acres on the island, an option on 3,600 additional acres of adjacent land, and a copyright for the name "Platinum Coast." The initial development plan envisaged a five-phase program, with separate permitting for each: Marco River, Roberts

Bay, Collier Bay, Barfield Bay, and Big Key. An additional area, called Unit 24, was reserved for later development. The entire project was to be completed in fifteen years. An announcement appeared in the local press with the banner headline, "$500 Million Development Planned for Marco Island."[3] The phase-in plan, devised by Neil Bahr, chief sales and marketing executive, allowed Deltona to amortize the costs by completing one section every three years, funded by selling undeveloped land in anticipation of the next phase. Many were installment sales with a small amount down and three years to pay the balance. Contracts had value, and banks were willing to lend against them based more upon the Mackles' reputation than the buyer's creditworthiness. As with many schemes in Florida, success depended upon escalating land values, constant sales pressure, and availability of money—a combination that would weigh heavily on Deltona five years later.

County and state permits for dredge-and-fill of the Marco River area were issued in October 1964. The Corps permit took only nine days. Working feverishly around the clock, the Mackles were able to open Marco Island to the public on January 31, 1965, and began selling lots for two model homes—one for an inland parcel and the second for waterfront. Nearly 25,000 people showed up for the opening. Many of them brought checkbooks tucked in their picnic baskets next to the fried chicken and coleslaw. And many belonged to a curious human subspecies prevalent in south Florida called *Flipper americanus*.

Things were going swimmingly. A grand hotel was opened, and in 1968 outside investors were bought out for $6.8 million in stock. Kice Island, with two miles of beach, was added. By 1970 Deltona owned more than 19,000 acres of mangrove forests, pristine land, and small islands. But while the company was busy gobbling up acreage in southwest Florida, the world was changing.

In 1967 the Florida state legislature passed two bills that would affect Deltona's plans for Marco. First was the Randall Act—named for a Fort Myers state representative concerned with the effect of human effluents on his favorite fishing holes—which required a pre-development biological survey to set a bulkhead line and create baseline data against which to measure post-development environmental impacts. It provided that any state permit affecting the life cycle of fish and wildlife must be approved by the (then) State Board of Conservation, which consisted of the Florida Cabinet. The second piece of legislation was the Florida Air and Water Pollution Control Act, which reasserted state jurisdiction over coastal tidal lands below the mean high-water mark already established by the 1957 Bulkhead Act. Like many regulatory reforms in Florida, the law had been largely ignored, but the 1967 law established a new threshold for pollution discharges in the form of a formal "water quality certificate," a change that would come back to haunt Deltona in 1971. Florida's tidal zones and estuaries were no longer at the complete mercy of the dredge-and-fill crowd and their pals in the state capital. At the federal level, permitting had become a joint responsibility between the Corps and U.S. Fish and Wildlife Service (USFWS), extending the time required for interagency approval and eliminating fast-tracking permits as in the case of Marco River.

Deltona applied for Roberts Bay development permits in 1967. Tallahassee and Washington delayed processing, and the following year the permit was denied on the basis of damage to the balance of nature. Deltona reacted vigorously by enlisting Florida's two senators, George Smathers and Spessard Holland, to petition Interior Secretary Russell Train to intervene. Train supported his staff's opposition, but in December 1969 the Corps, under intense political pressure, issued the permit over objections by USFWS, a pattern that would continue for the next forty years and come to a head in the battle over developing the Corkscrew Regional Ecosystem Watershed (covered in a later chapter). At that point, the fate of Roberts Bay lay in the hands of the state's Internal Improvement Fund, consisting of Republican Claude Kirk and elected Cabinet members, all of whom were Democrats favoring Deltona, with its vast holdings and political connections. Kirk, the first Republican governor elected since Reconstruction, consistently defied the wishes of other members of the IIF by pushing back hard and publicly on the extent of dredge-and-fill going on throughout the state. He eventually relented on this one, however, and permits were issued for Roberts Bay.

Deltona's owners breathed a sigh of relief, thinking they had a clear understanding of permitting requirements, but they had not reckoned with Joel Kuperberg, who had left the Conservancy for Tallahassee as executive director of the IIF. One of the first agenda items for fund trustees in 1971 was permitting for three remaining sections: Collier Bay, Barfield Bay, and Big Key, all of which had passed through the county process with little objection. The 9,000-acre Collier Bay (known as the Collier-Read tract) permitting area was of greatest significance because it was on the southern border of Rookery Bay and the northernmost extension of Marco Island development. The governor and Cabinet were expecting a settlement between the Mackles and environmentalists, but the bullheaded (when it came to environmental degradation) Kuperberg would have no part of a compromise. Negotiations dragged on as the *Miami Herald* cheered a settlement in May, again in July, and finally another time in October, when agreement was supposedly reached among all parties at interest. However, south Florida environmentalist groups, led by Audubon and the Conservancy, after working for seven years on buying small parcels in Rookery Bay and the Ten Thousand Islands, were determined to limit Deltona's growth to Marco Island. The company, on the other side of the equation, had completed most dredge-and-fill work in the two permitted areas; Marco River and Roberts Bay fill fingers had settled sufficiently to begin home construction. Collier Bay was 75% sold, Barfield/Blue Hill Bay 90% sold, and Big Key virtually sold out. Then, a "cessation of work" order came from the Corps in 1971, preventing any further dredging inland of Collier Bay, and Deltona was looking at a rapidly slowing economy combined with the changing political climate in Tallahassee.[4]

Two important pieces of legislation were passed in 1972 that would indirectly affect Deltona's development. The Florida Water Resources Act affirmed the right of the state to control the waters of Florida to "realize their full beneficial use." Oversight authority was vested in the Department of Natural Resources. The United States Congress, realizing that development was beginning to stress the coasts nationwide, passed the Coastal Zone Management Act, directing states to make detailed plans for the preservation of coastal ecosystems while finding ways to provide public access to beaches. More importantly, the federal act created the National Estuarine Research Reserve (NERR) system and made federal funds available for research and education.[5] These laws did not have a direct effect on Deltona's decision to suspend land sales in June 1973, but the economy was not improving, and in order to meet the requirements of newly passed state and federal laws, a briefing session was convened in Tallahassee at the Department of Pollution Control to study the impact of development on Florida's coastline. Among the scientists invited was Bernie Yokel.[6] His presentation was a "review of information presently available regarding the effects of dredge-and-fill activities on water quality."[7] He had been studying mangrove ecology in Rookery Bay at the Norris Research Center for more than two years. His paper, along with others from the scientific community, was based on the effect of dredging for existing projects; Deltona's experts testifying at the hearing were using unproven predictive models. Yokel realized he had a powerful tool to argue against further dredge-and-fill on Marco Island. And he would use it to slow the process to a crawl.

As Deltona's operations were grinding to a halt, the state legislature passed the Environmental Reorganization Act of 1975, transferring staff of the semi-autonomous Internal Improvement Fund to the Department of Natural Resources. With this change in Tallahassee and the "cessation of work" order from the Corps still in effect, the company decided it needed clarification since lack of clarity was anathema to the development industry. It began with the highest hurdle: the Jacksonville office of the Corps, which had issued the "cessation of work" order. The district engineer, Col. Donald Wisdom, scheduled a hearing for September 2–3, 1975, at Lely High School. His decision to take personal control buoyed the hopes of Yokel and Kuperberg. Known as a "green colonel," Wisdom was in the vanguard of an environmental awakening within the Corps. The Conservancy and its nineteen partner organizations would be represented by James Tripp, an attorney from the Environmental Defense Fund. Skilled at cross-examination, he'd leave you sitting in your own blood without knowing you had been cut. But there would be little blood spilled at the hearing because Wisdom was a man capable of controlling difficult situations with a courtly manner and gentle humor. He would need both again a year later, when he presided over hearings that resulted in the Corps withdrawing most of its support for the controversial Cross Florida Barge Canal, supported by Jacksonville business leaders and the state legislature.[8]

As the hearing date approached, the Conservancy and its partners were preparing for the worst. With typical thoroughness, Merrihue was working with Charles Callison of National Audubon to devise a series of fallback positions should additional dredging be approved. In a comment letter on the environmental impact statement already submitted, Merrihue noted: "It is the conclusion of our Board of Directors that the permits should be denied and that Deltona should be asked to submit a new design for completion of the main island." Hoping to open the door for negotiations, the letter went on to describe the Conservancy as "one of the largest and most successful independent county-wide citizens' conservation groups in America. The twenty-six men and women on our Board are retired or active leaders of business, industry and finance and our 1,500 members are primarily men and women who are moderates rather than 'no compromise' environmental extremists."[9]

By August, with the hearing less than one month away, the Conservancy tried to enlist the support of Nathaniel Reed, who by then had left Tallahassee to become Assistant Secretary of the Interior for Fish and Wildlife and Parks under President Nixon. In a letter, Merrihue pointed out Deltona's heavy hand in the environmental impact statement released by the Corps to the public: 59% of the citations came from Deltona's hired guns. "The heavy dependence on Deltona-produced information . . . gives further support to the contention that a rational balanced evaluation of the impact of these permits has yet to be produced."[10] Four days later, Yokel laid out to Reed alternatives for a compromise. He ranked the three subdivisions in order of environmental importance: Big Key first, then Barfield/Blue Hill Bay, and lastly Collier Bay. His favored position: "Grant the Collier Bay permit and reject the others" because Collier Bay had already been heavily comprised by nearby dredge-and-fill activities and had few remaining viable wetlands.[11] But all attempts at compromise failed; Deltona was willing to roll the dice with Wisdom.

Among partner organizations testifying at the hearing were the Nature Conservancy, Florida Audubon, and the Sierra Club, along with representatives from the U.S. Fish and Wildlife Service and the Bureau of National Marine Fisheries. Deltona's case hinged on three points: The company had a long record of environmental responsibility; mangroves involved in the latest round of permits amounted to less than one half of 1% of Florida's coastal forests; and denial of the permits would amount to an unconstitutional "taking" of Deltona's land without due compensation. Yokel and Tripp discounted Deltona's first two claims but left the last argument for the courts to decide. However, at the conclusion of his testimony, Yokel once again opened the door for compromise by suggesting moving the development elsewhere or redesigning the existing plan. Yokel's notes show the Conservancy and its allies were still depending on back-channel negotiations through Nat Reed, but Deltona showed no inclination to change its position, so Yokel took one last shot in a post-hearing brief:

> It is well known that [Collier Bay] is platted and largely sold and that the 7,500-acre area is also subject to development. To proceed into the present decision without knowledge or consideration of the environmental, social and economic impacts of development of nearly 10,000 additional acres in the same general area by the same developer is to ignore an overwhelming part of the land management problem and to prevent a consideration of the full array of alternatives that could very well benefit both society and the developer. I believe this represents piecemeal planning and permitting, and

leads to poor use of natural resources and
is clearly not in the public interest.[12]

The Corps issued its decision the following April: permits denied for
all but 1,400 homes in the partially developed Collier Bay. Frank Mackle Jr.
was "shocked and outraged at the injustice of the decision by the Corps"[13]
and promised an immediate appeal. He said the decision eliminated transfer of Kice Island and canceled deeding of an additional 4,000 acres of
wetlands to the state. His determination was obvious when the next day
Deltona ran a full-page ad in the *Naples Daily News* advertising the latest
Marco Island model home, the Marco Polo. For $52,050 a buyer could get
three bedrooms, two and a half baths, vaulted ceilings in the living room
and dining room, a tile roof, and a kidney-shaped swimming pool in the
backyard—all with a ten-year warranty. The *Naples Daily News* quickly
jumped on the bandwagon by running a news article with a photo showing a phalanx of bulldozers pushing piles of dirt around in Collier Bay. The
editorial page remained silent. Not so, Deltona's lawyers.

Four years of legal maneuvering followed, and in 1980 the U.S. Court
of Claims ruled that denial of the permits did indeed constitute a taking
under the rule of "inverse condemnation." Either the Corps should reverse
itself or pay Deltona an unspecified (at that time) amount in compensation. But by then Deltona was in serious trouble. The company had sold
some 4,000 lots worth approximately $45 million in Barfield/Blue Hill Bay
and Big Key. It would have to refund the money or trade for other land,
but buyers, expecting waterfront property, had little desire to trade and
move inland. Plus there was the matter of another 3,700 lots in the Collier-
Read (Unit 24) section worth about $34 million. The company established
an escrow fund of $15 million—increased in increments to $58 million
by 1982—but was overwhelmed by cancellations and withdrawals. Deltona was forced to sell some of its prime properties, and in 1982, after the
United States District Court overturned the claims court decision and the
United States Supreme Court refused to hear an appeal, the company entered into what is known today as the Deltona Settlement.

The agreement was entered into on July 20, 1982, between Deltona and the conservation interveners, including National Audubon Society, the Collier County Conservancy, Florida Audubon, Environmental Defense Fund, and the Florida Izaak Walton League. Government parties to the agreement were the Florida Department of Environmental Regulation, Trustees of the Internal Improvement Fund, Florida Department of Veterans and Community Affairs, the South Florida Water Management District, and Collier County.[14] As *de facto* approval for development of eligible lands by the signatory agencies, it bound conservation groups to allowing an airport in Unit 30, an undeveloped area. It gave Deltona the right to finish Marco Shores with an additional 14,500 units. The state agreed to trade 36 acres located to the west of Miami International Airport for 12,400 acres of wetlands adjacent to Marco Island for eventual preservation.[15] Deltona gave up all dredge-and-fill permits previously issued by the Internal Improvement Fund in Barfield Bay, Big Key, and the Collier-Read section. Finally, and perhaps most significant, Deltona agreed to submit any "modifications" and final drawings for the 14,500 additional units to the Conservancy as appointed representative of the conservation alliance for approval. The definition of "modifications" specifically mentioned wetlands impacts; this would remain the key element in the settlement agreement.

On March 25, 1985, a ceremony was held at the Conservancy's Nature Center in Naples. Attended by Governor Bob Graham, the affair had the aura of a social gala. Plans were carefully vetted by Bill Merrihue, who beamed as Graham thanked the parties. "The Department of Environmental Regulation, the Deltona Corporation, and the Collier County Conservancy have accomplished a historic achievement," he said.[16] And so they had. The *Naples Daily News*, beneficiary of Deltona's advertising dollars, adopted a conciliatory attitude: "It's entirely fitting that the Conservancy, which has been a tireless guardian of the ecology for so many years, also recognized the practical benefits of arriving at arrangements that developers with sensitivity to environmental concerns—such as Deltona—can live with."[17] Nicely put, within the spirit of the moment. However, the reality was somewhat more somber. The Deltona controversy had extended over a period of fourteen years. Settlement negotiations took three years and occurred only after thousands of hours of foot-dragging, influence-peddling, public hearings, back-channel maneuvering, and court battles. Deltona was forced into settling and did so only after pursuing and exhausting all means of achieving its goal: to maximize the number of rooftops south of Rookery Bay.

Epilogue

Celebration of the Deltona Settlement was followed by a decade of relief from controversy on Marco Island, but in 1996 the games began anew. The Collier County Airport Authority, responsible for managing the local airport, obtained permission from Florida's Department of Environmental Protection (DEP) to cut up to 467 acres of mangroves adjacent to the runways and taxiways. An explicit violation of the 1982 settlement agreement, it was never brought to the Conservancy's attention as lead agency for conservation signers. In August 1998, the DEP notified the Conservancy that the airport had requested a major expansion request for more parking spaces and a new taxiway, which would encroach on the lands conserved by the settlement—one of only two nesting sites in the state occupied by the endangered American crocodile. After several meetings, airport authority chairman Michael Williams sent Environmental Policy Director Michael Simonik a fully drafted resolution for the Conservancy board to rubber-stamp. The science division worked up a biological opinion recommending that any taxiway expansion be directed away from the reptiles and twenty-three acres of protected mangroves. The idea was presented to airport management, whereupon the Conservancy learned that the airport had been trimming mangroves all along without first obtaining a legal opinion as to whether the practice violated settlement terms. The Airport Authority took cover by citing Federal Aviation Administration (FAA) regulations, but the trimming affected conservation lands set aside in the settlement agreement. Debate continued over the next twelve months, and finally the airport agreed to limit expansion and purchase 150 acres of mitigation in exchange for a parking area. The final agreement was expanded to include three state agencies, including the DEP, to prevent further misunderstandings.

The era of cooperation was interrupted a decade later when a debate over native habitat trimming erupted on Key Marco, also known as Horr's Island. The island was platted with 134 lots. By 2010 the island had been through three years of declining real estate values, ownership changes on a number of lots, and twenty-four homes built with little oversight. According to the Deltona Settlement agreement, Conservancy employees had the right to inspect areas set aside as native habitat parks, where upland vegetation and archaeological sites would remain untouched. One resident of the island called the Conservancy to report that trimming and clearing of native vegetation was occurring in one of the fifteen designated habitat parks on the island. After receiving no response from code enforcement officials on Marco Island and a preliminary denial of entry from the homeowners association, permission to enter was granted. Two Conservancy employees sent to inspect the damage were greeted at gunpoint and quickly departed. An agreement was reached the following year, setting forth respective rights of both Horr's Island property owners and Deltona Settlement signatories, but the incident highlighted, once again, the level of vigilance required to enforce the original agreement signed twenty-five years earlier.

Deltona began its Marco Island project at the birth of Florida's environmental consciousness. The Cross Florida Barge Canal and Miami Dade Jetport were meeting with determined resistance in central and south Florida. People like Nathaniel Reed, Donald Wisdom, and Joel Kuperberg occupied critical positions in government. Preservation of coastal resources was coming into focus with the Coastal Zone Management Act of 1972 and Florida's Water Resources Act. Each of these elements created extraordinarily difficult permitting hurdles. The economic recession of 1973-1975, caused by a quadrupling of oil prices, combined with Deltona's decision to finance the project from anticipated cash flow, placed great financial stress on the company.

Marco Island remains a highly clustered oasis on the edge of hundreds of thousands of acres of public land. Unlike the smaller villages of Goodland and Everglades City, it is a destination resort and home to thousands of winter visitors. It is suffering the problems of age: Canals are beginning to fill in, and older septic systems are failing. Both spell problems for the numerous bays and productive estuaries surrounding Marco. The Conservancy remains an interested party as solutions are proposed and debated, but they are primarily municipal matters because the boundaries of development are clearly delineated—boundaries that exist because of the work of the Conservancy, Audubon, and surprising stoutness by the Corps of Engineers in denying permits.

Two other projects were in early planning stages when Florida and Washington began to focus on coastal protection. Looking north of the City of Naples, two large developments were proposed with potentially dire consequences for pristine estuaries. Unlike the situation at Marco Island, the Conservancy was in at the early permitting phases of both, but the development trajectory over the ensuing years was divergent in both time and emphasis. We now turn to the cases of Pelican Bay and Barefoot Beach.

CHAPTER 7

PELICAN BAY AND BAREFOOT BEACH

T̲he first case in this chapter profoundly altered the Conservancy's future. First, it demonstrated that the organization could have a dramatic impact upon development in Collier County. Second, the presence of a scientist in helping set boundaries around a sensitive ecosystem was proof positive that the science component from that time forward should expand beyond pure research to become an integral part of the organization's tactical approach toward land-use planning. The Conservancy would take a more active role in the formulation and refining of zoning regulations in southwest Florida, particularly those affecting wetlands and expanses of mangrove forests fringing the Gulf of Mexico. As Governor Reubin Askew's environmental agenda was gaining traction in the state legislature, two large coastal developments were in the works, spanning much of southwest Florida's coastline from Lee County down to the City of Naples. Both dealt with similar ecosystems—bays and estuaries protected by coastal barriers—but the methods were entirely different. The first was Pelican Bay, immediately to the north of the Naples city limits. Above Pelican Bay lay Big and Little Hickory Bay, where Lely Development Corporation had big plans, but we will start with the example of how to do it right: Pelican Bay (see Map 5).

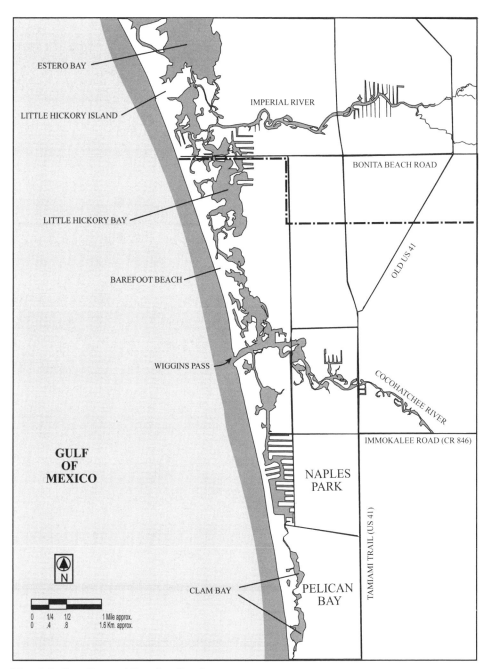

Map 5: Pelican Bay and Barefoot Beach.

Pelican Bay

Westinghouse Communities, Inc. (doing business as Coral Ridge Properties), fresh off successes on the east coast of Florida, purchased 2,104 acres of land in 1972 from the Collier family along the Gulf, running for three miles from Pine Ridge Road on the south to Vanderbilt Beach Road on the north and east for nearly one mile to the Tamiami Trail. The land was bisected by a ridge running north to south at an elevation of about seventeen feet. It was 40% wetlands with a coastal mangrove fringe forest surrounding a tranquil backwater known as Clam Bay. With tidal flushing at multiple openings, fed by interconnected winding tributaries that allowed water to flow freely, the ecosystem was healthy and productive.

To the south, a 760-acre tract called Park Shore was being developed, with a series of high-rises running along the sandy beach. Houses fronting internal bays were protected by hardened seawalls. Westinghouse presumed it could do the same once it filled in the Clam Bay estuary. The president of Coral Ridge at the time (and later of Westinghouse Communities) was Joseph Taravella, who had developed the City of Coral Springs and Galt Ocean Mile in Broward County. Heading up the effort in Collier County was Ross Obley, a thirty-five-year employee of the parent company in various capacities. In an interview, he described himself as having dealt with everything from weapons systems to operations outside Westinghouse's core businesses, a generalist rising through the ranks who eventually found himself assigned to head up planning and building Pelican Bay—a job destined to become the greatest test of his career. Despite his credentials, Obley had no prior experience in real estate development.

Because of its size, Pelican Bay was designated a "development of regional impact," subject to a higher level of scrutiny by permitting agencies. Obley, a trim, meticulous, and thoughtful man, reached out to Bill Merrihue at the Conservancy for guidance. The two men hit it off immediately. Merrihue had been a career man at General Electric, moving from the training program to high office on a path similar to Obley's at Westinghouse. He agreed to become involved in the planning process early on and convinced Bernie Yokel to sign on as lead scientist. Yokel was happily gathering baseline data at the Norris Marine Research Laboratory in Rookery Bay and knew his expertise was in biology and not land-use planning. Westinghouse covered that base by bringing in John Simonds, a nationally regarded expert in community planning who immediately saw that the fundamental problem was water. Pelican Bay could not locate a well field within its footprint without compromising the City of Naples' wells and potable water supply.

Simonds' plan for Pelican Bay was a stroke of genius. Accepting as a given the Conservancy's opposition to any attempt to dredge-and-fill the mangrove forests in Clam Bay, he envisaged high-rises on the western perimeter of with low-rise housing clustered in smaller communities to the east of a three-mile berm separating the estuary from the development. The berm had two purposes. It would operate as an inflow and outflow buffer with six pinch points where control elevations would allow normal drainage to flow into the estuary while protecting buildings along the (inside) edge of the berm from storm surge. Additionally, it would become a tram roadway and interpretive walking trail for environmental education. Commercial centers, normally at the hub of most planned communities of this era, would be located at the northern and southern peripheries.

Another innovation, at Obley's urging, was a dual water system separating potable from non-potable (used primarily for irrigation purposes) water. By recycling rain and drainage runoff for landscape irrigation, less demand would be made on potable water well fields, which would have to be drilled ten miles to the east of Pelican Bay and piped to the coast under Immokalee Road. There it would be stored in a three-million-gallon reservoir for treatment by reverse osmosis, the first application of this technology in the State of Florida. The University of Florida in Gainesville had done pioneering work in reverse osmosis since the 1950s, convinced it was the most efficacious method of desalinating seawater.[1] The technique was time consuming and expensive, but the result was a reliable supply of drinking water for Pelican Bay residents.

The Conservancy, particularly Yokel, appreciated efforts made by

Westinghouse to both avoid mangrove destruction and create an innovative water management system. Many of the permitting agencies at that time had faith in the Conservancy staff's ability to work through issues to create an outcome with the highest possible level of environmental protection. The feeling, as expressed by Obley, was that the Conservancy was straightforward, tough, and honest in its approach toward environmental preservation and that it was better to work with them than against them. "They couldn't be bought; everyone knew that. At the same time, so long as our plans were meeting the needs of the environment they would be flexible and supportive. The government agencies were not well staffed and Yokel understood that."[2]

Staffing was only part of the problem at the government agencies. The permitting process for Pelican Bay involved eighteen different agencies and was becoming an obstacle course for Westinghouse, ridden with delays and conflicting conditions. Anything as large as a "development of regional impact" would get mousetrapped in the back-and-forth between different levels of government.

It took nearly three years, but by 1977 most major issues had been resolved. Building would proceed on the condition that 98 acres of low-grade wetlands would be filled in exchange for the rezoning of 570 acres of "sensitive treatment" lands—representing 25% of Pelican Bay—into conservation. The coastal barrier would remain untouched with the exception of thirty-five acres at the south end and five acres at the north end given over as public parks with full beach access. The estuary, nearly 200 acres of mangrove forests with a navigable channel, ended up being conveyed to Collier County. At the time, county code required beach access seventy-five feet wide at half-mile intervals, but the "sensitive treatment" designation got around that.

Westinghouse and the Conservancy had preserved part of the bays and estuary temporarily. The southern inlet to Clam Bay was closed by construction of the Seagate subdivision. The northern inlet was cut off later by Vanderbilt Beach Road and Bay Colony Drive, which Pelican Bay could have challenged but did not. The central and only remaining outlet to the Gulf of Mexico was Clam Pass. Terminus bays to the north and south would become hydrologically stagnant, allowing detritus to accumulate without any flushing. Abundant sea grasses in the upper and lower bays began to die off from the imbalance of saltwater and freshwater. The mangrove ecosystem in Clam Bay was partially preserved as the biological etiology of those forests was just beginning to be studied and understood.

The evolution of Pelican Bay gave Conservancy scientists and Merrihue firsthand experience working with community planners on the complex problems posed by large-scale coastal development. The value of that newfound expertise would be immediately tested in the form of a proposal to build in another ecologically sensitive area just south of Estero Bay called Little Hickory Island.

Barefoot Beach

Little Hickory Island stretches northward from Wiggins Pass up to Estero Bay. Narrow and nearly five miles long up to Big Hickory Pass, before development it varied in width from 300 feet to 2,500 feet, with white sandy beaches fronting the Gulf of Mexico. On the landward side lay two environmentally important mangrove-lined estuaries, Little Hickory and Fish Trap Bays, with classic wetlands and shallow tidal flats regularly flushed with freshwater from the Cocohatchee and Imperial Rivers. Plant and animal communities had taken hold and thrived there for hundreds for years, creating an exquisitely complicated ecosystem. Of the island's 1,400 acres, approximately 1,200 were wetlands (see Map 5).

Most of the island was owned by Lely Estates, Inc., with big plans for development. The State of Florida had begun purchasing land immediately north of Wiggins Pass in 1972 in an area known as Gulf to Bay Estates to create what would later become Barefoot Beach State Preserve. By 1974, however, Lely decided to begin building on land north of the preserve area and requested a setback variance from the Coastal Area Planning Commission. The Conservancy board offered a lukewarm endorsement of low-density development on the island with the following caveat:

If the proposed Barefoot Beach concept is

> at variance with present state statutes, the
> resulting judgments should be based on
> the immediate local findings and recom-
> mendations of the technical staffs of the
> Bureau of Beaches and Shores of the De-
> partment of Natural Resources and of the
> engineering department of the University
> of Florida, upon whose detailed techni-
> cal studies the new setback line has been
> based.[3]

With the nation in an economic slowdown, little activity took place over the next two years, putting pressure on Lely's finances. Then in February 1976, Christiaan Duvekot, Lely's president, approached the Conservancy with a scheme to turn a quick buck. He paid a visit to Tom McDonough, who held the title of administrator, to explain that when Lely Estates had purchased a large part of Little Hickory Island, it had invested $5 million, having ponied up $1 million cash and borrowed the balance, due to be called by the lender in five months. Duvekot felt he had made a good deal at the time because the county assessor's office had originally valued the land at $8.6 million and he had managed to negotiate the price down to $5 million. He thought Tallahassee might purchase the land for $8 million, and knew the Conservancy had a relationship with the Internal Improvement Fund from its work in the Ten Thousand Islands. Fund trustees would probably look more favorably upon a proposal brought to them by the Conservancy than by Lely Estates.

He laid out a plan saying he had three independent appraisals in hand, ranging from $8.5 million from John R. Wood to $10 million from an unnamed Tampa appraiser. Lely Estates would sell the land to the Conservancy for $1.5 million cash and assumption of the loan balance, which the company believed could be repaid at sixty cents on the dollar because it was held by the financially imperiled GAC Corporation. McDonough was interested. He believed the Conservancy could borrow $5.5 million from the national Nature Conservancy and flip the property to the state for a quick $2.5 million profit (based on an $8 million purchase price), split down the middle between the Conservancy and Duvekot's company. Although the numbers worked, the transaction would be carefully scrutinized by the Conservancy's board.

IIF trustees were scheduled to meet in March, and Duvekot was shrewd enough to remind McDonough and Merrihue that a quickly turned buck could raise enough money to build the new nature center they were desperate to finance.[4] He also knew the Conservancy had been pressing for state purchase of Little Hickory Island, which added legitimacy to the effort. Despite these temptations, the deal was nixed by the Conservancy's board, and while it might have been a bit malodorous, purchase of the entire 470-acre parcel would have made a great deal of sense at the time since it would have preserved a large part of the entire island for public benefit and use.

After the deal fell apart, Lely Estates negotiated an arrangement with its creditors and filed a development application with Collier County in 1977 nearly identical to the petition filed in 1974.[5] As a negotiating ploy, the company offered the county 600 feet of public beach with a 100-car, paved parking lot after the first 100 housing units or lots to the south were sold. In exchange, Lely wanted the county to void the code provision requiring seventy-five-foot wide beach access points at every half-mile interval. This would make the beach virtually inaccessible to the public, and the plan moved forward with little opposition. When Lely's consultant, Bill Vines, appeared before the county commission, he made no presentation and asked if there were questions. After a single irrelevant question from one commissioner and no public comment, a rezone of two miles along Little Hickory Island beach passed unanimously. Why the Conservancy remained passive and defaulted on the Department of Natural Resources coastal setback line[6] was mystifying; its quiescence was uncharacteristic of the organization. The most likely explanation, unsubstantiated by any records, is that a long-standing relationship between Bill Vines and Bill Merrihue worked in favor of the developer and kept the Conservancy temporarily out of the fray.

After gaining approval, Lely did very little between 1977 and 1985.

The nation fell into recession again from 1982 to 1985, and Lely was struggling financially. Coastal development was coming under increased scrutiny at the federal and state levels. The company was in a tough spot. It had established an entitlement but did not want to run afoul of evolving regulations. One impediment was the Federal Coastal Barrier Resources Act of 1982, which discouraged any development of barrier islands susceptible to storm surge during tropical cyclones.[7] Before the act, there were few restrictions beyond coastal barrier lines drawn by county politicians and their developer cronies. Florida's counties jealously retained jurisdiction over the bulkhead line but saw the handwriting on the wall when the governor and Cabinet, after careful scientific study, decided to ban coastal shoreline armoring, i.e., seawalls and riprap, because of the impact on beaches.

By March 1985, the company had worked its way out of financial difficulties by selling most of its beachfront home sites at the northern end of the island—more than 100 lots—and had turned its attention back to Barefoot Beach by filing an amendment to its approved 1977 development plan. The company wanted to obtain legacy rights before the local building code was tightened, but in an abrupt change of heart the new plan was immediately and vigorously opposed by the Conservancy's board, which voted unanimously to oppose all zoning changes.[8]

While publicly opposing the amendments and zoning changes, the Conservancy was holding behind-the-scenes talks with Lely. In June 1985, the new plan was approved despite impassioned pleas by the Conservancy and the Voters League of Collier County, but the victory was only temporary. Shortly after commission approval, the state Department of Community Affairs intervened in a letter to Bill Vines stating that the scope of changes required resubmission as a "development of regional impact" and not an amendment to the existing plan. The number of housing units was one issue, but the main problem stemmed from a traffic analysis showing dramatic impacts on Estero Bay Aquatic Preserve, Barefoot Beach State Preserve, and Bonita Beach Road, used as a main thoroughfare and hurricane evacuation route.

Later that month, the Conservancy filed the first lawsuit in its history against Lely Estates, Inc., and Collier County, challenging approval of a development with significantly increased density in a critically threatened area. "We regret having to take this course of action," said Toivo Tammerk, president of the Conservancy in a press release. "Our firm policy is to work out solutions to environmental problems associated with developments through negotiations and alternative design. Repeated efforts in this matter have failed."[9] He pointed out that the commission had approved development plans for more than 80,000 units in the prior sixty days without hearing objections or reservations from the Conservancy because environmental issues had been satisfactorily settled in negotiations with applicants.

Lely had walked away from the table, but once the lawsuit was filed, settlement talks began immediately, and by December an agreement was reached. The number of residential units would be reduced to 1977 levels.[10] Setback would be at the State Construction Control Line, not the more forgiving county line. A community recreation facility would occupy no more than 10% of available uplands. The agreement set specific development standards and, more importantly, required Lely Estates and its heirs, successors, and assignees to obtain the Conservancy's written approval of any changes, except minor ones, to the site plan, development plan, water management plan, landscaping, and tree removal as long as approval "shall not be reasonably withheld."[11] As in all legal documents, the devil would be in the details, particularly as to what "reasonably withheld" really meant.

After digesting the agreement, Richard Klaas, new president of Lely Estates, wrote the chairman of the Collier County Commission to propose that the southern 1,800 feet of the island be purchased by the State of Florida and that a 9-acre parcel at the northern tip be purchased by either the state or the county as a parking lot. Klaas wanted $5.5 million for the two and stated in his letter, "We would not accept less."[12]

Discussions continued for six months. At one point Klaas suggested the company might be willing to trade 600 feet of the northern tip for identical beachfront on the southern strip, and this led the Conservancy to believe additional frontage might be on the auction block. The

Izaak Walton League and Audubon of Florida commenced a carefully orchestrated campaign to pressure the Florida Department of Natural Resources to use Save Our Coast funds, while George Vega pushed the Conservancy to take action. "We need the support of the Conservancy as the State desires that this become a community matter. It certainly will not become a community matter if the Conservancy doesn't take a position."[13] The board responded by reiterating its support and asked Merrihue to contact Elton Gissendanner, chair of the Land Acquisition Selection Committee in Tallahassee, to urge the state buy 3,100 feet of beachfront. This was the second encounter with Gissendanner, who was a central player in the acquisition of Cannon Island and in the later controversy over the Villages of Sabal Bay. But the story ended well. After the state finally refused to buy the land, Collier County stepped up, swallowed hard, and acquired the frontage for $3.1 million in late 1987.

Public ownership of the beach did not sew up all of Little Hickory Island; it was targeted for development one last time. The remaining private parcel, 1.69 acres at the south tip, was owned by Ricky Stouffer and leased to Paul Harvey of Naples who, in the fall of 1989, proposed to build a combined public and private beach access facility to include a three-story building with restaurant, locker rooms, horseshoe pits, barbeque grills, and bocce ball courts, along with living quarters for a park ranger (as a *quid pro quo* for approval of his project). A private beach shuttle for members would depart from a 100-foot-long dock, with another vessel available to the public (for a small fee). Beachgoers would have an elevated walkway over coastal barrier dunes separated from a "members only" private walk. The Conservancy was appalled at the proposal and suggested to Harvey that he sell his land to the state. But the land was never his to sell.[14] In the final chapter of Little Hickory Island, Collier County commissioner Pam Mac'Kie negotiated purchase of the property from Stouffer for $4.75 million in October 2001, a record price at the time of nearly $3 million per acre.

Barefoot Beach continued to be a problem for the Conservancy. In 2003 the DEP issued a permit to allow the trimming of mangroves. The order extended to both private property and county land. Trimming would allow units facing east to have a better view of the bays. Changes to vegetation were part of the landscaping and tree-removal provision over which the Conservancy had the right of veto, but when asked for an explanation, the DEP stiffed Conservancy scientists as non-interested parties, i.e., not property owners. Terms of the 1986 settlement agreement, when brought to the department's attention, were dismissed with the wave of a hand, bringing on a suit filed in district court. As settlement, both sides agreed to minor trimming as long as it would not affect the forest's health and productivity, and Conservancy scientists were allowed to use the area as a test bed to determine the effects of minor modifications to mangroves over time.

Thoughts

This final twist highlighted a major difference between the two projects. Pelican Bay was owned by a large, well-financed corporation using experts with a record of adeptly managing development in sensitive areas. The Conservancy was brought in during the early planning stages of the project because Westinghouse was facing a permitting nightmare. The company understood the value of having an influential local environmental ally in moving its plans through federal, state, and local agencies caught up in a fitful muddle of regulation. The Conservancy found it easy to cooperate with a sophisticated and well-heeled company. Finally, a close working relationship was established between two men who, by similarities of nature, background, and careers, were able to develop a high degree of trust and see the project through.

Barefoot Beach, on the other hand, dragged on much longer. Both Lely and the Conservancy underwent a series of management changes, making it difficult to establish stable, ongoing relationships at the level enjoyed by Ross Obley and Bill Merrihue. Lely Estates was financially stretched at times. Had Barefoot been developed within the same timeline as Pelican Bay, the outcome might have been different, but by constantly changing development plans over the years Lely flew into the squall line of increasing federal and state scrutiny of coastal development.

The story of Barefoot Beach also chronicled Bill Merrihue's declining influence within the organization and the rise of Ned Putzell, whose interest lay more in pressing for growth management than land preservation. Both men knew the Conservancy needed to adapt. How they guided the organization during those years of increasing citizen participation and government involvement, with a new emphasis on managing growth, is where we now turn.

CHAPTER 8

CHANGING OF THE GUARD

*B*ill Merrihue, having been in the thick of battles over Marco and Cannon Islands, Pelican Bay, and Barefoot Beach, could see that the cozy relationship between local government officials and the development industry was coming to an end and that public participation was going to inevitably increase. He knew his organization, narrowly committed to buying land, would require a portfolio of broader capabilities, so he cast about for a model environmental organization for the future. And right up the Tamiami Trail was Sanibel-Captiva Conservation Foundation (SCCF) in Lee County, structured much like the Conservancy but with significant differences.

SCCF was launched in 1967 as a successor to the Jay N. (Ding) Darling Memorial Committee. Its first president, Roy Bazire, had requested of Joel Kuperberg copies of the Conservancy's charter and bylaws, and the two men quickly became good friends. At the time, Kuperberg was the national Nature Conservancy's designated representative at regional conferences. In February 1968, he attended a meeting on Sanibel Island at which Dr. Joseph Shomon, an adviser to the National Audubon Society, presented his idea that nature center buildings with exhibit spaces were integral to educating the public on the importance of environmental issues, even at the expense of diverting resources from land acquisition.[1] Kuperberg was shocked and reported to Tom Richards, Nature

Conservancy president: "Shomon indicated that they could do whatever they want and need to do in land preservation through scenic easements or the like. It is my opinion that scenic easements in South Florida are not the way to stop the developers. I may be speaking out of ignorance, but I can't see how scenic easements can do the job in an area that is urbanizing at the rate we are."[2] So there it was. Kuperberg firmly believed Sanibel Island's unique ecosystems would be wiped out by careless development but was reluctant to be publicly critical because Audubon was a willing partner in acquiring parcels in Rookery Bay and the Ten Thousand Islands to the south.

Vainly hoping SCCF would follow in the Conservancy's footsteps by using its financial resources to acquire and protect sensitive lands, Kuperberg asked Richards to intervene with the National Audubon Society, but the effort came to naught. Sanibel-Captiva proceeded with its construction of the nature center, and the Conservancy's focus remained temporarily on land preservation.[3] The two organizations took different paths from that point on but remained united on one objective: to protect the coastal environment of Lee and Collier counties.

Big Cypress Nature Center Enters the Picture

Discussions between Bazire and Kuperberg were being carefully monitored by a concerned Bill Merrihue. Ever since taking over as chairman, he had been hearing buzz that the Conservancy was little more than a group of rich folks from Port Royal who wanted to protect their backyard, Rookery Bay. Well connected with a small group of wealthy families and individuals who had retired to Naples, Merrihue felt the organization lacked support within the larger community. His determination to change that had begun with hiring Bernie Yokel to run the Norris Research Center in Rookery Bay. The science component within the Conservancy would expand over the years to become a robust and essential element informing policy positions and educational programs, but Merrihue also believed science lacked direct community impact. He concluded that education was the key to garnering broad support, and there was an exceptional institution located in Collier County, the Big Cypress Nature Center (BCNC). When Kuperberg moved to Tallahassee in 1971 to become executive director of the Internal Improvement Fund, Merrihue felt free to pursue the idea of a nature center without having to deal with Kuperberg's singular concentration on acquiring land.

The center was well run and respected. It had a $25,000 annual contract with Collier County schools to provide state-mandated environmental education. Reaching deep into the community, it had a long history stretching back to the 1950s, with support from individuals, businesses, and organizations such as the United Fund. In the black with a six-figure budget, it was located on a five-acre campus in Naples at the southeast corner of Goodlette-Frank Road and Golden Gate Parkway. Its director was Gary Schmelz, PhD, an ichthyologist from the University of Delaware who had come to the center after a brief stint with Deltona. Programmatically robust, the center had programs for kindergartners on reptiles and south Florida wildlife, after-school activities, and high school programs designed to develop an understanding of the interrelationship among humans, wild creatures, and the habitat they share. The center also had a student ecology club, weekly evening lectures from November through April, and weekend field trips into Corkscrew, Estero, and Rookery Bays. Junior Audubon ran an animal recovery program at the center, taking in injured birds, mammals, and reptiles. Finally, the center ran natural history tours for adults to the Galapagos, Caribbean Islands, and Central and South America. All of this fit perfectly into Merrihue's plan to move the Conservancy into environmental education.

Merrihue knew the center's facility was beginning to burst at the seams. Supporting this was a February 1973 National Audubon study concluding that the "current land area (is) much too small to satisfy present and future needs."[4] The existing site was inadequate for self-guided walking trails designed to demonstrate the ecological diversity of south Florida. The one-classroom building was inadequate for the center's existing programs. And, most importantly, the site was landlocked because the center did not own its access road. Audubon recommended that long-range curriculum planning efforts be postponed until a suitable location for expanded operations could be found within Collier County. On the Conservancy's board at the time was John Blair, who had made his fortune brokering advertising between local television station groups and large national accounts. Interested in education, he had privately expressed interest in supporting programs at the Big Cypress, stating that he would be willing to fund a more robust education component. Merrihue was always ready to run with a good idea, particularly when a major donor was involved.

Merrihue first approached William Webb, superintendent of Collier County schools, about a cooperative effort with the Conservancy. Webb replied that the district already had an environmental curriculum through the BCNC. It is possible (although not certain from Merrihue's notes of the conversation) that the subject of a combination of the two organizations arose at the time because immediately after talking to Webb, Merrihue approached Duane Julian, chair of the Big Cypress board, with the idea of a merger. Julian jumped at the opportunity to tap into the fund-raising capacity of the Conservancy and agreed to take the idea privately to selected members of his board. Merrihue was delighted. He realized that the school programs, trips to the Bahamas and Caribbean, and the center's broadly representative board of directors—beyond Port Royal—were exactly what he needed to fill the Conservancy's dossier. However, he wasn't terribly fond of the wildlife rescue and rehabilitation program.

Merger talks between the two boards progressed throughout the summer and fall. It was decided that the Conservancy would build a new auditorium and classroom building at the Big Cypress site, but right-of-way into the property was a problem. It was controlled by Julius Fleischmann's estate, and the existing Big Cypress building was Fleischmann's old beach house, disassembled and trucked to the Goodlette and Golden Gate location, where it was painstakingly reassembled. Merrihue liked the site because it would locate the Conservancy near his existing donor base, but the right-of-way issue loomed large so he began looking for other locations. After turning down a number of sites in the county, he approached Charles M. Long, executor of Fleischmann's estate, about partially cleared land south of Jungle Larry's zoo. The property had 13.8 acres, including a small bay from which to launch electric boats for Gordon River tours. Long was interested because in a swap he could regain five acres to the north where the nature center building was located. Merrihue wanted an entrance to the new campus directly off Goodlette-Frank Road, but Long insisted on retaining frontage. Merrihue eventually relented, creating an entrance off 14th Avenue North by purchasing one platted lot, but he always regretted not having direct access to the main artery, an issue partially resolved in 2009.

Before closing on the real estate, the merger needed to be finalized. Merrihue wrote Duane Julian a long letter outlining his vision for the combined entity, stressing the Conservancy's ability to provide additional financial resources to relocate the combined organizations, aggressively build membership, and provide staff at the Big Cypress with an appropriate salary and benefits structure.[5] The membership approved the merger in March 1976 by a vote of 370 to 5, with the Collier County Conservancy as the surviving corporation. The Big Cypress board also voted to approve the merger in March with one holdout, Bob Anderson, who questioned the Conservancy's motives and advised his colleagues that the deal would mean the end of the BCNC board. His prescience was largely ignored.

Merrihue was effusive in his praise of the merger: "Rather than duplicating the fine work being carried on by Big Cypress, it seemed far more sensible to invite it to become part of our organization. A merger will give more financial security to the nature center and increase its expertise. We have tremendous business leadership. So, a merger will be a beneficial transfusion for the center. But it will also bring younger people into the Conservancy."[6] Papers were filed with the Secretary of State one month later. Merrihue had a tiger by the tail but didn't know it.

New Campus for the Conservancy

At this point, the Conservancy had to find money to build the new nature center. It was also occupied with challenging a spate of coastal developments including Pelican Bay, Barefoot Beach, Little Hickory Island,

and Key Island. Merrihue's board had turned down a deal with Christian Duvekot of Lely Estates, Inc., to turn a quick buck by flipping property on Little Hickory Island to the state (covered in the previous chapter), so fund-raising had to start from scratch. Charles Long saved the day. He was willing to sign a three-year lease on the existing BCNC facility, which bought the Conservancy time. In a moment of typical optimism, Merrihue closed with the Fleischmann estate in 1978 and turned, as was his wont, to his major donors. In a remarkable series of letters and phone calls, Merrihue convinced his old friend Arthur Godfrey, who had worked wonders in raising money for Rookery Bay, to chair a fund-raising committee. Bill Allyn and Ross Simonds were vice-chairs, and Sam Ross, executive director for the Green Chimneys Farm Center in Brewster, New York, and a seasonal resident of Marco Island, was Godfrey's informal advisor.[7] Merrihue's seasoned solicitors went to work, and by August 1979 the Conservancy had pledges in hand of $1.2 million toward a goal of $2.5 million.

Site planning had begun in 1977 when board members Stuart Douglas, Duane Julian, Jack McElroy, and Bill Oberhelman visited the Sanibel-Captiva campus. Impressed by what they saw, the group recommended wooden buildings on stilts surrounded by nature trails populated by volunteer docents at every important stop.[8] Design of the new buildings began under the aegis of architect William R. Tracy; Kraft Construction Company was chosen to be the general contractor. Initial drawings showed a "mini-university of the outdoors" using local native cypress sheathing for the buildings, which included an auditorium financed by a gift from the Norris family, an education facility donated by the Benedum family of Pittsburgh, a shell exhibit supported by the Drackett family (who would buy Key Island in 1989) and the Naples Shell Club, a science lab, and an administrative facility given by Dorothy and John Blair. The campuslike setting would be surrounded by native trees; interpretive cruises on the Gordon River would launch from an elevated gazebo and landing dock donated by the Thomas Campbell family. A small wildlife hospital and animal rehabilitation center funded by the Naples Women's Club was included, despite Merrihue's mild objections.

The opening of the new campus marked the high point of Bill Merrihue's long and distinguished tenure as chairman of the Conservancy. He had raised more than $2.25 million. He even personally designed a new flag for the occasion: It was royal blue with a gold border and two eagles. Both had gold beaks, and the male had white tail feathers and a white head. Members of the city council, the county commission, the school superintendent, and major donors found their placarded seats in the front rows. After the invocation, Jim Dupree rose as master of ceremonies to introduce dignitaries to the assembled crowd. Every word he spoke had been carefully written and edited in longhand by Bill Merrihue, who originally had intended to have six speakers follow his own presentation but thought better of it and scrapped that part of the program. Putting six politicians in front of 300 people was a bad idea, he thought.

Merrihue's talk began by "thanking the Lord that he gave us the courage to dream no little dream—to plan no little plan—to dare to build for tomorrow, today."[9] In a somewhat shaky hand, he had written on the bottom of his speech that this moment was his "ultimate dream." The address of the new Conservancy facility was 1450 Merrihue Drive.

Merrihue still had to raise an additional $200,000, but his wife was in failing health. He announced his retirement as chairman in January 1982, six months after the death of his friend Lester Norris, then vice-chairman of the Conservancy, in a Miami hospital in July 1981. Norris's wife, Dellora, had passed away in 1979. The organization had lost its two greatest benefactors. The Norrises, in their quiet and unassuming way, had given more than $500,000 toward the purchase of sensitive lands. In addition to support for the Conservancy nature center, the couple had been responsible for saving vast tracts of land for public use, including Delnor-Wiggins State Park, Lowdermilk and Cambier Parks in Naples, and the Big Cypress Bend, as well as restoring Naples City Pier after Hurricane Donna. They were primary donors to the modern Naples Community Hospital and a driving force behind the creation of the 110,000-acre Rookery Bay National Estuarine Research Reserve.

With the new campus open and fund-raising drawing to a close, the merger with Big Cypress was faltering. Merrihue had appointed Jim

Dupree, a Princeton graduate and retired Procter & Gamble executive, to a six-person Big Cypress Liaison Committee in January 1977, but the committee had a relatively short life. It was replaced by a twenty-member "advisory council," composed primarily of former Big Cypress directors and supporters. Minutes of this group's meetings indicate a growing and vocal dissatisfaction with the Conservancy based on the perception that issues important to the advisory group were being ignored by the parent board. Resentment smoldered for some years. Although it had little impact on fund-raising, it flared up again after the new campus was dedicated and open to the public.

Matters came to a head when the BCNC board had to deal with new leadership at the Conservancy. The board elected Dupree as chairman and Ned Putzell, an energetic man whose star had risen rapidly, as president. Dupree was a logical choice. He was known to the Big Cypress board and had been on the Conservancy's executive committee for a number of years. Putzell's selection as president was a surprise. In the 1981 annual report to members, his name was nowhere to be found among the 11 officers and 32 directors, but his lack of involvement within the organization was understandable: He had his hands full as chairman of the Naples Airport Authority.[10] He was a lawyer, having retired after a distinguished career at Monsanto in St. Louis and a stint with "Wild Bill" Donovan's Office of Strategic Services (OSS) during World War II, when he parachuted into occupied France a number of times. He was blunt and direct. Accustomed to adversarial proceedings, he wasn't always concerned with reactions to changes he instituted; he was eager to move the Conservancy forward because of his conviction that land acquisition was only part of the essential mission of a regional environmental organization. His first act was to put the Big Cypress board on notice:

> Six years ago, the BCNC was legally merged into the Conservancy and thereupon ceased to exist as a legal entity. It is a division of the Conservancy. However, certain members of the BCNC and of the Conservancy have continued to think

> and act as though they were two separate
> organizations with different member-
> ships, different membership dues, differ-
> ent publications, different letterheads and
> arm patches, different volunteer groups,
> different publicity—and, indeed as a re-
> sult, different public images. . . . Yet, we
> are in legal theory and in fact only one
> private organization.[11]

The collision was inevitable. The two were culturally distinct. The Conservancy's core support lay in Port Royal. Its board was tightly controlled in the early years by men (and a few women) who knew each other socially. It had begun as and continued to be a successful and powerful acquirer of land. Big Cypress's support was more broadly based. Its board consisted mainly of people who lived and worked in southwest Florida and who were concerned about the quality and content of public education for their kids. Its mission, with a focus on youth and education, was carried out on a more methodically planned basis than the Conservancy's opportunistic acquisition activities. The nature center had been operating on a tight but balanced budget; the Conservancy could call on wealthy donors to support its efforts virtually overnight. The takeover was painful and created long-standing ill will among a number of committed environmentalists, but in the long run those differences were dwarfed by the need for a large and well-financed advocacy organization devoted to environmental protection. The Conservancy was to become just that.

Once the Big Cypress situation was settled, at least in Putzell's mind, he decided to move the Collier County Conservancy out of the shadow of its larger national cousin. By dropping Collier County from the Conservancy's name, he felt the organization would be identified as a more regional organization. When Putzell advised the national group of his plan, Bill Blair, then president of the Nature Conservancy, was adamant that the new name not be "The Conservancy," which would create confusion, but should include some reference to either Collier County or south Florida. His plea was brushed aside, and in November 1982 the organization officially changed its name to The Conservancy, Inc.

Wildlife Rehabilitation

One of the long-lasting legacies from the BCNC merger was the wildlife rehabilitation facility. In the beginning, the program was run in cooperation with Collier County Audubon. The staff created a temporary one-year junior program for young people from 10 to 18 years of age, hoping it would turn into a permanent, self-sustaining activity. Students worked for two hours after school. Advised by paraprofessionals, they participated in special lectures and field trips to help them better understand treatment protocols and the native environment of their injured patients.

The program was created after visits to similar facilities at the Crandon Park Zoo in Miami and the Suncoast Seabird Sanctuary in Pinellas County and was licensed by the Florida Game and Fresh Water Fish Commission in 1975. The rehabilitation clinic handled more than 100 wounded animals and birds in its first year. As word of mouth spread throughout the community, the facility was virtually overwhelmed with birds and animals dropped off for care and treatment. The Big Cypress had no place except a single room in the Nature Center building, but it had sixteen willing student volunteers and a great deal of community goodwill, most notably from Naples City Councilwoman Virginia Corkran. The Big Cypress board, delegated to an advisory role in the merger with the Conservancy, had continued to support the wildlife program with small donations from local residents and small foundations; no funds were requested from either the city or the county despite the fact that the Nature Center's wildlife program was performing some functions normally given over to local governments to deal with sick, injured, and sometimes rabid mammals. Merrihue and the staff had always been concerned with potential liabilities associated with students handling sick animals, but that soon became secondary to fund-raising pressures associated with the new campus, because in 1980 the Conservancy board decided to locate a new receiving and treatment building at the northeast corner of the new campus. The reason? It became abundantly clear to Merrihue that a number of large contributions were coming from wealthy members—many, his friends in Port Royal—interested primarily in wildlife treatment and rehabilitation. The wildlife program was a financial magnet, but had it not been for the persistence of the Big Cypress board and notably Franklin Adams, Duane Julian, Sewell Corkran, and Jim Deupree, the program would never have survived.

By 1981 the program was turned over to college interns, and as the opening of the new campus loomed, Conservancy staff built fencing and flight cages, a swimming pool, and a comprehensive freshwater and sewer system for the long-term residence of injured birds and animals. The board, looking at contributor dollars flowing into the program, hired a full-time director for the operation, Julie Wasserman, who brought new energy to the effort by installing night-deposit cages and a separate telephone system to facilitate handling injured animals. Working with Sally Richardson, the new volunteer coordinator, Wasserman began to integrate trained adults into the operation. They expanded educational programs into local fishing venues, particularly Naples pier, where pelicans were being hooked almost daily by fishermen. The future of wildlife treatment, a wellspring of financial support for the organization, and a hands-on educational platform were ensured a permanent place in the Conservancy's array of services.

The Conservancy's evolution into environmental education with a demonstration campus was as much a matter of expediency as design. The Big Cypress Nature Center provided structure and staff in place, making the expansion a much simplified process. The outcome of the merger, spanning the next thirty years, allowed the organization to broaden its base of support from a few wealthy families and individuals into a constituency numbering more than 5,000. The campus offered a platform from which to engage generations of residents and visitors, educating them to make informed choices about environmental quality.

This was all very much in line with Ned Putzell's thinking. The science staff had convinced him that ecology worked systemically, that rivers and canals were indifferent to local geopolitical boundaries, and that growth had to be viewed through a wide lens. With keenly tuned political instincts, he agreed with Merrihue that public awareness was essential as government assumed more responsibility for environmental protection. Putzell was a realist. Local politicians tended to be highly parochial in defending constituents' interests, particularly when money was involved. He knew state government was the most logical polity to deal with growth management and the health of coastal estuaries and other natural resources abundant in southwest Florida.

Formation of the Environmental Advisory Committee

In another move calculated to change the image of the Conservancy, Putzell decided to host a large luncheon in April 1984 for the Naples and Marco Island boards of realtors. "The Conservancy works closely with developers to protect the aesthetic and environmental characteristics of a project site while maximizing the beauty and appeal of the development. This way everyone wins and no one loses," he said.[12] From 1984 on, all Conservancy donor solicitations were careful to emphasize that the organization worked "with" developers to minimize impacts, reflecting Putzell's supreme political sense that broadening the Conservancy's approach was essential to its future growth.

In a touch of indigestion following the luncheon, Putzell heard from some of his members that they preferred a cautious courtship rather than a hasty embrace of the development community, so he formed a review subcommittee to deflect the criticism. Each project would be brought to a group of three directors for approval: "a. if the developers and promoters have a good . . . record of dealings in the community; b. if their past projects have been compatible with the ideology of The Conservancy, including this particular project. (This must meet approval by Bernie Yokel)."[13] It was clearly stated that recommendation was not an endorsement for the project, but rather a decision to file no objection.

The review committee was not a new idea within the Conservancy. It had first come up in June 1979 when Frederick Spiegel, a developer from Miami Beach, applied for a Corps of Engineers permit to dump 90,000 cubic yards of fill into fifteen acres of tidal wetlands at the confluence of the Gordon River and Rock Creek. Dumping would destroy mangrove forests in favor of another shopping center. Bernie Yokel had been aware of the proposal since January and, with plenty of time to prepare his case, used the Naples Bay Study to argue that the few acres of mangroves left were critical to the ecosystem and any further destruction would have a "serious and adverse biological and water quality effect."[14] Merrihue, who was preoccupied with raising money for the new nature center at the time, formed a Development Review Committee (DRC) to meet with Spiegel. He knew Yokel could hold his own but wanted to put a little more muscle into the effort by bringing in some of his heavyweight board members like Elmer Wavering, retired chairman of Motorola, and George Orr, retired chairman of Miles Laboratories. The strategy worked. After a meeting in November with the committee, Spiegel agreed to pull the development boundary back to a line that would exempt mangroves and wetlands from infill. Only uplands would be impacted.

Over the years of its existence, the committee grew to seven members who met with developers to negotiate environmentally meaningful modifications. Progenitor of the modern-day Environmental Affairs Committee (EAC) at the Conservancy, the group met with developers like Spiegel to fully explore the scope and outcome of each project. While development was the driving engine of southwest Florida's booming economy, it was also the single greatest source of environmental degradation. The committee consisted mainly of former business executives who understood the importance of residential and commercial construction to the local economy. Their intent was never to chill development, rather to minimize its impact on natural resources.

Toivo Tammerk Takes Over

When the garrulous and respected Bernie Yokel left the Conservancy to become head of Florida Audubon Society in the fall of 1984, it became obvious that to place so much responsibility on the shoulders of a single person had been a mistake. With Yokel's departure, the organization would lose its chief scientist and most articulate spokesman, as well as the power behind the classic Naples Bay Study. Yokel's loss placed added strain on Putzell, who was already choking with administrative duties after his first two years as chief executive officer. He misjudged the amount of detail that passed across Merrihue's desk when he took the unpaid position. While he was comfortable in the larger arena of strategic analysis, he felt the Conservancy needed an experienced administrator to take over the day-to-day running of the organization as it moved deeper into environmental education and advocacy. And he had the exact person in mind, Toivo Tammerk, a graduate of Rutgers University and executive director of the Naples Airport Authority. Putzell felt that Tammerk—athletic, active, and intelligent—was ideally suited to manage the organization.

Tammerk inherited a fiscal nightmare. Budget problems had been building for some time until coming to a head at an executive committee meeting in April 1985. The organization was facing a massive deficit. The cost of running the new nature center was unexpectedly high. The education division alone, now staffed by nine full-time employees and four interns, was peering into a $100,000 abyss. Abrupt termination of the BCNC advisory committee had created ill will among some local residents; a number of small donors were falling away. After toying with the idea of selling assets (mainly land) and closing the school system's education program, the committee reversed course and decided to bring on a full-time development director to increase membership and provide professional fund-raising capability.[15]

Despite financial pressures, Tammerk moved to quickly fill Yokel's position with Mark Benedict as director of Environmental Protection and Natural Resources Management. Benedict, tall and intelligent, was a good scientist (with a PhD) and a good environmentalist. Working as head of Collier County's environmental division, he was well known and respected by public officials. With the arrival of Benedict, Tammerk instituted a series of changes in implementing policy positions, depending more upon scientific analysis and less upon the high-touch ability of the DRC and members of the board to work out differences with individual developers. This was illustrated, at best and worst, by the way the Conservancy handled a dredging controversy.

Gordon Pass

Since 1982 the City of Naples and the Corps had wanted to build a new jetty on the southwestern shore of Gordon Pass. The project lacked support in Congress and was dropped until 1985, when the Corps issued a permit for dredging the pass with sand and shell to be spread along the northwestern tip of Keewaydin Island. But in 1986 a Port Royal property owner, Jack Donahue, filed suit in U.S. District Court to enjoin further dredging, complaining that spoil should be deposited on public beaches to the north of the pass and not on privately owned Key Island. Donahue had purchased land called The Point on the north side of the pass, which, due to winter storms, was eroding at a rapid rate, and he wanted to build three replacement rock groins. Lavern Gaynor publicly questioned the wisdom of these structures. Toe to toe were two powerful families: Donahue of Pittsburgh, founder of the enormously successful Federated Funds, and the Norris/Gaynor family, inheritors of Texaco stock with an unparalleled legacy of environmental commitment to southwest Florida. The Conservancy, mindful of its tenuous financial situation, had no desire to offend either party in the dispute but attempted to slow down approval of the project with a letter to the city manager. "This proposed project does not represent a typical CCL (Coastal Control Line) variance request affecting only one upland property owner. The project has potential widespread implications with respect to shoreline stability. . . ."[16] At its February 1986 meeting, the newly elected city council, with support from city staff and in defiance of the Conservancy's mildly stated concern, voted 5–1 in favor of Donahue's petition.

While Donahue won at city council, he lost in court; U.S. District Judge John Moore in Jacksonville refused to grant an injunction and allowed dredging of the pass to continue. But Donahue would not give in. He convinced the state to convene three days of hearings in Naples City Hall with the same outcome. The hearing officer refused to stop dredging and deposition of spoil on Key Island but noted that the question raised by the Donahue case had substance beyond the immediate: Should a public agency (Corps of Engineers) perform work for the exclusive benefit of a private property owner, or should the Corps be required to deposit spoil where it benefited the public? To this question the answer went begging.

With the dredging issue decided, reconstruction of groins off Donahue's property took center stage. The three existing structures were anchored at the northwest entrance to Gordon Pass, swinging out from the shore like the dorsal spines on a gaff sail catfish. Designed to catch sand erosion from storms blasting in from the Gulf, the groins would backwash sand and shells on to a beach at the bottom of Gordon Drive. The third one, which Donahue was most concerned about, had deteriorated to the point it was barely functioning.

Mark Benedict was asked by the city to conduct a study of hydrological impacts. He knew powerful families were involved and, to keep the Conservancy out of the fray, suggested that the city hire Gordon Hine, a professor of Marine Science at the University of South Florida, to provide an independent opinion. Hine's 1982 report showed that the pass, 140 feet wide in 1968, had expanded to 500 feet due mainly to runoff pulses from the Golden Gate Canal combined with extensive dredging of the Naples Bay channel.[17] Widening had created erosion on Keewaydin Island, while the north side of the pass had suffered as tidal outflows scoured the backside of the groins. Benedict maintained neutrality on the issue. "In summary the EP [Environmental Protection] Division has not publicly battled Mr. Donahue over his proposals. Instead, in what I believe is a much more efficient and productive way, we have sought to inform and educate the proper people on the issues involved and on our professional opinion. I presume I will continue to be involved in this issue, in this same fashion over the next few years."[18]

Donahue's contractor then rebuilt the terminal groin higher and wider than permitted and applied later for a 65-foot variance. The

Gaynor family pleaded with Tammerk and Benedict to get involved, but the Conservancy turned a deaf ear by requesting a two-year moratorium to study the hydrologic effect of the overbuilt groin. This infuriated the Gaynor family, creating hard feelings that lasted for many years.

The battle over Gordon Pass illuminated two larger points. First, for more than two decades the Conservancy had relied almost entirely upon volunteers and board members to identify projects and carry each one through to conclusion. Now it was moving from volunteers to professional management, adopting a corporate model rather than the loosely constructed partnership of the past where individuals used the organization to pursue their own interests. The budget crisis required tightly prioritized use of resources. Costs had been cut to the bone. Financial pressures began to force the Conservancy to seek the middle road on issues it might have approached with partisan vigor at an earlier time. Second, while internal changes within the Conservancy created a more formal and methodical process for adopting policy positions, it was not easily accepted by families who had supported the organization during the "hands-on" era of Bill Merrihue, when every detail was attended to personally. In the process, something had been lost: the enthusiasm and *espirit de corps* upon which the Conservancy built its early reputation. It was becoming a burgeoning bureaucracy in order to align itself with changes at the regional, state, and federal levels. Specialists were replacing generalists, formal procedures were replacing handshakes, and more deals were being made in the front parlor than in the back room.

The Merrihue era was fading away. His legacy of land preservation was unparalleled, and his acquisition of the Big Cypress Nature Center set the stage for the Conservancy to grow into a major regional organization with more than 5,000 members to engage and influence growth management legislation and land development regulation. He introduced the concepts of stewardship and education as coequal elements in creating broad public awareness of environmental issues in southwest Florida. And his influence reached well beyond his years into the future, as we shall see in the next chapter.

CHAPTER 9

VILLAGES OF SABAL BAY AND HAMILTON HARBOR

T he next case came to public attention in 1986. It was called Villages of Sabal Bay (see Map 6). To be built mostly in the county, the central element was a fifteen-acre marina in the City of Naples with water access at the southeastern end of Naples Bay. Understanding the depth of the Conservancy's opposition to this relatively small piece of real estate is a critical piece of the history of southwest Florida. It became one of the longest running confrontations between environmentalists and landowners in Florida's history, holding up development of more than 2,000 acres for 13 years. Of greater importance, the confrontation alienated half of Collier County's founding family, creating smoldering enmity that lasts to the present day.

In order to fully probe the root causes of the conflict, we need to be reminded of the Merrihue era and the Conservancy's study of water quality in Naples Bay, which had as its central focus the effect of freshwater inundation and nutrient loading on the bay's benthic habitat but little about the surrounding mangrove fringe forests. There was little research at the time about the role mangroves played as a buffer in intertidal zones, and while the study highlighted problems in Naples Bay proper, the science of mangrove functionality was just beginning to come into its own. But by 1985, well over half of the historic mangrove fringe in the bay had been ripped out by dredge-and-fill (mainly in the 1950s and

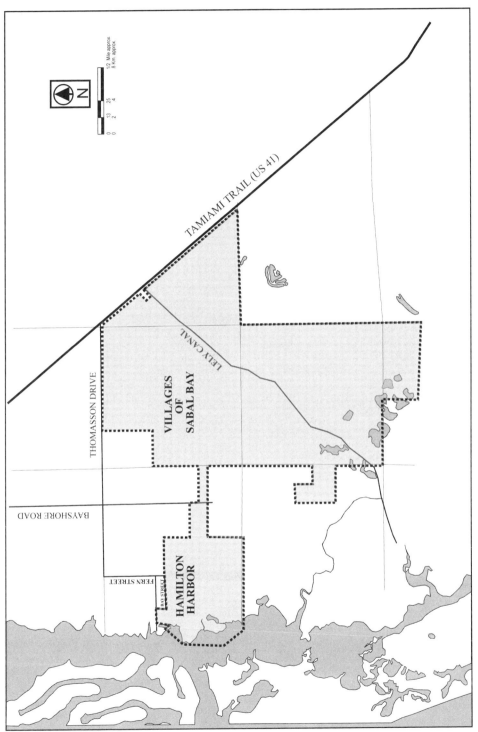

Map 6. Villages of Sabal Bay and original Hamilton Harbor.

1960s) and the remaining forests were in serious jeopardy.[1]

Villages of Sabal Bay

In 1980 the Collier family interests were divided into two separate corporate entities: Barron Collier Companies and Collier Enterprises. Certain shared interests were maintained in oil exploration through Collier Resources. Collier Enterprises went heavily into cattle, citrus and row-crop agriculture including tomatoes and market vegetables. Then, in 1986 one of its subsidiary corporations proposed a massive development stretching from highway US 41 to Naples Bay.

The plan first came to light when, after being quietly shepherded through the regulatory and review process, it whizzed through the Collier County Commission in November. Sabal Bay would be built out over 1,968 acres with 4,000 residential units, 45 holes of golf, a convention center with 600 hotel rooms in two towers, a spanking new marina with 200 wet slips and 610 dry slips, a harbormaster's facility, and a private yacht club. In addition, at the entrance to the development on Thomasson Drive and highway US 41 there would be (and is today) a shopping center. The total developed footprint would be approximately 2,200 acres.

Collier Development had covered all of the bases, submitting its plan to local officials, the Regional Planning Council, and the Department of Community Affairs in Tallahassee. In addition, Collier had obtained approval from the Internal Improvement Fund in July 1986 based in part on an offer from the company to donate 512 acres adjacent to the Rookery Bay National Estuarine Reserve as mitigation for destruction of roughly thirteen acres of mangroves in Naples Bay.[2]

The Conservancy and Florida Audubon immediately filed suit for violation of county ordinances, alleging commissioners approved the project without benefit of an environmental impact statement. The Conservancy then filed a second suit alleging that the county had violated its own rules. By attacking procedural violations, the plaintiffs had a greater chance of success because courts in Florida had a difficult time dealing with litigation involving scientific opinions but tended to favor arguments based on violations of process.[3]

During the interim, Collier Development's request of the City of Naples to approve dredging a channel in Naples Bay to accommodate projected marina boat traffic was met with vocal opposition from conservation groups. The request was delayed until city planners could review the project, and it is impossible to tell if the Conservancy's lawsuit against the county played into the city's wariness, but the possibility was there. The Conservancy's primary concern was the hydrodynamics of the proposed marina channel. Its internal scientific analysis showed that by dredging the channel deeper, polluted water from Naples Bay would breach the tidal barrier formed at Gordon Pass and begin to leech into Rookery Bay National Estuarine Research Reserve. The city spent the next two years reviewing the proposal. A revised configuration for the channel, proposed in November 1988, was rejected because it lacked adequate flushing capacity.

The city then was faced with two options: stick with the terms of the existing comprehensive plan or amend it to conform to specifications for the proposed new marina. The choice was complicated by two sections of the Conservation and Coastal Zone Element of the city's comprehensive plan: to "maintain mangrove forests in their natural state" and to ensure that "residential, commercial or industrial development shall not be allowed to replace key wetlands."[4] Those were both high hurdles, but the highest hurdle was a requirement that the "public benefit" of additional recreational facilities had to outweigh destruction of environmentally vital areas.

While the debate raged in Naples, the state notified Collier Development of its intent to issue a permit for the overall project including the revised marina channel. Initially opposed by staff at the Department of Environmental Regulation (later to become the Department of Environmental Protection), the project had gradually gained staff support. It is tempting to speculate that earlier approval by the IIF might have chilled lower-level opposition, but the most likely explanation is that the project did, in fact, fall within the state's guidelines and was helped along by offers of mitigation. But when guidelines for "Wetlands Preservation as Mitigation" had been issued in June 1988, there was an important note of caution: "Recently, the Department has had several situations in which applicants have offered to donate off-site wetlands to the State . . . as mitigation for dredge-and-fill impacts. The need for sound rationale and policy to evaluate these proposals has become apparent."[5] This was a critical point. For years, mitigation had been widely accepted as a means of compensating for environmental impacts. It worked when the destruction was not site critical, but in the case of mangroves fringing Naples Bay—already seriously compromised—any amount of mitigation at a remote location would be meaningless to the overall health of the bay's ecosystem. It was an admission, by the state agency most responsible for natural resource protection, that mitigation was not always a suitable alternative.

By January 1989, City of Naples Natural Resources Manager Jon Staiger issued a staff report framing the issue: "The decision concerning approval of the Collier DRI or Sabal Bay Project hinges on this one simple thing: acceptance or rejection of the developer's premise that a regional marina is an integral, unalterable part of the whole project." If acceptable, Staiger continued, the project should be approved. If not, it should be rejected because the developer had admitted that dredging 110,000 cubic yards of material would "not be environmentally sound, nor would (it) satisfy the area needs for marina space."[6] Despite this cautionary note, staff joined the state in coming down on the side of Collier, and the city's planning board approved the project with minor conditions at its February meeting. As the city council hearings approached, a Conservancy attorney, Joe Fleming, appeared at a workshop[7] and commented that during the review process "staff of Department of Environmental Regulation was overridden . . . not because of environmental concerns, but because of the realities of political permitting."[8] When Mark Benedict repeated the same claim, it angered Collier Development. The company, through one of its lawyers, John Radley, vehemently denied the charge. Radley went on to request an affidavit from the state to the effect that political pressure had not influenced its decision, arguing that the staff, initially opposed, had changed their minds after seeing a redesign of the project.[9] This was quickly ratified by the state: "We find no basis for these allegations and do not intend to spend any more time investigating them. In our opinion this (project) is in keeping with the statutes and rules under which we operate, and the result of this was, in our opinion, a permitable project."[10]

After two public hearings at which opponents dominated the podium, Naples City Council rejected the plan for Sabal Bay's marina on first reading, overriding the recommendation of its staff and planning board. This forced Collier Development to request a delay of the second reading to deal with council's objections. Not an easy task. The accumulated impacts of mangrove destruction (which had been going on for decades) had become a matter of growing concern in the 1980s. According to the 1979 Naples Bay Study, some three-quarters of the euryhaline plants, mostly red mangroves, had been destroyed by the construction of canals rimming the bay. Dredging during the 1960s had been haphazardly executed, with the depth of each canal based upon the volume of shoreline fill needed to create fingers upon which homes could be built, resulting in deep siltation traps. This—combined with the Golden Gate Canal, draining 130 inland square miles, and numerous leaky septic systems built in the 1960s and early 1970s—had compromised peripheral forests.

The council had a second concern: The impact of increased boat traffic to and from the marina. To answer this, Collier retained Henigar & Ray Engineering Associates to do an exhaustive study of boating in Naples Bay. The report did not whitewash the problem: "Because little has been accomplished toward bay resource management in the decade since The Naples Bay Study so thoroughly defined needed actions, plans to begin a bay management program must be made carefully and competently."[11] However, the matter never really hinged upon boat traffic. It always came down squarely on the marina's importance to the development as a whole. As Collier Development's lawyer put it: "Why must there be any marina. . . ? The answer: without the marina project the Villages of Sabal Bay project is simply not economically viable."[12]

Mayor Ned Putzell convened the June 1989 city council meeting at Naples High School, the only venue large enough to hold the number of speakers expected to weigh in on Sabal Bay's marina. Despite the mayor's plea that speakers not be repetitive, the meeting went on for more than fourteen warm hours until 10:30 P.M., when the council voted unanimously, with one member absent, against the development but opened the door a crack by setting forth twelve conditions to make the project more acceptable.[13]

Collier would have none of it and took its case to Tallahassee, first appealing to Governor Bob Martinez and the elected Cabinet. The company felt this was a safe approach since Martinez was a Republican, elected with generous support from developers, and most of the Cabinet members had been seated around the table when the project was first approved by the IIF in 1986. But Martinez was a pretty good environmentalist, particularly when it came to protecting the West Indian manatee, which would be further threatened by increased boat traffic in Naples Bay. When attempts to pressure the governor failed, Collier Development changed tactics. Its Tallahassee lawyer, John Aurell, filed a request with the State of Florida Division of Administrative Hearings for a review of the city's decision, citing the fact that Ned Putzell had been "a director, president and/or chairman of The Conservancy, Inc. from 1981 until December 1986" and that the "Naples City Attorney represented The Conservancy, Inc. in opposing the Sabal Bay DRI when the project was under consideration by Collier County."[14] The effort came to naught, and the case dragged on through the spring and summer.

By October the administrative law judge rendered his decision supporting the Conservancy and Florida Audubon (which by this time had been joined by Sierra Club and Citizens to Protect Naples Bay as intervenors). The ruling took into account Collier Development's offer to donate land to the state as mitigation and to improve drainage and flood control in Lely Canal running through the center of the Sabal Bay project. However, the decision pointed out those two public benefits did not outweigh the hard fact that flushing of the marina basin would be inadequate to meet required water quality standards for dissolved oxygen and copper, and would further endanger the West Indian manatee, fish habitat, and peripheral wetlands. Collier Development appealed for a second hearing, only to be denied. The next six years were taken up by a series of court actions, all of which went against Collier Development. The company's final appeal, to the Florida Supreme Court, resulted in a July 1996 ruling affirming an appellate court's decision to not rehear the Collier pleadings.

State of Florida Enters the Picture

Meanwhile, another front opened up with broader implications when the state filed an action against Collier County in 1998.[15] Commissioners had just approved a 500-home golf course project in eastern Collier County in the urban/rural fringe—an area of great concern to the state. The urban/rural boundary had been set at highway CR 951. East of the line was primary Florida panther habitat and some of the most precious water resources in Florida. The new secretary of the Department of Community Affairs, Steve Seibert, was highly critical of the county commission's open defiance of the state's growth management plan—with its fast-track approval of rezone petitions—and recommended a moratorium on development. Seibert was a former Pinellas County commissioner who had firsthand knowledge of the implications of unmanaged growth. The moratorium would affect Sabal Bay and other Collier Enterprises plans. But a flat-out moratorium was never a real option for Governor Jeb Bush and the Cabinet. They preferred to manage growth by clustering developments to avoid compromising environmentally sensitive resources. Nonetheless, the unsettled situation in Tallahassee did not sit well with Sabal Bay's investors.

Sabal Bay Becomes Hamilton Harbor

While Seibert's criticism was aimed at creating long-range planning for the eastern lands, it did nothing for Collier Enterprises' immediate concern: how to overcome opposition to developing its property on the east side of Naples Bay. The company returned to the drawing board and in 1998 gained the support of Fred Coyle, who had been appointed to fill a vacant seat on the city council. He claimed his interest was in creating a powerboat fueling station and construction loading facility to take pressure off water traffic in north Naples Bay. A new marina would do just that. So with the blessing and backing of Coyle, the company unveiled its plans for the newly rebranded Hamilton Harbor in March 1999.[16] It would encompass 124 acres, 103 in the city. The built-out portion would occupy only about fifteen acres, five being mangrove fringe forests. The remaining acreage would be zoned conservation as mitigation and deeded to the city. What was not mentioned in the plan, by either Coyle or Collier Enterprises, was the 2,000 acres to the east of the marina designed to have more than 10,000 dwellings.

Coyle believed the project, reduced in size, now had a demonstrable public benefit. This was a critical element going forward, because if the public benefit somehow outweighed environmental damage, regulatory bodies and politicians could find cover for their acquiescence. The Conservancy had always been chary of such arguments because alleged future benefits tended to be difficult to value against immediate destruction of irreplaceable natural resources. It took a dim view of mitigation as well, but the real problem was that, unless and until Collier Enterprises unveiled its plans for the 2,000 acres east of the marina, the cumulative effects would not be evident.[17] But that acreage lay in the county, not the city, and the company was staying mum.

Naples City Council, guided gently by Coyle, asked Collier Enterprises to produce a document setting forth the public benefits and to go back through the planning board. The company quickly obliged. Its presentation was memorialized in a slick leave-behind done by WilsonMiller, the developer's chosen land-use consultant. This was mentioned in the introduction: "We appreciate the opportunity to have participated in this work with Councilman Coyle and gratefully acknowledge his leadership as City Council's designated representative in developing these proposals."[18] The planning board heard the proposal at its May 1999 meeting. After Collier attorney George Varnadoe agreed with member Ken Abernathy's request to plant an additional five acres of mangroves as mitigation for destruction of a little less than three acres, Abernathy became the swing vote, commenting, "I'm going to vote for it . . . but I'm going to hold my nose while I do it."[19] The plan was recommended by a vote of 4–3.

One week later, with Coyle again leading the charge, Naples City Council took the matter up. The motion to rezone property to the east and south of Bay View Park from "Conservation" to "Planned Development" passed 5–2. The debate was rancorous, with Mayor Bill Barnett accusing Councilman Fred Tarrant of "slandering" the powerful family for whom Collier County was named. Environmentalists—including Citizens to Preserve Naples Bay, Florida Audubon Society, Save the Manatee Club, the Environmental Confederation of Southwest Florida, and the Responsible Growth Management Coalition—all spoke against the marina except Guggenheim, who left the door open for further negotiations with the Collier interests. Attorney Varnadoe squashed that idea quickly: "The juice has already been squeezed out of this lemon."[20] So be it.

A lawsuit was filed immediately by Citizens to Preserve Naples Bay and other environmental groups to invalidate the proceeding, while the Conservancy, despite Varnadoe's bluster, stood aside in hopes of beginning negotiations. Those discussions took place later, beginning with a series of letters between Guggenheim and Jeffrey Birr, president of Collier Enterprises, in May 1999. The Conservancy made it clear that joining the suit was an option if negotiations failed and was adamant that there be absolutely no adverse environmental impact from the project. There had to be a net environmental gain, and to get there wasn't going to be easy. As a starting point, the Conservancy proposed three options. The first was to purchase the entire development through the CARL program. The second was to exert efforts in Tallahassee and Washington for a land swap in which Collier would trade the development footprint as well as mineral rights in the Big Cypress (which Collier had retained when it sold that land) in exchange for Homestead Air Force Base as a site for development.[21] Finally, the Conservancy and Collier would jointly redesign Hamilton Harbor to minimize effects on mangroves, water quality, and manatees. Guggenheim knew the first two were weak reeds to cling to but hoped the third might interest Birr. And it did, after Birr set three conditions for future negotiation: that the Conservancy abandon its "not one mangrove disturbed" principle; that the subject relate only to Hamilton Harbor and not to the larger development or land purchase/swaps; and that the meetings include scientists from both sides to evaluate proposals and counterproposals.

After their first meeting, Birr wrote Guggenheim an optimistic assessment of the proceedings, but the very next day the Conservancy board, in a contentious meeting, voted to join the suit against Hamilton Harbor with the understanding that it could withdraw at a later date to file an independent action if necessary. The board's rebuke stung Guggenheim. He argued that the development company would see this as double-dealing and finally convinced directors to let him reach out to the Collier interests to let them know that negotiations could, and should, continue despite the decision to join litigation. This was a good call, for two weeks later Birr wrote Guggenheim suggesting that a meeting or two might be productive. The executive committee of the Conservancy agreed. Meeting dates were set for July, and Guggenheim was instructed to keep the tone positive. But the seeming goodwill between the two reached a flash point with an incident in the state capital.

In early July, Collier Enterprises scheduled a conference at the Department of Environmental Protection offices in Tallahassee. Mimi Wolok, general counsel of the Conservancy, showed up as a member of the public but, after vigorous protests by Collier attorneys already seated in the meeting room, was turned away at the door by department personnel. Since public business was being discussed, Wolok felt she had a right to be present. After being denied access, she requested, under the state's Sunshine Law, copies of any minutes of the meeting along with all exhibits regarding Hamilton Harbor. Her request was met with stony silence. This provoked Guggenheim; he was ready to throw in the towel. He wrote Birr: "At this point, given what we understand to be your minimum goals, we are at a loss to advance ideas that are likely to be acceptable to both of us."[22] But his board and primarily the chair, Ellin Goetz, were emphatic about the need to continue talks despite the Conservancy's joining in the lawsuit.

Goetz, a local landscape architect, had risen quickly in the organization. She explained it this way: "After John Fitch left, they were trying to make the board more diverse. To be honest, it was mostly retirees then—a 'good old boys' network. David Highmark, who was chair at the time, recruited me to come on the board with other working people. David was a working guy, running Northern Trust in Naples." She continued: "When I became chair right after David, I was leery of the expense of legal proceedings. It was important to find a way to continue to talk, instead of drawing guns and starting to shoot."[23] There may have been another reason to "continue to talk." Goetz was part of a group that had set up a Florida land preservation trust as a way to get large parcels into public hands. On the committee was Miles Collier. The program never gained traction. "Even with Miles there, it just didn't work out," said Goetz. "But, it did lead to Conservation Collier which turned out to be a great program, so I never felt the time and effort was wasted."[24] (Goetz was chair of the political action committee running the campaign).

The Conservancy then abruptly changed direction. Both the Environmental Affairs Committee and Executive Committee had become uncomfortable with litigation counsel and recommended that the Conservancy pull out and go it alone.[25] With help from Dick Grant, a respected land-use attorney in Naples, Guggenheim selected Tallahassee attorney Steve Pfeiffer to prepare motions for filing after Guggenheim took one last shot at settling with Birr. Grant told Pfeiffer that the Conservancy would like to find a way to work with the Collier family if possible but could not countenance destruction of mangrove forests with no offsetting environmental gains. "We do not want to challenge and litigate just to 'blow smoke' and stall things in court or the administrative process. If we did it would not succeed and we would lose all credibility. The Conservancy has credibility and we want to keep it."[26] Pfeiffer was cautious: "I am not wildly optimistic that we can reach accord for several reasons. First, there is a level of acrimony in this case. Second, Collier Enterprises appears married to the plans they have already developed."[27]

In late July, the Conservancy mailed two notices of "intent to sue" on its own. The first was addressed to the mayor, alleging that the city had violated its own comprehensive plan and requesting it rescind approval and issue no permits to Hamilton Harbor. A second was sent to the Department of Administrative Hearings in Tallahassee, asking the state to disallow the project based upon the city approving development on land already designated as environmentally significant.

The letters had no effect. A first complaint against the city was filed and assigned to state administrative law Judge Lawrence Stevenson. In its brief, the Conservancy argued that Hamilton Harbor's application should have been adopted as a regular comp plan amendment, requiring review by the Department of Community Affairs and other agencies, and that the plan adopted was based upon insufficient data. While the marina within the city limits involved a little more than five acres and the upper limit for small-scale amendments to local comp plans was ten acres, it was the Conservancy's position that the project should not be looked at by itself but rather in terms of its *use,* which was to serve a much larger "development of regional impact." When county land was included, the fully developed project would consume much more than fifteen acres, which would place it into large-scale amendment review process. And, if the mangrove preserve was considered, total *use* would exceed 100 acres. Collier Enterprises' position was that the storage, fueling station, and loading dock, comprising a little more than five acres, lay within city limits and was therefore subject to city approval only (after public hearings). The balance of the project was in the county, and it believed the county would rubber-stamp the plan.

Judge Stevenson's first act was to disqualify Collier Enterprises' attorney Ken Oertel because he had represented the Conservancy and other groups in the initial proceedings to stop Villages of Sabal Bay. Oertel, with more than six years' experience representing conservation groups, had proprietary information that might be used against them in court. The next day, the Conservancy filed an action in circuit court against the City of Naples and Collier Enterprises, keying in on a central question: Did the city's approval of a private comprehensive plan amendment in May involve a "small-scale development" consistent with the city's comprehensive plan?[28] The logic behind this second filing was somewhat different than the first: Approval of a "Planned Development" by the city could not become effective until the plan amendment itself was final. In other words, the second case was contingent upon the outcome of the first. Then efforts to settle the dispute took on new energy, moving from Guggenheim and Birr to attorneys Pfeiffer and William Williams, who had been hired to represent Collier Enterprises after Oertel's dismissal. Despite being a codefendant, the city was either uninterested or incapable of entering the discussions because there was an election in February that could upset the applecart. And it did.

In February 2000, three new candidates swept into office. According to rhetoric during the campaign, it was likely that Hamilton Harbor ordinances would be repealed. Collier attorney George Varnadoe wrote the new council to argue that reconsideration of a prior decision was probably illegal and would deprive his client of vested rights and due process. It was a thinly veiled threat. The letter infuriated Guggenheim, who alleged Varnadoe had engaged in unethical conduct by asserting meritless claims in an attempt to intimidate the public and its elected representatives. A phone call to Dick Grant, by then board chair of the Conservancy, produced a written apology from Guggenheim, but the exchange was an indicator of the level of frustration on both sides.

The Conservancy pressed for repeal. It contended that neither the plan amendment nor the rezone was "effective," and there were no statutory provisions prohibiting repeal prior to the "effective" date of an ordinance. Two weeks later, after a raucous meeting, the city council voted 4–3 to repeal both the small-scale amendment and the rezone of the 124 acres from "Conservation" to "Planned Development." At second reading, Collier Enterprises brought in John Passidomo, a Naples attorney renowned for his skill in dealing with administrative and elected bodies. Joined by a former mayor and two former city council members (including Fred Coyle, who had played a pivotal role in negotiating the fueling station as part of the revised Hamilton Harbor plan), Passidomo made an impassioned plea to reconsider the first vote. Despite his efforts, Councilman William MacIlvaine summed up his feelings before voting for repeal: "I think it's a good day for the environment, I think it's a good day for the majority of residents in the City of Naples, and I think it's a good idea to repeal bad ordinances."[29] Repeal sustained on second reading 4–3.

Satisfied, the Conservancy withdrew its two lawsuits. Collier Enterprises immediately sued the city in Circuit Court for $25 million on eleven separate counts. But in this case, two council members who had voted against repeal, Gary Galleberg and Tamela Wiseman, vocally opposed having face-to-face meetings with Collier Enterprises representatives. Wiseman was a real estate attorney; part of her concern was that city officials might say something during discussions admissible as evidence in court. A second action was filed by Collier under the Bert Harris Jr. Private Property Rights Act of 1995, requiring the city to make a settlement offer, but the city was unable to agree on an attorney, which dragged matters out until fall.

The second suit had significant financial implications for the city. The Bert Harris Act was passed after Governor Chiles appointed a Property Rights Study Commission II[30] in 1993 to look into ways to establish relief for property owners from unduly burdensome development orders. Based on some of the study commission's recommendations, the act allowed property owners compensation or other forms of relief when a government regulation, ruling, or action overly burdened a vested right or "existing use." This second phrase was defined as "reasonably foreseeable, nonspeculative land uses which are suitable for real property and compatible with adjacent land uses."[31] The act, written by more than a dozen lawyers, reiterated property rights case law almost to the word but attempted to make the adjudication and award process simpler and less costly. While putting local government on notice that it must carefully examine any action before placing an unfair burden on a property owner, the act established a one-year statute of limitations and required the losing party to pay all legal fees, a provision calibrated to chill plaintiffs. Some pundits thought it was an opportunity to scare the pants off local elected officials with fatuous claims, but the law did not overwhelm the courts as expected. More than 200 cases were filed during the first ten years after passage; only six went to trial and the others were settled out of court.[32]

Now removed from the courtroom, the Conservancy and its environmental partners saw a way to clarify critical areas for preservation. Working with city staff, they managed to introduce a city charter amendment to make a practical distinction between "conservation vital" and "conservation transitional" lands.[33] Mandated for "developments of significant environmental impact," the definition would make it easier for all parties, mainly property owners, to distinguish between critical areas and adjacent buffer zones (which would be subject to rezoning on a case-by-case basis). Much of the drafting was done by Gary Davis, a skilled and articulate lawyer from Tennessee, a former university professor, and part of a new team at the Conservancy headed by Guggenheim's replacement, Kathy Prosser. The move was a signal by Prosser to the development community that the atmospherics had changed at 1450 Merrihue Drive. She realized that capitulation would infuriate a small, powerful cadre of Conservancy supporters, so she opted for clarification of a previously murky area instead.

Prosser, like Ellin Goetz, felt Sabal Bay litigation was draining both staff time and financial resources. "Prior to my arrival, the organization's oft-used policy tools were litigation and saber-rattling. They were necessary tools to gain attention and respect from regulated communities. However, based upon my experiences running a 'command and control' regulatory agency, and then heading an environmental dispute resolution organization, I believed the country at large was ready for an additional approach, one built on partnerships and finding common ground where possible."[34] Her "experiences" included a position as Cabinet secretary in Indiana, heading up the Department of Environment from 1989 to 1996. She moved from there to become Secretary of the International Joint Commission, a U.S. and Canadian environmental organization, and on to a dispute-resolution group in Colorado before joining the Conservancy.

As the Conservancy's new chief executive, Prosser entered the Hamilton Harbor controversy more directly by offering to assist the city in its settlement discussions, but the mayor declined, citing complications from multiple lawsuits.[35] She had well-developed political antennae and, while being introduced to the Naples community, discovered deeply held feelings of animosity toward her organization. She met with Parker and Miles Collier at their house in Port Royal to learn from them that the Conservancy's opposition was a source of great tension throughout the community. Looking further into the matter, she became convinced progress could be made if she worked personally with Tom Flood, the new chief executive for Collier Enterprises. She and Flood quickly established a working relationship. Giving staff members on both sides time to work out details, they reserved the right of final approval of any agreement. Prosser credits Flood with breaking the logjam. "I believe Tom's leadership in this way sent strong signals to his team that the time had come for these issues to be resolved."[36]

In September 2002, the first steps toward resolution came with a revised plan moving the marina to a location south of city-owned Bayview Park. Collier attorneys and the city finally reached an accommodation based upon a report by biologist Samuel Snedaker. Well known to the Conservancy, having testified on its behalf against the earlier Sabal Bay marina in June 1989, Snedaker suggested that affected mangroves be placed into the "conservation transitional" category because of their stressed condition. The city council was scheduled to hear details of the compromise agreement at its September meeting, but when the agenda was published, no mention was made of the deal. This would have deprived the public of an opportunity to comment, and it was Mayor Mackenzie's plan to add the item to the agenda at the last minute. Citizens to Preserve Naples Bay, headed by Harry Timmins, protested that a conditional settlement agreement to litigation was a quasi-judicial matter and that in order to effectively present their case, all affected parties needed time to prepare. Mackenzie backed off and the matter was postponed.

Collier Enterprises used the postponement to weigh in privately with another plan that reduced mangrove destruction to half an acre and built in 36 wet slips and a little more than 300 dry slips. With that, the city executed a conditional settlement agreement in October. The proposal squeaked through the planning board 4–3 and was scheduled for council approval in March 2003. To tighten things up, the Conservancy and Citizens to Preserve Naples Bay entered into an agreement with Collier that February, stipulating set-aside of an additional thirty acres of mangroves along the Gordon River as mitigation. The city would incorporate certain conditions into the development order in exchange for the Conservancy's promise not to oppose a finding that the marina was "in the public interest," but the Conservancy continued to maintain the long-held position that the marina violated the City of Naples Comprehensive Plan.[37] When the details went to Tallahassee, the state cited inadequacies in the manatee protection element, forcing another revision to the settlement plan, but the deal finally went through with the withdrawal of all suits, including the Bert Harris action.

In August 2003, Collier Enterprises announced it had negotiated an option agreement for WCI Communities to take over the Sabal Bay property. WCI Communities was a somewhat modified version of the same company that had developed Pelican Bay; it was riding the crest of a growth wave in south Florida. WCI partnered with the Conservancy to create an acceptable site plan, and the two organizations submitted a rezone request, asking the county to change from Planned Unit Development to Mixed Use Planned Unit Development. This was the first step leading to a plan the following year encompassing 2,416 acres, with 1,999 varied housing units, a golf course, commercial and recreational centers, public facilities, and access to Hamilton Harbor Yacht Club. Terms of the revised plan included some impact on wetlands heavily infested with exotics in exchange for placing additional upland scrub habitat into preservation and creating a buffer between preserve areas and structures. WCI agreed to improve drainage by widening the Lely Canal, offered to include affordable housing in the development, and gave the Conservancy right of review on conservation easements. The project went on a fast track; final approval was granted by the county in 2005. The water management district issued a permit later that year, and the Corps was in the midst of reviewing a Section 404 permit[38] for the property when the roof caved in. WCI pulled out in September 2006, citing rapidly deteriorating conditions in the southwest Florida real estate market. The company's net income was down dramatically; it was trying to adapt to changed conditions by laying off employees and cutting back on commitments. Collier Enterprises was left holding the land, but the project's approvals are still in effect.

In the fall of 2011, Collier Development Corporation filed an amendment to the approved WCI plan, converting acreage set aside for a golf course into a series of interconnected lakes, but the county planning commission balked at giving the Conservancy the right to review conservation easements as part of the revised development plan. That matter was settled by a side letter between Collier and the Conservancy.[39] In July 2012, Collier Enterprises sold building rights to Minto Corporation, a Canadian company that had begun operations in southwest Florida. Preliminary plans showed much of the development would remain in a natural state, featuring hiking and biking trails as well as kayaking throughout the 2,300 acres, with 1,600 homes and no golf course. High-rise condominiums were mentioned but not within the first phase of building.[40] Minto had a green image, and its purchase of rights from Collier raised very few eyebrows within the environmental community. Hamilton Harbor Yacht Club was not included in the deal.

The Importance of Sabal Bay

Thirteen years in various courts until disposition of the last case, Villages of Sabal Bay and Hamilton Harbor was one of the most significant challenges ever faced by the Conservancy. Numerous developments were opposed by environmental groups over the years, but none were as protracted as Sabal Bay, complicated by shifting sands in Tallahassee and at 1450 Merrihue Drive. A lack of predictability is anathema to most businesses, especially southwest Florida's development community. During the controversy over Sabal Bay and Hamilton Harbor, Collier Development was attempting to contend with local opposition, a process complicated by Governor Martinez's apparent reversal of support for the project. It led Collier, the largest landholder in the county, to press for explicit land-use planning rules—as few as possible but clearly set forth. The company's dealings with the Conservancy pointed out another problem: leadership transitions. The Sabal Bay project spanned five Conservancy presidents.[41] Apart from Guggenheim's attempts to negotiate with Birr, it was difficult for Collier Enterprises to develop a relationship with someone on the other side of the table. The same situation applied within the environmental groups fighting Sabal Bay. At times the Conservancy would stand with its partners and other times stand aside. The Conservancy, through all of its leadership changes, was an unpredictable element during the thirteen years until Prosser came in and attempted to stabilize relationships on both sides of the dispute. The one constant in the process was the Conservancy's implacable opposition to any further destruction of mangroves in Naples Bay. The marina was always the key piece of the development plan; if it resulted in a net loss of mangroves, it was unacceptable.

The battles over Sabal Bay and Hamilton Harbor created a residue of ill will between the Conservancy and one side of the founding family of Collier County that continues to this day, despite the fact that Collier Enterprises built the world's first Audubon Signature Sanctuary golf course at Collier's Reserve in 1995 and Old Collier Golf Club near the Cocohatchee River without objection from the larger environmental community.[42] Miles Collier was part of a large effort to create a land trust for southwest Florida. Tom Flood has publicly stated his interest in making the company's legacy one of sustainability with environmental safeguards, but to this day the two organizations still regard one another with a wary eye.

CHAPTER 10

EBB TIDE

*D*uring the protracted battle over Villages of Sabal Bay and Hamilton Harbor, changes in Tallahassee marked a gradually diminishing commitment to environmental protection in the increasingly conservative legislature. After passage of the Local Government Comprehensive Planning Act of 1975, little activity took place for nearly ten years, but by 1984 the issue of growth management was heating up again. The state's first attempt at a comprehensive plan, after being turned down in 1978, was revised and rejected again by the legislature in 1980. Local governments, floundering with no approved state plan to guide them and little experience in planning, slogged through multiple iterations, producing documents that were internally inconsistent and nearly always unenforceable. Governor Graham, fed up with the situation during his second term, appointed another Environmental Land Management Study committee (ELMS II) to evaluate progress (or the lack thereof) toward statewide integrated planning.

Growth Management in Retreat

After two years of study, the bipartisan committee worked with the legislature to enact the State and Regional Planning Act of 1984, requiring regional councils to produce plans coordinated upward with state plans (adopted in 1985) and downward with local plans. Many of the loopholes in earlier efforts were closed with two dramatic results. First, each state agency was mandated to produce and act upon a plan consistent with the state plan. Second, regional councils moved out of an adjudicatory role; they were given the authority to force better planning at the local level. But in the process, regional councils' power to review DRIs was cut back. Local governments could be certified to perform reviews of projects within their jurisdictions, and all projects were to be given equal treatment regardless of size. Command and control was being replaced by incentives at the local level.

A second piece of legislation, the 1985 Local Government Comprehensive Planning and Land Development Act, went another step beyond simply clarifying parts of the 1975 act. It created state-mandated concurrency. The principle was straightforward: Development should not be approved at the local level until infrastructure serving population growth was in place, including water supplies, drainage and waste disposal, transportation, public schools, parks, and recreational facilities. By mandating concurrency, the state became a target for criticism both from developers who had to front-end money to local governments in the form of impact fees for the improvements and from local governments resenting the fact that Tallahassee was dictating rather than merely suggesting.

While command and control aspects of earlier legislation were being softened, the 1985 act strengthened the Department of Community Affairs (DCA), the state's land planning agency. Its role was no longer to simply "review and comment" but to definitively approve local plans and impose conditions when necessary.[1] The state could amerce noncompliant counties and municipalities by withholding state grants and matching funds. In order to involve citizens in the process of creating local comprehensive plans, elected officials began to rely less on overworked staff and more on consultants with the time and expertise to study critical issues in depth. The law also encouraged local residents to participate in formulating land-use policies and expanded the right of citizens to challenge local plans and seek injunctive relief. This last change gave the Conservancy standing to challenge what it viewed as inconsistent application of zoning and building codes in the case of Villages of Sabal Bay and later Hamilton Harbor.

To the surprise of many, Republican Governor Bob Martinez, in office from 1987 to 1991, made oversight of growth management one of his priorities with the appointment of Tom Pelham, a Tallahassee lawyer, to head up DCA. Pelham would become a key player for the next twenty years, having a critical role in the formation and revision of Collier County's Rural Lands Stewardship Program in 2002 and again in 2007. During Martinez's term, Florida was becoming increasingly Republican with the influx of retirees, particularly military families retiring to the Panhandle. But Martinez remained a strong environmentalist, as borne out by his actions in the Villages of Sabal Bay case.

Planning for the 1990s

While growth management laws were being overhauled in Tallahassee, the Conservancy was dealing with change too. As his tenure unfolded, Toivo Tammerk's political skills were obvious, but the organization lacked a coherent, overriding vision. It had grown into an organization with multiple functions, each with a different constituency, all competing for finite resources. Tammerk's background was in single-purpose organizations with specific missions. Adding to his difficulties, the board had become restive when Deltona's lease for operational control of the Marco Island Airport—home to the state's largest endangered American crocodile population—was about to be terminated and the State of Florida offered it to the Conservancy. Tammerk, with his experience in managing airports in both Naples and Tallahassee, jumped at the opportunity. The board pushed back. Ownership of an airport would be completely off-mission, and some members resented Tammerk's insistence on such a "harebrained scheme" with incalculable liabilities. The board turned it down flat; the airport eventually came into the custody and oversight of Collier County.[2]

Tammerk survived the airport debacle, but the incident created lingering questions about his judgment. To calm the troubled waters, Tammerk assigned Mark Benedict the task of producing a conservation strategy for the coming decade. Benedict was described by a colleague as "very bright. His heart was in the right place, and his specialty was more in environmental planning than in pure science. But he knew what he was doing and ran a good shop."[3] Having worked for the county, Benedict had spent his first weeks at the Conservancy separating science from policy and, as much as anyone in the organization, was responsible for convincing Tammerk to take on a more public role while leaving scientists to remain untainted by the venal compromises required by political realities.

Tammerk was lucky to have Benedict handling both science and policy because Benedict understood how to relate the two. He created an agenda for the 1990s with a broad, visionary approach. Based on a staff review of the organization's first two decades, his report concluded that local growth management and regulatory efforts had failed to protect critical natural resource areas because regulators were always looking at projects on a site-by-site basis. Little or no thought had been given to the broader picture of cumulative impacts and sustainability (known as a bioregional strategy), which attempted to balance growth with environmental concerns. This was a critical conclusion by the Conservancy at an important moment in its history; the issue would arise again and again as federal and state permitting bodies openly ignored the broader ecosystem implications of their decisions.

The report set forth three goals: to identify, map, and rank natural resources; to promote acquisition and conservation easements to protect resources; and to create a Collier County Natural Resource Protection Program. The first goal—the easy one—was accomplished with grants from the Laurel Foundation using the national Nature Conservancy's computer modeling system for data compilation and analysis. Two large ecosystems in need of protection were identified: Rookery Bay (the focus of the Conservancy's attention for more than two decades) and Corkscrew Regional Ecosystem Watershed (CREW), the last undisturbed watershed in the north end of Collier County. Benedict and his staff had selected as the core issue the need to carefully regulate and monitor development activities in areas on the periphery of sensitive CREW lands that would lead to interference with historic water flow patterns, a natural flood-control mechanism that allowed water to spread out and eventually either sink into the surficial aquifer, evaporate, or ooze away to the south and west.

Rookery Bay Redux

In the case of Rookery Bay, the concern was nutrient pollution causing imbalances in the ecosystem. Benedict had reliable long-term data to back this up, going back to 1967 when Joel Kuperberg had convinced the Conservation Foundation in Washington to do a demonstration study of the 4,000 acres comprising Rookery Bay at the time. The study, funded by the Ford Foundation, was designed to establish recommended management practices once the entire estuary was purchased for public use. The Conservation Foundation's president was Russell Train, later to become second head of the U.S. Environmental Protection Agency under President Nixon. The study was initiated with great fanfare and public input. Even Norman Herren, general superintendent of the Collier Company, which owned thousands of acres in Rookery Bay, expressed support: "The Collier interests have always been concerned about the preservation of the unique natural features of our area, as attested by the several gifts made to various government and private natural area groups over the years. We would give sincere consideration to any information provided us that would tend to create harmonious development of the Collier holdings in the Rookery Bay area."[4] That closing clause was not well received by Kuperberg, who preferred preservation to "harmonious development."

Train was interested enough in the future of Rookery Bay to personally hold a public meeting at the Naples Yacht Club in January 1968. He remained deeply involved in the project, which he saw as a template for future studies of estuarine ecosystems. The report, known as the first Rookery Area Project Study, was presented to Collier County commissioners and a group of major landowners in May 1968. There were five recommendations: (1) create a single governmental entity to control development of lands adjacent to Rookery Bay sanctuary; (2) control waterborne pollution at the source by protecting against sedimentation from dredging and unnecessary land clearing while strictly regulating pesticides and fertilizers; (3) design meandering arterial waterways surrounding Rookery Bay to allow natural tidal forces and mangrove fringe forest flushing; (4) cluster any development and create large, contiguous common spaces rather than urban sprawl; (5) ensure that islands in Rookery Bay remain accessible only by boat.[5] This last point was clearly aimed at preventing another "road to nowhere" from emerging as a driver of coastal development.

The county commission, in a stunning departure from past practice, passed a resolution "that the developmental objectives and general recommendations set forth in the publication Rookery Bay Area Project published in 1968 by the Conservation Foundation, Washington, D.C., are hereby endorsed."[6] Commissioners went on to iterate specific steps, including regulations to ensure "strict enforcement of county regulations and (to) take immediate action to correct any violations of county regulations which may now exist within (Rookery Bay)."[7] Warm embrace of this first study by political powers gave the environmental community heart, particularly the admission that enforcement was a necessary concomitant of regulation. But the study was also cautionary in concluding that wildlife, commercial fishing, and water-centered recreation were dependent upon *early* adoption of sensitive design principles to preserve the downstream impact on the estuary. The first study was so well received that Collier Development Corporation, Van der Lely Development Company, and the Fleischmann family, owners of the vast majority of acreage in northern Rookery Bay, requested the study team prepare development plans for their private lands.[8]

The success of this first effort led to a much larger study, seven years in the making, on the future of Rookery Bay. Its timing was impeccable because the Institute of Marine Science at the University of Miami had just established a Laboratory for Estuarine Research headed by the eminent Arthur Marshall, a coastal zone ecologist who attracted funding from the National Science Foundation and U.S. Department of the Interior.[9] He wanted to use the Conservancy's new Rookery Bay facility "to develop methods of protecting this valuable 4,100-acre estuary from the effects of urban development which is planned for the land surrounding it."[10] Marshall assigned one of his people, Bernie Yokel, to design the more expansive study. Yokel was highly motivated. He cared deeply about the subject; it also gave him a research basis for his doctoral dissertation. As described by a colleague: "Some people have it, and some don't. Yokel was one of those who had it. He would make you listen. It wasn't always what he said, it was the inflections. He had a way of saying things that would just catch your attention."[11]

After Yokel compiled baseline data, the second study was issued in December 1974. It was authored by ichthyologist John Clark, a senior research associate with the Conservation Foundation and a former employee of Woods Hole Fishery Laboratory in Massachusetts. The study was a model of simplicity. In eighty-eight pages, it presented "primary standards" for maintaining mangrove fringe ecosystems but in a nod to reality also included a set of "contingent standards" to fall back on should there be a compelling reason to abandon the preferred criteria, such as an irreversible prior commitment to a given use or an adverse court decision. The white paper concluded that Rookery Bay could not be protected in isolation from surrounding lands. The hydrodynamics of watershed drainage from upland acreage called for an integrated approach to management of the entire ecosystem. Recommendations were straightforward: Freshwater should exit boundaries of a development with the same chemical characteristics and in the same quantities that it entered; any significant alteration of natural drainage patterns should be avoided; water levels may be raised but should never be lowered below seasonal levels; the salinity line must be maintained.

The second study provided good baseline data from which scientists could assess the health of the estuary fifteen years later, when Mark Benedict realized that the environmental threats raised by the first and second studies were, in fact, taking place, as they are to this day, forty years later.

Plan for the 1990s Poses Problems

While the plan for the new decade was scientifically sound, it was politically perilous. Broad responsibility for resource management posed
a dilemma for the Conservancy. Collaborative efforts with developers
would be essential to directing growth away from critical natural areas.
It would require a dramatic change in the organization's direction because for two decades the focus had been on raising sufficient funds and
involving other parties to purchase critical resources. The underlying
goals were to wrestle land away from private hands into public ownership or conservation easements, and to create a natural resources protection program involving the county, which was known to be tight with
developers.

After much debate, the Conservancy board was unable to agree
on a new direction. When the strategy for the 1990s was announced
in the March 1991 annual report, it remained tightly wedded to political boundaries. "The geographic scope of The Conservancy, Inc. will be
primarily focused on Collier County except where actions in adjacent
counties . . . directly impact or are related to the success of its missions
and goals."[12] This was an unfortunate but deliberate mistake. By restricting its activities to Collier County, the Conservancy missed an opportunity to approach natural resource management from a larger systemic
perspective. It would shadow the Conservancy for years to come as the
Cocohatchee Slough in Lee County was fragmented by developments
that would eventually destroy the watershed. Dealing head-on with
threats to the CREW ecosystem (the main aquifer recharge area for Lee
County) was not in the plan.

When the plan for the 1990s backed away from challenging developments, the Conservancy began to lose financial support from members
who felt the mission had been watered down. Some malcontents were
on the board of directors; others were large contributors. The opposing
faction on the board, convinced Governor Martinez and the legislature
were backing away from earlier growth management laws, suggested the
organization take a more conciliatory approach toward development.
Ned Putzell had been elected mayor of Naples in 1986, and his legacy

of attempting to work more closely with the real estate community carried over with some of the directors. Meeting minutes from this period
indicate growing dissatisfaction and ominous divisions within the Conservancy's board, volunteer leadership, and donor base.

Despite the grumbling, the Conservancy continued to nibble away
at every opportunity to preserve public spaces. After purchase of Cannon Island in November 1988, the Conservancy had turned its attention,
in conjunction with the Nature Conservancy and staff at Rookery Bay,
to purchasing Johnson Island. It negotiated a conservation easement on
more than fifty acres on Horr's Island, which was being developed into
high-end houses by its new owner Ronto, to create a series of native
habitat parks within the development footprint.[13] The new agreement
created a rigid development code for dwellings on the island as an extension of the 1984 settlement with Deltona Corporation. For example,
the first home in Key Marco, scheduled for completion in 1993, would
be limited to clearing no more than half the lot's acreage. The agreement
also provided that "upland vegetation . . . shall remain predominantly
uncleared and in (its) natural state except for exotic vegetation removal,
water management uses, pedestrian access . . . utilities and archaeological investigations."[14] It explicitly permitted Conservancy personnel to
inspect the island periodically.[15]

But these were isolated instances as development pressure continued unabated. In May 1991, the county planning office received preliminary application from a West Palm Beach builder named Robert
Malt for a seventy-eight-acre development along CR 951 east of the
Conservancy's Briggs Nature Center[16] and Norris Marine Laboratory.
Accessed by Shell Island Road, it would be called Sunset Bay. In its earliest incarnation, the project consisted of two four-story buildings with
236 units and parking built on upland fill covering about sixteen acres.
It was the first project south of Henderson Creek, and it was smack in
the middle of Rookery Bay.

Malt had purchased the property in the 1970s. Realizing his development plan would meet stiff resistance, he approached Gary Lytton
(environmental administrator for the state's Department of Natural Re-

sources Rookery Bay facility) a year before filing the preliminary application to inquire if the state would entertain either a sale or swap for his land. Malt originally had more than eighty-three acres but had lost a few acres in 1987 when CR 951 was four-laned into Marco Island. Lytton, who would later head up the Rookery Bay National Estuarine Research Reserve, knew state funds were fully committed through the CARL program and filed a plea with the national office of the Nature Conservancy to buy the property.[17] Malt's preliminary development application to the county, mainly intended to put pressure on the state, went nowhere. Although Sunset Bay was inside the urban boundary and wetlands impact would be minimal, it was the first baby step in compromising Rookery Bay. In 1993 Malt had the land appraised at $435,000. Lytton was still searching for funds, to no avail. The project would return in the late 1990s and again in 2001 but caused remarkably little active opposition from the Conservancy in its early phases because Tammerk had resigned and the organization was looking for a new president.

Finding a new chief executive was difficult. In September 1991, the board finally settled on John Fitch, a PhD who had been with Massachusetts Audubon and was serving as president of Mainewatch Institute, an organization devoted to education and research in the eponymous state. Fitch had strong academic ties in the Northeast and was the polar opposite of the mercurial, forceful, and political Toivo Tammerk. He was a thoughtful, cautious man who felt that good science could win political arguments and that confrontation generally led to bad outcomes. While that may have been true in Maine, Fitch now found himself in wild and woolly south Florida, where politics ruled and confrontation was simply part of the game.

Soon after Fitch came on board, Bill Merrihue passed away, one day shy of his ninetieth birthday. Merrihue's loss was an emotional and financial blow; he was without peer as a fund-raiser. One anecdote recalled a lunch at Naples Yacht Club with one of the Conservancy's major donors. After a few minutes of small talk, Merrihue piped up. "You know the purpose of this lunch; I'm going to ask you for money." The guest took out his checkbook and wrote out a check for $2,500, passing it across the table. Merrihue looked at it and passed it back. "I was thinking about a lot more than that." The guest turned crimson and tore up the check. He reached into his jacket, pulled out the checkbook, wrote another one, and passed it across the table to Merrihue. It was for $25,000.

Merrihue's love of southwest Florida and record of land preservation was unparalleled; he often referred to Rookery Bay as "sacred waters." He loved people as much as he loved the landscape and was at ease with almost everyone he met. A good friend of both Lawton Chiles and Bob Graham, he corresponded with both over the years when they were in positions of power and when they were not. In his later years, he was never a major force in policy issues but was a daily presence at his desk in the Nature Center. He, more than anyone else, molded the Conservancy into the large and influential environmental organization it is today.

Transitions

After Merrihue's passing, the organization continued at a somewhat diminished level of activity because Fitch was cautious in his approach to environmental policy. He was comfortable staying within the strategic framework set forth for the 1990s. This was reflected in January 1994, when the emphasis was on institutional identity, history, philosophy, and planning. Strategic goals were broadly brushed: "encouraging and demonstrating conservation stewardship," "increasing environmental awareness and literacy," and "fostering conservation networks."[18] While these various nostrums read well, southwest Florida was being developed at a breakneck pace and the Conservancy was beginning to lose its edge. Policy initiatives, intentionally limited to Collier County by Benedict's strategic plan, ignored the rapid, uncontrolled development immediately to the north in Lee County. Few new science initiatives were begun; activity in public policy slowed to a crawl. But one department in the organization thrived under Fitch's leadership: education. Fitch was determined to remake the Conservancy into an organization with a broad environmental education program. Policy goals had their place but, in his mind, could not supplant or overwhelm his overriding goal to expose a broad range of south Florida children, residents, and visitors to the unique ecology of the region through lectures, trips and tours, and classroom visits. When the organization merged with Big Cypress Nature Center, it had begun the process of creating an educational curriculum that Fitch embraced and expanded during his tenure.

Fitch resigned in June 1996 to take a position with Florida Gulf Coast University, and David Highmark, board chairman, took over as interim president. Highmark was head of Northern Trust for southwest Florida and a graduate of Dartmouth College with an MBA from Indiana University. A former major league pitcher whose arm lasted only one season, he needed to find a new chief executive quickly. After a brief search, 42-year-old David Guggenheim was introduced to the board as new head of the Conservancy in September. He had beaten out Ellie Krier for the job. A former board chair who had joined the staff as vice president in 1993, Krier was known as a highly organized woman capable of running complex operations,[19] but the search committee was composed mainly of men and Krier ended up in second place.

Guggenheim's credentials were varied and unusual. He had won the Ojai (California) triathlon three years in a row and once completed the Lake Tahoe "Death Ride," a 144-mile bicycle race that included elevation changes up to 15,000 feet. He had a master's in biology from the University of California–Santa Barbara and was working on a doctorate at George Mason University while working as a partner at Eco Analysis, an environmental consulting firm, when Highmark called with an offer to take over as president of the Conservancy.

Pushing Beyond the Urban Boundary

Guggenheim started out with a conciliatory approach, a strategy quickly tested when two developments, TwinEagles and Fiddler's Creek, challenged Collier County's urban boundary (see Map 7). Both projects— out beyond that line in the county's comprehensive growth plan where water and sewer services were not available (generally east of highway CR 95)—were being pushed through the approval process with unre-

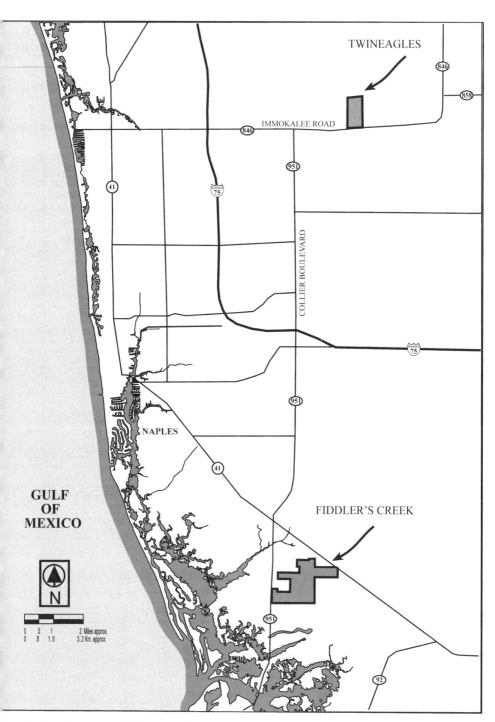

Map 7. TwinEagles and Fiddler's Creek.

lenting pressure.[20] County commissioners had mildly affirmed support for the line when, in April 1996, they turned down a proposal for a four-square-mile development east of the northern extension of CR 951. But during debate, they gave passing thought to extending services beyond the existing boundary. As a compromise, county staff proposed, one year later, that the commission assume approval rights to all private water supply and treatment facilities in the rural area. The county planning commission considered the idea but rejected it for fear it might run afoul of state regulations. It did.

In July 1997, the Department of Community Affairs came down hard, warning the county about violating its own growth management plan by assuming such powers. The Conservancy was strangely silent on the issue, mainly because it was working behind the scenes with county staff to draft a redefinition of the urban boundary to keep growth away from irreplaceable natural resources. Guggenheim, in a desperate attempt to gain broader traction, proposed a symposium at which all parties of interest would sit down together to draft new guidelines for dealing with development in what had become the hottest real estate market in the United States. His suggestion was met with grudging support from commissioners and complete disdain from other environmental groups intent upon fighting TwinEagles and Fiddler's Creek, so he went public, issuing a policy statement called "Criteria for a PUD Outside Urban Boundary Along a Designated Immokalee Road Corridor."[21] In it, the organization stated its mild opposition to development outside the urban boundary up to TwinEagles on the east, carefully conditioned on five points: (1) that one half the acreage of a development remain in natural areas; (2) that development of natural areas carry a mitigation two-for-one with lands purchased within the boundaries of the CREW trust; (3) that golf courses, mowed lawns, and constructed lakes be excluded from the definition of natural areas; (4) that all preserved lands be internally interconnected; (5) that density remain at one for five acres (clustered). If all of these criteria were put into Collier County's comprehensive plan, opposition might be withdrawn. It was, to the dismay of other environmental groups.

Unwilling to criticize the Conservancy publicly, the Florida Wild-life Federation and Collier County Audubon hired Richard Grosso of the Environmental and Land Use Law Center at Fort Lauderdale's Nova Southeastern University to represent them at hearings on TwinEagles. Grosso was a fabled lawyer, having devoted his entire career to support-ing environmental organizations. The issue for him and his clients went well beyond TwinEagles. It became a broad defense of plain language in the county's growth plan, which Grosso believed should be applied uni-formly and unambiguously. In his opinion and that of his clients, allow-ing a large development to sprout up outside the urban/rural line would make the statutory boundary irrelevant. But TwinEagles had already cranked up bulldozers at the development site on the north side of Im-mokalee Road, claiming it had permission from the water management district and Collier County to rip out trees and dig holes in the ground even before site plans were fully approved.[22] In addition, the water dis-trict's permit had been issued despite objections by the Florida Game and Fresh Water Fish Commission (FWC) on the impact to threatened and endangered species. This gave Grosso the sense that he had another valid argument to make before the commission because state agencies rarely disagreed publicly.

Aside from providing encouragement to Grosso, this highlighted a significant weakness in the permitting process in Florida. When two agencies disagreed, it was always assumed the final resolution would fa-vor construction. The system was biased toward fast-tracking develop-ment even if it meant overriding environmental safeguards or, in this case, the urban boundary. To neutralize the conflict between the water district and FWC, TwinEagles' attorney, Bruce Anderson, defended the process in a July hearing before county commissioners by arguing that the project should continue because it was better than current zoning of one home per five acres. Besides, he had the Conservancy on his side, having gained its support by agreeing that more than 50% of the devel-opment would remain in its "natural" state, although what specific parts of the development would be classified as "natural" had yet to be agreed upon. But Grosso would have none of it. He argued the main point at issue was "the clear intent of the comprehensive plan was to keep urban development out of areas classified as agricultural."[23] Despite Grosso's plea, the skids had been adequately greased, and Anderson, one of a small group of established land-use attorneys who understood how to get things done in Collier County, got his way with TwinEagles.[24]

Then, three months later, Fiddler's Creek cajoled the CCPC into recommending approval of a private comprehensive plan amendment adding 1,385 acres to its footprint.[25] The Conservancy, now being openly criticized by other environmental groups for caving in on the TwinEagles controversy, was more circumspect this time around. "This is premature," said environmental manager Michael Simonik, "because we are still having conversations with the county about rules for development in rural areas."[26] Those "conversations" were critical because the added acreage fell outside the urban boundary. It put the development into the same "leapfrog" category of subdivisions in rural lands as TwinEagles, which essentially made the outermost development a marker past which the urban/rural line could later be pushed, making more lands available for development.

By February of the following year, the Conservancy decided to issue a statement in support of the Fiddler's Creek expansion. To win the organization's support, Fiddler's had agreed to construct a series of swales and water diversion canals to duplicate predevelopment flow patterns. This was important because receiving wetlands south of Fiddler's Creek had been filled and replaced by detention ponds, periodically flooding the adjacent Port-Au-Prince neighborhood. The developer agreed to maintain 450 acres in their natural state and eschew rights to develop a 63-acre parcel extending into a research reserve area.

However, records indicate there may have been more to the Conservancy's support. In a letter to Guggenheim, attorney George Varnadoe, representing 951 Land Holdings Joint Venture, wrote to "memorialize" an agreement between the Conservancy and his client that would make a $185,000 contribution toward purchase of the Malt property. Payment was "conditioned upon, and will not be made unless and until all of the pending petition approvals for Fiddler's Creek . . . have become final. . . .

This pledge is made in recognition of the Conservancy's cooperation on the previously referenced Fiddler's Creek amendments."[27] It isn't known if word of this arrangement made its way to other environmental groups fighting Fiddler's Creek, but opposition by the Florida Wildlife Federation and Collier County Audubon remained vocal and unyielding. According to Nancy Payton, southwestern Florida field representative for the Florida Wildlife Federation, the county couldn't approve the amended project without moving the urban boundary again, a prescient observation when the county commission approved the project, amended the urban/rural boundary, and gave Fiddler's four additional years to complete the project.

By 1998 Robert Malt's project on the west side of CR 951, which the Conservancy was hoping to buy with funds from the Fiddler's Creek agreement, reared its head again. One corner of Malt's property included Shell Island Road, and he decided to turn up the heat by having his attorney write the Department of Environmental Protection office at Rookery Bay asking it to "arrange for alternate access onto its property."[28] The letter mentioned that Malt was proceeding with plans to develop the property because he had been unable to reach agreement with the State of Florida to purchase the land under the CARL program. This time around, the Conservancy jumped into the fray with both feet because access to its Rookery Bay laboratory and Briggs Nature Center was via Shell Island Road too. David Addison, who was overseeing the center at the time, was concerned. "Remember we are an effected [sic] party if he decides to go through with the development. Operation of the Briggs Nature Center could (be) impacted with a couple of condominiums overlooking the pond for our boardwalk. . . ."[29]

Guggenheim began to research Malt's history on the east coast of Florida. He turned up a number of code enforcement complaints filed against Malt's properties in Palm Beach County, including citations for overgrown lots, failure to obtain permits for building modifications, and a number of lawsuits beginning back in 1988. The local newspaper reported that Robert C. Malt Co. had filed for bankruptcy in June 1992, identifying Malt as plaintiff in a lawsuit against Masonite Corporation for selling his company a faulty product. (The suit was dismissed).[30] When the new plan for Sunset Bay, now called Rookery Bay Towers, emerged, it was shocking. The original design for the property contemplated two four-story buildings but now would comprise two ten-story high-rises peering out over Rookery Bay. Malt applied for a rezone of the seventy-nine acres, asserting a right to build at three to four units per acre despite the fact that the land was zoned agricultural, arguing that other high-rises were near his site. He offered to place a conservation easement on sixty-five acres of undevelopable wetlands in exchange for the right to build on only five acres. Guggenheim's notes show that Malt had decided to ask for $4 million as the "developable" value of the property. The state had offered only $300,000–$400,000 during negotiations, but Malt made it clear that he was a willing seller. He simply wanted to maximize his price, and it is likely that the new plan was a negotiating ploy.

The U.S. Fish and Wildlife Service turned the project down in April 2001, but its biological opinion was ignored when the Corps issued a 404 permit despite a lack of alternatives analysis required as part of the permitting process. This episode is momentarily instructive. At the federal level, only the Corps had the power, beginning in 1999, to permit destruction of jurisdictional wetlands. There was an agreement in effect, dating back to 1967, that gave USFWS the right to appeal a 404 permit if the affected wetland was an "aquatic resource of national importance." The process, called "elevation," was rarely exercised partly because the Corps had blown off every appeal since 1992. Fish and Wildlife staff were accustomed to being overridden, so they always attempted to negotiate with the Corps before seeking to "elevate" a project. The fact that they so openly opposed Malt's towers was an indication of the agency's deep disapproval of the project.

Then, despite approval by staff planners, the county Environmental Advisory Committee voted 7–0 in November against recommending the project to county commissioners. "This is unquestionably the most damaging to the environment I have ever seen. What birdbrain that has lived here any length of time would believe this?" asked council member Mickey Coe.[31] Among the birdbrains was the SFWMD, which approved the project, subject to some minor changes, in February 2002. The CCPC turned it down 4–2 after chiding staff and other agencies for approving the project. Malt decided to temporarily withdraw the application because discussions with Conservancy officials, Rookery Bay manager Lytton, and the Nature Conservancy were continuing. Malt preferred to sell the land if he could get a fair price, which he eventually did.

Urban Boundary

Fuss and feathers over TwinEagles and Fiddler's Creek—and to a lesser extent Sunset Towers—provoked the county into a series of moves to reduce density in rural Collier County. Against stout resistance from bankers, developers, and their lawyers, the county considered reducing density to one dwelling per twenty acres in the rural areas. Having been badly burned, Guggenheim was now adamant: "The economics are like a freight train—unstoppable. We need zoning that keeps agricultural land in preserve, and current standards aren't enough to stop golf course communities."[32] He subscribed to the concept of transferable development credits, allowing landowners adjacent to or nearby the urban boundary to be compensated if they wished to give up their rights. Nancy Payton of the Florida Wildlife Federation was initially opposed because, in her opinion, the three areas selected for transferable rights were simply a sly way of moving the urban boundary. Besides, one of the areas north of Immokalee Road near TwinEagles was targeted for state purchase. It was a critical part of the Corkscrew Swamp watershed, where endangered wood storks foraged during nesting season. Commissioner Tim Hancock agreed with her, calling transferable rights a "mitigation bone" to avoid lawsuits from irate landowners. But as it turned out, Payton was right. By moving the urban boundary further east, Collier County was doing planning in reverse. The urban/rural "bright line" was following development rather than guiding it. Developers argued that keeping the line intact would restrict expansion. The environmental argument was harder to make: Maintaining the boundary would encourage infill and redevelopment and provide ample economic opportunities. But redevelopment was for the little guy, and the major players in southwest Florida wanted raw land.

This last argument came back to haunt the Conservancy. TwinEagles, at the terminus of the already compromised Cocohatchee Slough, would become a placeholder on Immokalee Road, allowing infill to the west and multiple projects that would lead to some of the most furious battles between developers and environmental groups in southwest Florida. It would be followed by subdivision of a former mining area called Heritage Bay (later The Quarry), while the south side of Immokalee Road would become populated by a series of smaller subdivisions. Had the urban/rural boundary been maintained, code regulations limiting density might have prevented annihilation of the remaining watershed.

To fully appreciate the growing problem of choking the Corkscrew ecosystem—with Audubon's large sanctuary near its headwaters—we now turn to the story of Lee County's struggle to maintain the integrity of its primary groundwater recharge area just as the state legislature was beginning to rewrite growth management laws in an attempt to push planning down to the local level. We'll also look at the power politics of locating a campus for Florida Gulf Coast University and at a tale of sordid political maneuvering to build a subdivision that would threaten to inundate the City of Bonita Springs.

CHAPTER 11

WATERSHED UNDER SIEGE

*T*he stories in this chapter are important because they vividly illustrate the central weakness of the entire permitting process in southwest Florida: a wanton disregard by government agencies for the cumulative effects of projects authorized in isolation from one another, despite the fact that some properties shared abutting borders within a single hydrologic system. On the demand side of the equation, ferocious pressure was being applied by builders seeking to move less paper and more dirt. Sometimes openly flaunting the rules, other times operating in either ignorance or confusion, they rushed to get projects started. What follows—and makes it less excusable—took place well after the spate of growth management and environmental protection laws passed in the 1970s and 1980s and well after the long-term effects of projects like southern Golden Gate Estates and the Picayune Strand had been thoroughly studied and were well known. The Conservancy and its environmental partners battled against development in this geography for more than fifteen years as part of a larger consortium and, despite millions of dollars spent in staff time and legal fees, failed to save all but a vestige of the massive sheet flow feeding the Cocohatchee River out to Wiggins Pass in the Gulf of Mexico, once served by three major drainage basins running northeast to southwest.

To fully appreciate the magnitude of destruction, we need to go back in time when a vast landscape existed in southern Lee County and northern Collier County, capable of storing and handling water in a smoothly predictable way. It was called the Cocohatchee Slough (see Map 8). Closest to the Gulf of Mexico was the Estero watershed, draining into the free-flowing Estero River and Estero Bay (the state's first aquatic preserve). To the east lay the Imperial watershed, a narrow elongated system emptying into the Imperial River. Combined, these two fed Lee County's two major estuaries located between sandy Gulf beaches and mangrove forests, inaccessible to residents and visitors until the dredges had their day. The third basin was the largest, beginning in northeastern Lee and Hendry Counties, with sheet flow nearly eighty miles across. Part of the outflow fed into the twenty-mile-wide Cocohatchee Slough, a deeper and more noticeable conveyance within the system that drained slowly down across the Lee and Collier border, eventually emptying into the Gulf via the Cocohatchee River and Wiggins Pass. A secondary derivative of the tertiary basin went south through Lake Trafford, meandering through the Camp Keais Strand to the west of the Fakahatchee Strand. Historically, all three probably operated as one, with the headwaters hydrating the most significant element in the northeast section of the slough, southwest Florida's enduring but fragile treasure: Corkscrew Swamp Sanctuary, once home to the nation's largest population of endangered wood storks.

In the 1970s and 1980s, southwest Florida could boast of a mild winter climate and white sandy beaches—an irresistible combination for visiting tourists, many of whom would return as permanent residents. Lee County, with its large airport and a reputation for rolling over for developers, grew more rapidly than Collier County, which had been stymied by a lack of easy access until I-75 was opened. Both had allowed subdivisions to creep into the southern and western edges of the Cocohatchee Slough. The effect was to separate the once-unified sheet flow drainage system into three parts by diverting water with agricultural irrigation ditches and roadside canals, drying out the bulk of the land.

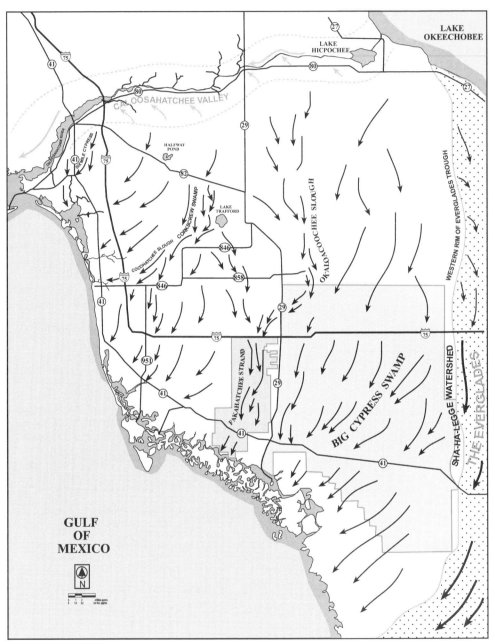

Map 8: Historic waterflow patterns of Southwest Florida.

But after Governor Bob Graham's ELMS II Committee set forth its recommendations, the legislature passed the 1984 State and Regional Planning Act, followed by the 1985 Local Government Comprehensive Planning and Land Development Act, forcing Lee County to begin to analyze land use based upon population projections and natural resources. Using community-based planning protocols, development would be directed to locations that took advantage of existing infrastructure to avoid (insofar as possible) compromising natural resources, but progress was glacial. Both acts took years to implement because the state provided little money to assist local efforts. When the county's new comprehensive plan first emerged, it was clear that little attention had been paid to areas critical to groundwater recharge of aquifers supplying much of the county's potable water to Bonita Springs and other communities. Part of the reason was that the complex drainage system, already altered by development, was not well understood. What was known was that the primary source of groundwater recharge lay in the southeastern quadrant of the county, and protection of that resource was an essential part of managing for future growth.

Enter the RGMC

In 1988 a group of citizens and organizations, feeling the subject of water recharge had been given short shrift by Lee County, formed the Responsible Growth Management Coalition (RGMC). Once the final draft of the county's comprehensive plan was forwarded to the Department of Community Affairs in Tallahassee for review and approval, the RGMC filed suit against the county and the State of Florida for violating guidelines set forth in the 1985 act. Lee County, along with many other counties in Florida, was breaking new ground by attempting to do the nearly impossible: establish consensus among a large group of stakeholders with diverse and sometimes opposing interests. The fact that water recharge was given short shrift in the plan was an obvious concession to development and mining interests, their sights set on the inland part of the county. In 1990, in settlement of the lawsuit, the state required Lee

County to set aside 96,000 acres to be designated as a Density Reduction/ Groundwater Resource (DR/GR) area, with no more than one dwelling per ten acres in uplands and one per twenty acres in wetlands. Other than low-density residential construction, other uses were restricted to recreation, agriculture, and mining.

Historically, as much as 86% of the DR/GR was once wetlands. Agriculture had dried out approximately 20,000 acres, but the damage was not irreversible; some wetlands restoration was possible. What could not be restored was turned over to development. The Conservancy, a partner in the RGMC, was marginally involved in the suit, having its hands full with Villages of Sabal Bay, acquisition of Cannon Island, and proposed development of Keewaydin Island in Collier County.

Once the DR/GR was reserved, there were few skirmishes over new subdivisions in Lee County until 1992, when the Florida Board of Regents, after looking at twenty-two alternate sites, decided to accept an offer of land and money from Ben Hill Griffin III and Alico Corporation to build a new institution, Florida Gulf Coast University (FGCU), on the western edge of the DR/GR. Alico owned 135,000 acres of land throughout the state. One of its major shareholders was J.D. Alexander, a powerful and well-connected state legislator (whom we will meet again in next the chapter). The university footprint would cover approximately 800 acres. It fit perfectly into Alico's long-range plans for its real estate holdings, some 11,000 acres in Lee County, much of it in mining. The new university, chartered in 1991, was highly desired by southwest Floridians. A number of smaller private institutions of higher education existed in the region for years, but none had risen to the level of a major university. FGCU filled a void that many people felt was holding back economic growth in southwest Florida. Enthusiastically embraced, the university quickly developed an innovative curriculum and promised to become a model of environmental sustainability by integrating solar panels into water heating systems, preserving 400 acres of green space, and creating lakes throughout the campus for water control. On the other hand, the school also attempted (unsuccessfully) to use preserve areas as parking lots and to support adjacent land rezone requests for what the RGMC regarded as incompatible uses. Those were withdrawn after threats of litigation.

State of Florida Returns Growth Management to Local Government

While FGCU was moving through the permitting pipeline, the growing Republican membership in the state legislature was having second thoughts about growth management laws passed during the prior decade. Lawmakers cooked up a series of initiatives in 1992 designed to reduce mangrove protection, a critical component of the Estero Bay ecosystem. These were opposed by the RGMC and quickly disposed of with a stroke of Governor Lawton Chiles' veto pen. Another issue was mandated concurrency, one of the central elements of the 1985 act. It came under attack because developers lacked the patience to wait for roads, sewer and water systems, and schools to be nearly in place before they could start ripping up the landscape, but as long as Chiles sat in the governor's chair, most growth management laws would remain intact. That is, until he received the report from his blue-ribbon ELMS III committee.

The committee concluded that economic development should be the state's first priority. While affirming the underlying concept of managing growth at the state level, the committee wanted a more strategic approach at the local level. Regional planning was regarded as superfluous. Tiering the effort at three levels, the committee recommended local governments be given greater flexibility in applying growth management regulations based upon the wide variation in topography, population, and potential land uses throughout Florida. To accomplish this, regional planning councils would have their powers cut back significantly and the DRI program—already eviscerated in 1985—would be severely restricted despite the fact that eighty major projects had been approved during the prior 12 years.[1]

ELMS III recommendations, based on the assumption that local planning efforts had become increasingly sophisticated, contained an explicit reminder of the need for clustering housing and services in large

developments, such as FGCU, to maximize green space. The committee's report, with minor modifications, became the Growth Management
Act of 1993, which was quickly signed by Chiles. By returning state-
mandated concurrency to local control, the act marked a turn toward
strengthening property rights and represented a step back from the 1975
and 1985 acts, both of which had treated environmental protection as a
central element of regional planning.

Nowhere was the effect of this new law more apparent than in the
transportation network surrounding FGCU. Existing access roads were
inadequate, forcing local authorities to react quickly and without guidance from the state. The 1993 legislation mandated a growth management component to the state comp plan in an attempt to pull together
transportation, land acquisition policies, and water management, but
this piece of the bill was never implemented so Lee County was forced
to go it alone, a task made slightly more difficult when the legislature
ignored one important piece of the ELMS III package: a 10-cent-per-
gallon gas tax to help support transportation improvements in local
plans. But failure to enact the gas tax increase would have little effect on
booming southwest Florida. As FGCU's enrollment grew, support services, housing, big-box stores, small retail shops, and fast food joints
sprouted around the hub of the campus. Local officials, with the school
offering diversification to the tourist- and construction-based economy
of southwest Florida, gave virtual *carte blanche* to development around
the campus periphery. An environmental ethic remained strong as long
as it didn't interfere with growth.

As Lee County assumed control over its own destiny, it gave the
RGMC a reason to look more carefully at environmental issues in estuaries like Estero Bay because of past dealings with public officials. To further this end, the group negotiated a deal in 1995 that created an Estero
Bay advisory subcommittee of the RPC, an indication that the RGMC
was determined to assert more influence as southwest Florida's regional
oversight body was gradually being stripped of its powers.[2]

For example, when the state published its 1993 list of impaired water bodies, it identified Estero Bay as being freshwater to the mouth of

the estuary, thereby tolerating lower dissolved oxygen and higher levels
of nutrient pollution (mainly nitrogen and phosphorous) in the bay. The
RGMC, along with the Conservancy and other environmental groups,
filed an administrative challenge against the DEP for setting the freshwater line out too far and ignoring the mixing effect of wind and tide.
The resulting settlement moved the eastern boundary for freshwater
back inland to US 41. The DEP also agreed to set maximum pollution
limits for all four main tributaries into Estero Bay. Environmentalists felt
this would improve Estero Bay over time, a critical point in the case of
Edison Farms and Agripartners, when politics ruled and common sense
went out the window.

Agripartners

The story began in 1991 when a company called Gulfview Communities
proposed a DRI for a 7,100-acre development. The project failed to turn
a spade of dirt. A portion of Gulfview's land, 2,500 acres running along
I-75 north of Bonita Beach Road, was sold in 1999 to Daniel Aranoff's
company, Agripartners Ltd. Partnership. Much of the rest was sold or
leased to various entities for agriculture or other purposes. Aranoff was
determined to rid the property of wetlands and went about it using every
trick in the book. First, the company applied for a Corps permit to drain
more than 1,000 acres for "agricultural purposes." The Corps, which had
a record of approving 99% of the permits to come before it, shocked
Agripartners with a denial based upon its conclusion that destroying
wetlands had nothing to do with agriculture and everything to do with
building houses and golf courses. It also had to do with Lee County's
water supply, because some of Agripartners' land was in the Flint Pen
Strand of the DR/GR (see Map 9), which had a moratorium on large developments. In response to the Corps' decision, Agripartners then commenced a series of political maneuvers with Sisyphean determination.
In 2002 and again in 2004, the company applied to the City of Bonita
Springs for annexation that would have allowed density up to six units
per acre rather than the existing DR/GR zoning of one unit per 10 acres

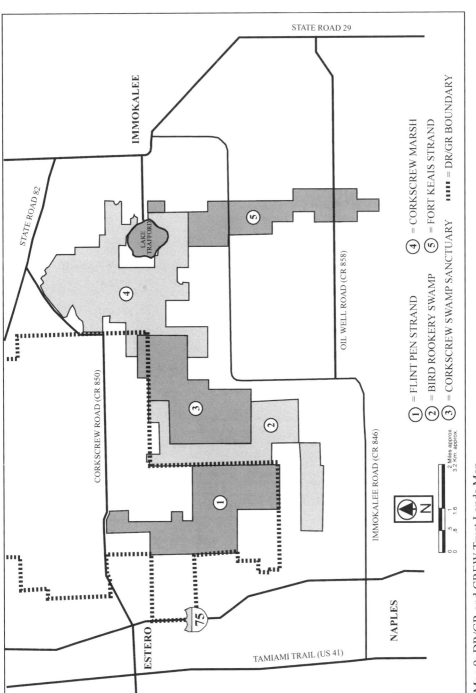

Map 9: DR/GR and CREW Trust Lands Map.

or one per 20.[3] The city turned it down flat both times. Agripartners also applied to the RPC for an I-75 interchange at Coconut Road to access its property. That was turned down flat too. By this time, publicity over the various proposals brought opponents out in force, but Aranoff wouldn't take no for an answer. He turned to a tried-and-true source for influence and favors: politicians.

After a fund-raiser in southwest Florida for committee chairman Donald Young (R-Alaska), a $10-million earmark magically appeared to study the feasibility of an I-75 interchange at Coconut Road. Forensic investigation showed that the earmark had been inserted *after* Congress had approved the bill but *before* it went to the president's desk for signature; the change was made by one of Young's staffers. An obvious payoff to a campaign donor, it created a field day for the media. "Remember the duck—if it looks like a duck, walks like a duck, etc., then chances are it's a duck. Forty grand in campaign contributions wrapped around an earmark inserted after Congress had already voted on a massive transportation bill quacks like Donald," opined Young's hometown paper, the *Anchorage Daily News*. [4] Southwest Florida's local congressman, Connie Mack, ran for cover, claiming he knew nothing of the earmark even though the interchange was in the middle of his district and Young publicly claimed he had Mack's support. The earmark got pulled, and an interchange would be a dead issue for as long as the land remained a wetland. But that was about to change.

In a stupefying series of procedural maneuvers, SFWMD staff looked favorably upon an application from Agripartners to cut a four-mile ditch alongside I-75, after concluding it would destroy only 16 acres of high-quality wetlands and impact fewer than 200 acres. The document made no mention of any land-use changes as a result of the canal. SFWMD forwarded its recommendations to the SFWMD governing board on December 12, 2006; it was distributed to the Conservancy and RPC the following day. A vote by the district's board was scheduled to be taken 24 hours later as part of the consent agenda, a package of routine items normally receiving little attention and no discussion. While not violating the letter of the law, it mocked the concept of public participation by giving opponents no time to marshal a response.

Infuriated by the underhanded tactics of SFWMD staff, the Conservancy, with vocal support by a citizens group from The Brooks, a high-end subdivision to the west of the Agripartners property, filed an administrative appeal based upon two contentions: outflow from the ditch would impact both the timing of inflows and overall water quality in the Estero River and Estero Bay, both of which were designated as Outstanding Florida Waters and would destroy foraging habitat for endangered wood storks nesting in nearby Corkscrew Swamp.[5] On the first point, SFWMD staff argued that water quality would not be affected because there was no accompanying information on a change in land use but admitted that the canal would truncate seasonal hydroperiods, leading to less forage for storks to nourish their chicks. The Conservancy's argument that the ditch would drain up to 1,200 acres of wetlands was not mentioned in SFWMD's response.

As litigation wound its way through discovery in 2007, the Conservancy caught wind of yet another scheme, this one floated from within Florida's Department of Transportation (FDOT). As part of the plan to widen I-75 from the Collier County line up to Corkscrew Road, the SFWMD proposed to FDOT that it install five culverts under the right of way to improve water management. The outcome of this maneuver would be to drop the water table in Agripartners' land by at least one foot, despite the fact that the existing downstream system lacked sufficient capacity to absorb additional water. The result would be to flood The Brooks during storm events. FDOT said its recommendation was based upon a 1997 study of hydrological patterns in the area by the water district. The Conservancy suggested creating an updated model to include the impact of five new culverts, to which all parties agreed except the water district. It insisted the culverts go in, at taxpayers' expense, but then be immediately plugged until the updated study was completed. The *Fort Myers News-Press* blasted the idea: "The county should not roll over for this," opined the editorial page. "(t)his is the land that was to have benefited from the sneaky funding of an I-75 interchange at Coconut Road."[6] Lee County Commissioner Ray Judah was adamantly opposed to the canal: "Whatever it takes," he said, and that included more litigation. This maneuver by SFWMD staff was incomprehensible unless there was more to the issue than met the public eye, but objectors eventually prevailed and the district board voted to restudy the project, which is where it sits today, gathering dust.

Protecting the DR/GR

In 2007 Lee County's commission, led by Ray Judah and Bob Janes, engaged Dover, Kohl & Partners, a town planning firm from Coral Gables, to study the traffic impact of mining trucks on the DR/GR, to map surface and groundwater flow patterns, and to do a land-use analysis of the area. After holding a series of workshops soliciting community comment, the firm recommended using transferable development rights as a means of encouraging clustered development to preserve and restore flow ways and wetlands. The report noted that mining was an "irreversible conversion" and should be limited to a corridor along Alico Road. Dover, Kohl projected the available supply of rock from mines in operation, with no new permits, would meet 80% of southwest Florida's needs until 2030.[7]

The county commission bought the argument and in 2010 decided to ban mining along Corkscrew Road, but it failed to adopt the change as an amendment to the comprehensive plan. This infuriated not only mining interests but also those in the agricultural community, many of whom had been preparing to submit mining applications in the DR/GR (in addition to the existing Lost Grove mine on 2,500 acres on the eastern fringe). The economics of mining were compelling when compared to growing row crops or doing low-density development, giving the landholder a significantly higher valuation if rezoning was denied.[8] Besides, aggregate was an important commodity for road building; local sourcing reduced the cost of transporting rock over longer distances. Mining interests, knowing this and assuming they would receive support from county transportation planners and Florida DOT, filed a series of complaints with the state. The argument was that denial constituted a partial "taking" of the land, which was reimbursable to the owner since the use was allowable under the operative (and unamended) comprehensive plan. But in February 2012, after three days of hearings, an administrative law judge upheld the county commission's decision. One month later, the Department of Economic Opportunity, a part of which contained the tattered remnants of the once-influential Department of Community Affairs, issued a final order limiting mining to the Alico Road corridor. Mining companies were denied virtually all of the exceptions they requested.[9] The issue was subsequently pursued in District Court by Resource Conservation Holdings. After being denied a rezone for 400 acres of mining, the company sued, "alleging it spent $47 million on the land, then spent more after its legal fight."[10] The decision was consistent with an earlier Circuit Court decision, which held that the company had options for land use other than mining.

Over the years, Lee County's elected leadership and staff have become more environmentally aware. Growth is now being managed. The DR/GR decision offers proof of the county's commitment to preserve the water recharge area. Part of the reason that permits were issued in the early years was the cozy relationship between officials and developers, and the other part was the fragmentation of environmental groups in the county. The Sanibel-Captiva Conservation Foundation had the broadest reach, monitoring the islands and ecosystem that is Charlotte Harbor. A number of smaller groups, protecting specific sites like Six Mile Cypress Slough Preserve (which is also a Lee County park), Lovers Key, and Cayo Costa, were fought by coalitions like the RGMC, the Conservancy, and Audubon of Florida (with its vested interest protecting the 13,000-acre Corkscrew Swamp Sanctuary and adjacent forage). Once combined, they formed a powerful alliance that would again align as activity heated up in the southern terminus of the Cocohatchee Slough.

Corkscrew Regional Ecosystem Watershed (CREW)
When Preservation 2000 was enacted in 1990, Governor Bob Martinez hailed it as "the most ambitious land acquisition program in the nation, which will enable Florida to lead the way in protecting the environment

for future generations.["]11 The measure was controversial at the time be-cause it committed the state to finance $3 billion in revenue bonds over the next decade.[12] But it was critical to southwest Florida because land prices were escalating and the state's ability to buy large parcels based upon annual collection of documentary stamp taxes was overly restric-tive. Part of the nearly two million acres acquired with Preservation 2000 funds was the southwestern end of the combined Imperial and Cocohatchee basins, partly within Lee County's DR/GR, a large part of which Audubon Florida had convinced the state to purchase. It account-ed for more than 15,000 of the 22,000 acres in the Corkscrew Regional Ecosystem Watershed (CREW), Land Trust territory. The balance, about 38,000 acres, ended up being controlled through conservation ease-ments by the water management district and Florida Fish & Wildlife Conservation Commission. Much of the trust's lands, clearly shown on Map 9 as Area 3, lay outside the DR/GR. Water flowing down the Fort Keais Strand leading to the Fakahatchee had a chance of making it to the Ten Thousand Islands, but most of the remaining drainage from CREW lands in the southern half of Lee County would end up in Collier County in the Cocohatchee Canal along Immokalee Road. With a placeholder sitting nearly ten miles to the east of I-75 on Immokalee Road, that ge-ography, at the south end of the once free-flowing Estero and Imperial watersheds, was perfectly positioned to become a prime target for more rooftops and golf courses.

Mirasol, Terafina, and Parklands Collier

At the edge of the CREW on Immokalee Road sat TwinEagles, which the Conservancy had supported in 1997 to the consternation of other south-west Florida environmental groups. By 2003 a trio of new subdivisions was planned on the southern edge of the compressed Corkscrew ecosys-tem: Mirasol, Terafina, and Parklands Collier (see shaded areas in Map 10). The water management district was interested in the terminus of what remained of the Cocohatchee Slough, having fretted over drainage in that area since the 1995 flooding in the City of Bonita Springs when

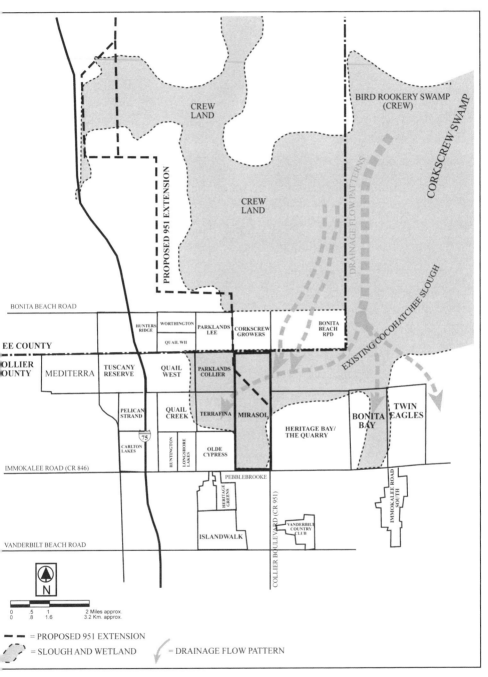

Map 10. Cocohatchee Slough and Developments.

the Cocohatchee, Imperial, and Estero basins reverted to a single historic watershed to overwhelm the storm water network.[13] The main outlet was a canal along Immokalee Road, already dumping water loaded with nutrients and high-coliform bacteria into a remnant of the Cocohatchee River and the Gulf of Mexico through Wiggins Pass, an Outstanding Florida Water (OFW).[14] The OFW designation carried with it a rule stating that no further degradation of water quality would be tolerated and that any discharges into Wiggins Pass must be "clearly in the public interest," pointed out frequently by environmentalists but paid little heed in the heyday of southwest Florida's overheated building boom. The district's answer? Create additional drainage capacity to direct storm water into the Gulf of Mexico.

One proposed solution to flooding in Bonita Springs had emerged in 1996: Build a six-foot-high levee running north-south from Corkscrew Road in Lee County along a proposed extension of highway CR 951 (shown on Map 10 as Collier Boulevard). It would cut the historic Cocohatchee Slough into two parts and divert water, both sheet flow and summer rains, directly south through the main Golden Gate canal system into Naples Bay. The levee would have dramatically altered the amount of water in conservation areas during the rainy season and destroyed the entire ecosystem. Known as the Tree Line Levee, it was received unenthusiastically by the Southwest Florida Regional Planning Commission (RPC) until it got to SFWMD headquarters in West Palm Beach, where, despite a staff report warning that backup from the dike would flood parts of Golden Gate during summer storms, it remained at a slow boil. Lee County didn't approve of the dike but decided to push for an extension of highway CR 951 further to the east from its northern terminus at Immokalee Road in Collier County to connect at Alico Road in Lee County, an alignment supported by developers wanting to open multilane road access to the agricultural lands in both counties. One study supported the extension under the pretext that I-75 could not accommodate projected 2020 traffic even with ten lanes. This gave Collier County Commissioner Jim Coletta, representing northeastern Collier County, a reason to push for the road as a means of regional connectivity. Lee County Commission Chair Ray Judah, normally a reliable vote on conservation issues, favored the realignment as well. But the Conservancy and Florida Audubon, unalterably opposed to any further invasion into the Corkscrew ecosystem, kept the idea bottled up. A later scheme surfaced to build a toll road adjacent to existing I-75 right-of-way, but it was scotched when widening of the interstate from four to six lanes was approved and funded.

The larger problem facing environmental groups at the time was a massive 2,562-acre development at a rock-mining site on the northeast corner of Immokalee Road and highway CR 951 called Heritage Bay (now The Quarry). It was divided into four sections, one within the urban boundary and three in the rural fringe. More than 400 acres had been dug up by 2002; an additional 1,285 acres was permitted for future mining. A conservation easement covered a little more than 500 acres on the property just south of CREW lands. Heritage Bay's developer was a powerful national corporation, U.S. Home, which suggested "blending," applying an average density over the entire development rather than the one-for-five zoning required in all three sections in the rural fringe, offering 300 additional acres of conservation land in exchange for the environmental community's agreement to sit on its hands when it came to challenging permits. The Conservancy was in a tight spot because it had endorsed blending as an acceptable practice. Aerial views of Heritage Bay confirm that blending was probably the right answer, given the location of various mining pit ponds on the site. Whether it was the right thing for the Cocohatchee flow way was a different matter.

After sitting out Heritage Bay, the environmental community realized that the last remaining vestige of the Cocohatchee flow way—a narrow corridor to the west running down the gut of Mirasol—was about to be choked off. Before human intervention, it was twenty miles wide, but when Mirasol began predevelopment discussions it was squeezed down to 2,000 feet. Alarmed, the Conservancy, Collier County Audubon, the Florida Wildlife Federation, and National Audubon joined forces to fight Mirasol's wanton destruction of wetlands. The Collier County Commission approved Mirasol's first plan in May 2002. The subdivision would occupy 1,700 acres, more than 80% being wetlands within the Cocohatchee flow way. Mirasol proposed a four-foot-deep, 200-foot-wide canal to drain nearly 600 acres, upon which to build 800 dwellings surrounding 36 holes of golf. A second subdivision, Terafina (originally Wildwood),[15] would occupy 646 acres, of which 537 were wetlands. The plan was to fill 280 acres and build an 850-unit subdivision. Finally, Parklands Collier would be a 645-acre development impacting 209 acres of wetlands. Taken together (as shown on Map 9), the three projects represented the largest destruction of wetlands in southwest Florida since Golden Gate Estates.

After the first Section 404 permit application was published in 2002, the Conservancy met with Mirasol consultants Turrell and Associates twice, insisting the golf courses be scrapped and building limited to existing uplands. After that proposal was summarily rejected, the National Wildlife Federation entered the fray with a request to Jimmy Palmer, regional administrator of the EPA in Atlanta, to veto the project pursuant to his authority under the Clean Water Act.[16] Palmer decided to sit it out and let the Corps make the call. The coalition braced itself. Shockingly, the Corps denied Mirasol's application in December 2005, based partly on its concern that Mirasol's ditch could dehydrate a portion of Audubon's Corkscrew Swamp Sanctuary. Coincidentally, the Corps issued a permit for Parklands Collier, which depended in part on Mirasol's proposed design just turned down for modification.

This created all of the elements necessary for confusion during the overheated building boom taking place at the time. The development consortium of Ronto Development Parklands, Inc., and Parklands Limited Development Partnership, after receiving a Section 404 permit for Parklands Collier, sent in the bulldozers. Discovered accidentally by Audubon wood stork biologist Jason Lauritsen while flying over the site, the SFWMD took umbrage at the work, which it alleged was undertaken without all permits in hand, voting unanimously to levy a fine of nearly $52,000 for filling in 18 acres of wetlands. It was further alleged that the developers had presumed Logan Boulevard would be extended but violated conditions in the former Terafina (now called Saturnia Falls) permits.

In addition, an investigation was opened because Ronto was accused of illegally excavating 400,000 yards of dirt from district property after cutting a deal with a district employee. The company claimed that it planned to restore the property but expressed frustration that permits received from a regional office employee were somehow invalid.[17] While the company offered a plausible explanation for its actions, the Ronto incident served to illustrate two things: a failure of intragovernmental coordination within the water district and a lack of analysis of the complex hydrological interrelationship between Mirasol and adjacent developments.

After the New Year was rung in, Mirasol proposed another wrinkle, an amendment to the county's comprehensive plan to redesignate 160 acres of land within the development from Sending Lands to Neutral Lands.[18] The acreage in question was wetlands and primary Florida panther habitat but, more importantly, had already been used by Mirasol's owners as mitigation to obtain an environmental resource permit from the SFWMD. To allow mitigation land to be used a second time would amount to double-dipping, and the coalition was ready to pounce. But Mirasol faced another obstacle: Its PUD authorization was about to expire, requiring the company to either go back to the county commission for an extension or run through the permitting gamut all over again.[19] The Cocohatchee Coalition believed Mirasol's development plan was so dramatically altered that it needed to go back through the entire permitting pipeline again. During the prior five years, watershed protection regulations in the county's comp plan had become much tougher, and when Mirasol applied for its extension, it had more than doubled the number of dwelling units from around 800 to 1,917.

In addition to doubling the number of housing units, Mirasol's ditch had also been reconfigured to meander through the thirty-six holes of golf, using a series of interconnected lakes for flood control.[20] This modification had a spillover effect on Terafina's project, which had integrated the original Mirasol conveyance into its own water management system, but when Mirasol went back to the SFWMD with the revisions, it showed only modifications to the original plan and not the full site plan. The district granted the change but failed to review the project as part of a systemic whole. Part of the reason for rushing through the process was that permits were being held up due to the complexity required to analyze the impact of filling wetlands in, and developers were complaining. To relieve the pressure, SFWMD and, later, the DEP and EPA adopted a simplified but somewhat imperfect mathematical model called the Harper Methodology, which, in its 2003 incarnation, assumed that wetlands were not nature's palliative kidneys and, under some conditions, could be a source of incremental pollution.[21] This infuriated environmentalists but gave the various granting bodies a means of quickly moving projects from the drawing board to reality.

The last approval of Mirasol's partial plan sent the environmental partners off to court again. In July 2007, to the delight of I.M. Collier Joint Venture partner Robert Claussen of Naples and primary investor J.D. Nicewonder of West Virginia, administrative law Judge Donald Alexander ruled against the coalition. The judge admitted that evidence was not uniformly favorable to Mirasol but that the "preponderance" lay in favor of the defendant. In his decision, Alexander avoided the issue of whether mitigation proposed by Claussen's group was adequate by focusing on the marginal impact to wetlands of the modified permit and ignoring the overall damage it would wreak. After reviewing a transcript of the hearing, executive director Carol Wehle and her staff in West Palm Beach were determined to push Mirasol's permit through at any cost, even the destruction of functioning wetlands. The judge, relying heavily on testimony by SFWMD staff, glossed over an unfavorable peer review of the Harper wetlands impact model used by the district in permitting, which would come back to haunt the Conservancy at another time and place.

Deflated coalition members decided to concentrate efforts instead on the Jacksonville office of the Corps. But the Alexander decision helped grease the skids for Mirasol's Section 404 permit issued that October. Then in a full-court press, lead counsel, National Wildlife Federation, moved for a preliminary injunction to stop Saturnia Falls, then being developed by G.L. Homes. Coalition lawyers believed an injunction against Saturnia would have a marked impact on the pending request for a summary judgment against Mirasol pending in another case filed against both the Corps' 2007 Mirasol permit and the USFWS. This case was for issuing a faulty biological opinion by another coalition attorney (and the Conservancy's policy director), Gary Davis. The court declined to grant the injunction and scheduled oral arguments for October 2008, so by Christmas 2007 there were only two avenues left: Fight the Mirasol PUD recertification at the county commission (which had been postponed for two years) or wait out Davis's case, sitting on the desk of Judge Jose Martinez of the U.S. District Court in Miami.

The first option was closed when, sixteen months later, the Collier County Commission approved Mirasol's amended PUD without making the company go back through the permitting pipeline. The last chance proved to be the best. On October 23, 2009, Judge Martinez issued his opinion. He ruled that the U.S. Army Corps of Engineers had violated the federal Administrative Procedures Act and the National Environmental Policy Act by failing to take a "hard look" at the cumulative impacts of Mirasol on nearby developments in its environmental assessment.[22] The U.S. Fish and Wildlife Service violated the Administrative Procedures Act and the Endangered Species Act when it issued a "biological opinion (that) was arbitrary and capricious based upon its failure to analyze the impacts of other federal projects in the area in analyzing the environmental baseline and based on the FWS's unexplained calculation of fish density in the opinion."[23] While it slowed the process down temporarily, the decision was, in reality, quite narrow. It hinged upon inadequate cumulative impacts analysis, a subject federal agencies had always struggled with. It also offered Mirasol a blueprint as to how to refine its application and obtain approval in the next round, and did little more than give the Corps and USFWS a slap on the wrist. Finally, since there were no Clean Water Act violations, it was only a matter of time before the Cocohatchee Slough was further compromised, giving Corkscrew Sanctuary's wood storks another good reason to move to Georgia.

Mirasol's consultants, Todd Turrell and Rick Barber, went back to work on a revised water management plan based upon the court's decision. A modified permit application was approved by the Corps in July 2011, but the underlying biological opinion remained flawed, according to Jason Lauritsen, Florida Audubon's respected wood stork scientist. By this time, Claussen had tired of the interminable wrangling, and management of the project fell to Dennis Gilkey, a veteran of the development wars during his years with Bonita Bay Group, an organization with a highly burnished green image. Known as a man willing to listen to both sides, Gilkey and the coalition reached a settlement in April 2012. The western edge of Mirasol would remain a natural wetland; the development line would be moved further east. In all, 1,100 acres of the once 20-mile-wide Cocohatchee Slough would be preserved. The build-out would be a little more than 1,100 units, down 800 from the revised plan approved by the county commission. Two smaller external preserves would be constructed. Water control outflow into the Cocohatchee Canal was widened from 200 to 450 feet, and the Cocohatchee Coalition was guaranteed a perpetual easement, which included the right of inspection to make sure the functionality of the outlet conformed to the developer's promises.

Lessons from the Cocohatchee

The first lesson from the Cocohatchee battles was that the Corps and SF-WMD was highly permissive when it came to wetlands destruction during the go-go real estate boom of the 1980s and 1990s. The Corps had been involved in south Florida for more than 50 years. The one agency with some control over Corps permitting was EPA, an agency rife with politics at its upper levels of appointees, depending upon who was in the White House. The agency could veto a Section 404 permit for "unacceptable adverse effects" but exercised that right only eleven times between 1979 and 2009. During the same 30-year period, the Corps issued 150,000 permits throughout the United States.[24]

The Corps is the go-to federal agency for water projects. Housed within the Pentagon, it is dependent upon Congressional appropriations from individual members for its budget. An example of the Corps' operating mentality was on display at a 2001 meeting in Nebraska City, Nebraska. The American Rivers board of directors was working on creating a string of "habitat beads" along the Missouri River for the 2004 Lewis and Clark Bicentennial celebration, and the district colonel at the time gave an opening speech in plenary session. "Today the Corps spends 75% of its money on new projects and 25% on remediation. In twenty years, I predict we will be doing just the opposite. We will be spending 25% on new projects and 75% on remediation." After a moment of stunned silence, a woman raised her hand to ask the obvious question. "Why don't you just not do all those new projects if you are going to have to remediate them in 20 years?" The colonel didn't miss a beat. "You have to understand the process. Each year the Corps gets a certain amount of money. If we don't spend it, our appropriation for the following year will be cut back. We don't want that to happen, so we do everything in our power to spend every dollar we have coming to us."[25]

In addition, the policy of "no net loss" of wetlands was being undermined by assessment tools, allowing state and federal agencies to base decisions on loss of function, not acreage. One might excuse Corps projects built early on as part of the Central and South Florida Project, but permitting in the Cocohatchee watershed occurred well after degradation of nearby forage areas was scientifically documented. One agency, the USFWS, holds the right to issue a "jeopardy opinion" if listed species could be materially affected by a Section 404 permit. The courts saw it that way when they slapped the wrist of the USFWS for failing to analyze cumulative impacts of that agency's approval of development in the Cocohatchee Slough, but the ruling was ephemeral. Jeopardy opinions remain few and far between, partly because the agency and its respected resident science staff, part of the Interior Department, is susceptible to pressure from higher level political appointees.

A second lesson was that administrative rulings and court decisions can cut two ways. Judge Martinez rebuked both the Corps and USFWS but failed to invoke the more powerful provisions of the Clean Water Act, which would have required reexamination of the entire protocol for permitting. One of the provisions of the act designed to deal with precisely the problem in the Cocohatchee drainage—creation of large volumes of storm water runoff from rooftops, parking lots, and overfertilized golf courses—remains unfulfilled. Whether the water management system designed for Mirasol further degrades the Cocohatchee River and Wiggins Pass remains to be seen. The one advantage of a carefully designed system, using modern technology and best management practices, is that the outflow can be continuously monitored and measured at a given discharge point, certainly preferable to the non–point-source pollution pouring down the Golden Gate Canal.

Another bitter pill was that the Outstanding Florida Waters designation of the Cocohatchee River/Wiggins Pass meant very little when it came to permitting, demonstrating that the State of Florida is at war with itself when it identifies a natural resource area as having special significance or value, then turns around and ignores the very criteria that made it so. This dysfunction in water planning was first apparent in the Cocohatchee watershed south and west of Corkscrew Swamp beginning with TwinEagles. Sheet flow became increasingly constricted by man-made ditches feeding into holding ponds and the canal on the north side of Immokalee Road. The water district and Corps couldn't—or wouldn't—say no. Decisions were being made in a helter-skelter manner, each separate approval sequestered from the next with little or no reticulation.

In addition, the story of the Cocohatchee, Imperial, and Estero watersheds demonstrated either unwillingness or inability by permitting agencies to fully consider the effects of multiple developments over time connected by geography. The outer borders of cumulative impacts generally conformed to ecosystems, i.e., clearly delineated watersheds and drainages. A federal court described cumulative impacts succinctly: "A better image is that of scattered bits of broken chain, some segments of which contain numerous links, while others have only one or two. Each segment stands alone, but each link within each segment does not."[26] Part of the problem was a lack of understanding of historic basin hydrology going back to the 1960s. Analysis was difficult because it involved both spatial and temporal considerations but was required by statute in the 1985 act. Despite improved local planning efforts, environmentally sensitive lands were still being chipped away piece by piece, with no overarching vision on a regional scale as to how nature functioned systemically.

The final lesson was that the Conservancy and the environmental partnership forged during the Cocohatchee battles took their chances when going to court. In the early years, litigation was used only as a last resort—as in the case of Barefoot Beach—since most southwest Florida conservation groups had a long history of being reasonable and cooperative, but as time went on litigation became an integral part of the toolkit, necessary to maintaining negotiating leverage. Some groups began to back down because of either a sense of futility or an unreasonable strain on financial resources. The Conservancy, on the other hand, had practicing attorneys in important staff positions for some years: Mimi Wolok in the Sabal Bay controversy and Gary Davis in the Mirasol battles. After Davis left, individuals stepped into the breach to support challenges on a case-by-case basis.

Looking back over the record of the last 50 years, cases brought on procedural grounds have been more successful than cases based on substance because the courts were able to deal with clear, statutory issues. Cases where science was involved were tougher. For example, in the hearing before Judge Donald Alexander, contradictory testimony was given by expert witnesses from both sides and may have confused rather than clarified the case, resulting in quiescent judicial acceptance of the controversial Harper methodology. The tendency was for courts to split the difference or, as in Judge Jose Martinez's court, make a conditional ruling. This would allow the losing party to cure defects in its case and try again. As a result, settlement was always the preferred option to the vagaries of the judicial system.

The bottom line is that the Corkscrew watershed should never have been developed. At its heart lay Corkscrew Swamp, nesting site for hundreds of wood storks. The slough, with seasonal hydroperiods, provided ideal foraging grounds for the birds within a reasonable distance of their nests, but between 2006 and 2011 only one season produced hatchlings. Environmental groups fought tenaciously against development. Audubon took a leadership role because at risk was the Audubon sanctuary. At the end of the day, the Cocohatchee Coalition and the Conservancy, despite the ten-year struggle and constant litigation, did little more than preserve a slight alluvium of the historic waterway. They were too late; the epitaph was already written with development of TwinEagles. It was the first place-holder for the entire area north along Immokalee Road, with the other projects becoming infill, each contributing its part to the demise of the ecosystem all the way out to the revised rural boundary. The Conservancy might have made a difference had its Plan for the 1990s not pulled back in both ambition and geography, but that is little more than conjecture .

The Cocohatchee struggle brought together a consortium that had been split earlier over TwinEagles and Fiddler's Creek. With occasional disagreements over litigation strategy, the group was single minded in its objectives, but that spirit of cooperation was only temporary. It would be tested—and eventually shattered again—in the case covered in the next chapter, the rural lands program of Collier County.

Chapter 12

RURAL LANDS STEWARDSHIP

W

hile the Cocohatchee watershed was slowly being strangled by development, support continued in Tallahassee for land acquisition when the 1998 Florida Constitution Revision Commission proposed, among other changes, an amendment to extend the state's commitment under Preservation 2000 (to be renamed Florida Forever) to purchase sensitive lands. Amendment 5, on the November 1998 ballot, merged two state commissions and parts of DEP into a single agency, the Florida Fish and Wildlife Conservation Commission (FWC). Overwhelmingly endorsed by a three-to-one margin, the amendment also further restricted the state's ability to dispose of conservation lands under its control. It was overwhelmingly endorsed by voters by a margin of nearly three to one. Lawton Chiles worked hard with the legislature during his last year in office to codify the amendment, and in 1999, with the encouragement of newly elected Governor Jeb Bush, the state legislature passed the Florida Forever Act, providing another $3 billion in land acquisition funds for the next ten years (with some reallocation of the money).[1] The legislature, with Republican majorities in both houses, pressed for greater accountability in the management of state lands for habitat preservation and water conservation, to be accomplished through an "objective, science-based analysis" of natural resource inventories of lands considered for purchase. Florida Forever projects would be given priority according to compatibility with the state's growth management plan. Overall, the program reflected an increasingly sophisticated approach by instituting measurement metrics, albeit at the price of more control by the legislature over the entire process.

Although money for land preservation was ensured by funding Preservation 2000, Jeb Bush's years as governor, from 1999 through 2007, were marked by a radical change in the state's growth management programs. After taking office, he appointed a Growth Management Study Commission to look at the role of each level of government involved in sponsoring land for acquisition. He also charged it with reviewing citizen input to the planning process and, most significantly, defining the public's role in enforcing comprehensive plans. Bush's 25-member commission was dominated by developers and their consultants, flavored with a few politicians and one environmental advocate. The chairman of the Rural Policy Subcommittee was J.D. Alexander, a state representative at the time, grandson of Ben Hill Griffin Jr., and great-grandson of Napoleon Bonaparte Broward, governor of Florida in 1905. Alexander, who is listed in Wikipedia as a citrus farmer, is also vice chairman of Alico Corporation, a 1960 spin-off of the Atlantic Coast Line Railroad company bought by his grandfather in 1972. Alico owns more than 135,000 acres of land in central Florida in Collier, Lee, Hendry, Glades, and Polk Counties, a small part of which was donated to build Florida Gulf Coast University in southern Lee County.[2]

The group's report began with the assertion that "there is a direct relationship between land values and the ability of rural landowners to keep their properties in agricultural production"[3] because land used as financial collateral was ultimately dependent upon the value of underlying rights. In other words, the land had layers of optional uses. The top layer was the right to develop, and in the group's opinion this right had been compromised over time by ineffective growth management and land-use policies. The report went on to emphasize that the state should encourage its agricultural economy with an incentive-based system to preserve land with high conservation and natural resource values balanced carefully against protection of private property rights. This was attuned to changes at all levels of government. The old method of com-

mand-and-control regulation was being replaced by incentive-based approaches that would be easy to administer, less costly to enforce, and
easier to understand, making them more politically feasible.[4]

The committee's vice chair was the lone environmentalist, Charles
Lee, a vice president of Florida Audubon. Lee was well known in Tallahassee as a knowledgeable and relentless man who bore decades of
battle scars. He headed a group tasked to look for approaches within
existing statutory provisions to preserve agricultural viability through a
vehicle called Rural Lands Stewardship (RLS) as an option available to
local governments. Originally recommended only for an area exceeding 100,000 acres, the threshold was later dropped to 50,000. The state
was willing to provide technical assistance but pushed planning down to
the county level to ensure that boundaries were drawn with cooperation
from affected landholders (although there was no requirement for 100%
participation). Recommendations for design of a statewide rural lands
program underwent numerous modifications in the legislature until it
was finally adopted in April 2004. This lag between the initial bill and
final legislative approval had a direct impact on Collier County.

Collier County Forges Ahead

The Department of Community Affairs had been pressing Collier County to comply with the state's growth management plan since 1998. The
main issues were excess density in areas zoned agricultural, the destruction of wetlands and natural resources in rural areas by overzealous road
building, and urban sprawl.[5] After receiving two warning letters, the
county was desperate to avoid a hard deadline. Prodded by the Florida
Wildlife Federation and Collier Audubon, the state's patience finally
wore thin. DCA filed an administrative proceeding against the county
for walking away from wetlands and habitat protection, clearing the way
for settlement discussions that included a proposal to reduce density to
one dwelling per 40 acres in environmentally sensitive areas and one
per 20 in rural lands beginning one mile east of highway CR 951. The
Conservancy wanted downzoning but was highly critical of the fact that

North Belle Meade, which was north of I-75, had been left out of sensitive lands on the county's maps.[6] The Conservancy also wanted the same criteria used in its 1997 settlement with TwinEagles to be applied to rural fringe and agricultural lands.[7] Finally, environmental groups requested that terms of the settlement be set forth in both the county's comprehensive plan and land development code, not detoured to a side letter. But the most incendiary issue was a moratorium on all new building in the county proposed by DEP secretary Steve Seibert. Pam Mac'Kie, chair of the Collier County Commission, was incensed by the overt criticism. "I just can't believe Secretary Seibert is going to allow this to go. Obviously, a moratorium is not a reasonable option—unless he's writing the check for that too."[8] Bruce Anderson, a local attorney accustomed to having his own way when representing developers, commented: "I can't imagine the state would force a moratorium down here. If they do it, they better get the checkbooks out."[9] Obviously, when it came to questioning development in Collier County it was all about the money.

The larger matter of the county's unwillingness to restrict development on rural lands was to go before Governor Bush and the Cabinet in June 1999. As the hearing date approached, a swarm of lawyers and lobbyists descended upon Tallahassee. The Conservancy's new president, David Guggenheim, supported the proposed course of action in his presentation to the governor and Cabinet. "DCA has proposed interim growth restrictions while a balanced community-based planning effort, to include DCA, environmental agencies, and a broad range of county stakeholders, work together to develop a sound plan for development in rural areas."[10] He was backed up by a Conservancy voter survey of Lee and Collier County residents showing that the majority favored tightening the state's growth management laws to further restrain sprawl.[11] By pressing for a "sound plan," the Conservancy's president acknowledged that development would occur but hoped for better than low-density development with zoning of one house per five acres, separating people from where they worked, shopped, and went to school. Bush and the Cabinet liked the idea. They believed that Collier could create a model for other counties throughout the state. If the plan proved viable, it would encourage county-level plans that, in Bush's opinion, would have a greater chance of being adopted and applied than efforts initiated at the state level. Besides, he knew it would be a tough sell to the legislature with its new Republican majority in both houses.

The state, temporarily mollified, withdrew its lawsuit to give the county time to harmonize its growth plan with the state's. To comply, the county divided the agricultural area into two parts: rural fringe and eastern lands. Planning for the rural fringe began immediately. Covering around 90,000 heavily impacted acres, the fringe had been compromised both by development creeping outward one subdivision at a time and by subdivisions east of highway CR 951. The main pressure points were along the Immokalee Road corridor with the TwinEagles subdivision,[12] all of North Belle Meade, and isolated pockets south of US 41 past the intersection leading to Marco Island. A county-appointed citizen's committee met weekly throughout the spring of 2000; the group was fraught with bickering and unable to reach a consensus. County staff stepped in and, with support from the Conservancy and other environmental groups, proposed a program to allow "transferable density allocations for rural property to be used for the implementation of clustered development." This method, commonly known as transfer of development rights (TDR), had been used in Collier County since the 1980s.[13] It was a simple system designed to compensate farmers and rural landowners for giving up development rights on their land. A governmental entity could establish a transfer program by identifying areas critical for conservation (sending areas) and those most suitable for development (receiving areas). The value of rights on sending lands would be determined by negotiation between seller and buyer and could be applied to receiving lands projects in exchange for additional density. The role of government was to grant and maintain conservation easements on protected lands. A developer could increase density in less sensitive areas from two to four dwellings per acre by purchasing development rights; the Collier program eventually resulted in a four-fold increase of available credits, from 4,500 to 17,500. While conceptually sound, the program was not significant given the size of the county. Large developers bought a modest number of sending land credits, but many went unused. Eventually the program fell into disfavor.

Rural Lands Stewardship Area (RLSA)

Planning for the eastern lands (see Map 11) was more complicated than working on the rural fringe, even though there were fewer landowners and most were engaged in agricultural production and livestock. The county commission, under pressure from DCA after allowing the controversial TwinEagles development, held an eight-hour workshop in 1999 to consider changes governing developments larger than 40 acres.[14] At the heart of the issue was a reduction in density. Commissioner John Norris commented: "What I see here are some good proposals for density reduction, but what I also see here is that this seems to have evolved into more regulations on the environmental side of things. I don't think that's what I ever intended." He then went on to reiterate a proposition dearly held among developers: Golf courses should be counted as natural areas. "It's hard to argue that a golf course is not green space," he said.[15] Of course, every acre of a golf course that could be counted as conservation land meant one less acre that had to be found elsewhere, and Norris was quite taken with golf courses. Not known at the time, he later was found to own a portion of a $100-million venture called Stadium Naples. He had put no money into the project but became a 12.5% limited partner with a lifetime membership and an $80,000 consulting contract. He cast a number of votes in favor of the project without revealing the conflict of interest and was later indicted on charges of racketeering and conspiracy. The largest scandal in Collier County's history, it marked the end of the overtly cozy relationship between developers and public officials.[16] Another commissioner, Tim Constantine, part of the effort to push back against the downzoning package, was also caught up in the net after receiving payoffs.

Commissioners were in a tight spot. They were divided on how far to take the changes. If they could not reach an agreement with DCA, they had a right to appeal to the governor but with little chance of suc-

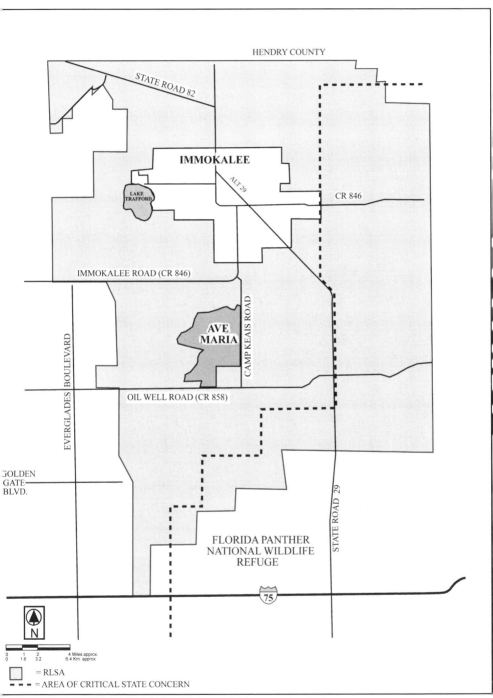

Map 11. Collier County Rural Lands Stewardship Area (RLSA).

cess. They knew a lawsuit by environmental groups was pending but had been held up. And they knew George Varnadoe, representing Barron Collier Companies, had threatened litigation if his client felt that the new plan was somehow in violation of its property rights. "I think you're giving us a lawsuit," he had said at a December consultants' presentation of initial recommendations.[17] To top it all off, commissioners could not rely upon their appointed planning commission to make recommendations because three members either owned land or had a direct financial interest in the outcome of a development rights plan.[18] Aside from showcasing the incestuous relationship between politicians and the development community, the compromised planning body deprived commissioners of a valuable source of advice, counsel, and, most important, political camouflage.

At the very end of the meeting, Varnadoe and Alan Reynolds, president of local consulting firm WilsonMiller, came to the rescue. Representing four landowners holding more than 150,000 acres east of Golden Gate Estates, including planning commission member Russell Priddy, Reynolds proposed a two- to three-year study that would map current land uses; inventory sensitive lands, water recovery, and retention areas; outline possible road configurations; and propose a method of moving development rights to appropriate lands. Varnadoe noted that the landowners involved would defer any development until after the program was presented to both the county and Department of Community Affairs, and he offered to meet personally with the governor if any department in Tallahassee refused to go along with the new timeline. Seeing a way out of the settlement mess and the potential conflict of interest they had created in appointments to the planning commission, commissioners jumped all over the proposal. It was also a means of pushing the issue off their plate until after the next election.

The study team, known as the Rural Lands Assessment Oversight Committee, was populated with agricultural, business, civic, and environmental interests. Business development and agricultural interests were in the majority. Ron Hamel, executive vice president of the Gulf Citrus Growers Association, was appointed chairman. Agricultural interests were represented by Alico, the company run by the Ben Hill Griffin and Alexander families, and the Baron Collier Companies and Collier Enterprises of Naples, both of which had large landholdings in the eastern county and experience in building large subdivisions. The study was funded jointly by Collier County and by a group called Eastern Collier Property Owners Association (ECPO). Selected by ECPO to do the design work was WilsonMiller, a large engineering firm located right up the street from the Barron Collier Companies' headquarters, well known to developers in southwest Florida as the go-to firm to maximize rooftops. The Conservancy had a seat at the table in the person of David Guggenheim. After he left, his successor, Kathy Prosser, was appointed to the committee and became its chair for a short time. A second environmental seat was first occupied by Andrew Mackie of Corkscrew Swamp Sanctuary and later by Mike Bauer,[19] representing both the sanctuary and Florida Audubon. The committee fairly represented all parties at interest.

The group met 30 times over the next two and a half years. Twenty of the meetings were for public discussion since the program itself was being designed almost entirely by the staff at WilsonMiller. The full plan was unanimously adopted by the committee in April 2002 for presentation to the county commission, and the unveiling in June was a fine affair. Chair Hamel's foreword was preceded with a quote by Thomas Jefferson extolling the value of science as applied to agriculture. He was properly appreciative of the efforts of volunteers, county staff, and WilsonMiller, which had produced the presentation as well as the plan.[20]

In summary, the program had four laudable goals: (1) to protect agricultural lands against ill-planned development in the RLSA; (2) to set aside water flow ways and retention areas in a natural state for human consumption and managed agricultural use; (3) to preserve critical wildlife habitat areas and corridors by directing development away from sensitive lands; (4) to discourage urban sprawl by encouraging compact, clustered development through a series of economic incentives. The last objective required a complex system of layered credits, beginning with lands kept in agricultural uses, conservation areas, and open space designated as Stewardship Sending Areas (SSA), with the value of credits determined by natural resources on each parcel. Credits could be transferred within the RLSA overlay to Stewardship Receiving Areas (SRA), designated as lands slated for higher levels of mixed uses, mainly residential and commercial. Lands with the highest ecological value were Flow-way Stewardship Areas (FSA) and Habitat Stewardship Areas (HSA). The committee estimated 67,000 acres, or approximately one-third of 195,000 acres covered by the overlay,[21] would fall into the latter two categories. Most importantly—and an issue that would become extremely contentious five years later—estimated developed land at build-out amounted to 16,800 acres, with only 6,700 acres required to meet the county's projected population growth by the horizon year 2025.[22]

When compared to the underlying zoning of one house per five acres, it was estimated that the WilsonMiller system would "not result in an increase in the total number of allowable dwelling units or population in the Eastern Lands area, but rather result in a reallocation of the density and population allowed under the baseline standards."[23] Given this conclusion and the fact that the plan proposed to convert barely 9% of the eastern lands to towns, villages, hamlets, and compact rural development, the Conservancy and other environmental organizations signed off on the deal. The county breathed a sigh of relief since the plan got it out from under the state's administrative oversight. ECPO was relieved to have some certainty as to developable acreage within the foreseeable future, but WilsonMiller knew that a mandatory review of the plan, scheduled for five years later, would allow another big bite out of the apple. In Collier County, apples were best eaten in smaller bites.

The first RLSA accomplished two very important things beyond the obvious objectives of the plan itself. It got environmental organizations on board with cooperative landowners. Some of those relationships would become vital to the review process in 2007, when landowners were able to splinter southwest Florida's environmental community in order to achieve a wholly different outcome in the second RLSA. Much more importantly, it prevented the County Commission from reducing density to one per 20 or one per 40, which would have locked landowners into a lower population number and made the second version of the program dramatically different. WilsonMiller and its clients were taking the long view by thinking well beyond the first five years, and the environmental community's willingness to back off density reduction dramatically reduced its own options. The first RLSA was palatable, accomplished most of the Conservancy's goals except for density reduction, and emphasized sustainable clustered developments at a level equal to or less than the baseline zoning of one dwelling per five acres. From the developers' view, it allowed a degree of certainty that their proposals would be favorably reviewed in a timely fashion provided the RLSA criteria were faithfully adhered to. Density would be higher in the western part of the county, which would not necessarily be equitable to all landowners, but the intention was to protect valuable water recharge source bases in the eastern county, notably the Okaloacoochee Slough. Finally, wetlands would receive more attention under the revised crediting system. Kathy Prosser-Bovard summed it up: "I was in favor of the big ideas proposed and felt we had an opportunity to effect meaningful change in Collier County and beyond. Like everything, however, the devil was in the details. And the details were mainly created and/or controlled by the development community."[24]

DCA's staff review proved to be substantial rather than a rubber stamp. It was clear they had read the report as well as minutes of the committee's meetings. They requested modifications to the original submission; once approved it went back to the Collier County Commission for a final blessing. But massive changes to the program occurred before final adoption. A number of new credits were introduced for "early entry" and "restoration." The original plan for 134,000 credits was inflated to a new and unpublished number. Immediately after the commissioners' approval, the first clustered development was announced by Barron Collier Companies. A new unincorporated town called Ave Maria would be located south of Immokalee and would be governed by a partnership between the development company and the Ave Maria Foundation, brainchild of Domino's Pizza founder Thomas Monaghan. The project would be built on land donated for a Catholic church and university surrounded by a town, based on the European model of an ecclesiastical edifice as the geographic and philosophical nexus of the community.[25]

The plan raised eyebrows. As mitigation, the Barron Collier Companies agreed to preserve more than 17,000 acres of SSAs within the rural lands at a ratio of a little more than three for one, but the original RLSA plan contemplated about 36,000 units housing a population of about 87,000 souls,[26] which meant Ave Maria would consume nearly one-third of the units at projected build-out of the county. Both the ratio and sheer size of Ave Maria concerned Conservancy officials, DCA, and conservation groups concerned primarily with wildlife and caused some necessary rethinking.[27] The state's main concern: "(it is) . . . questionable whether this very large amount of development is consistent with rural sustainability including maintaining the viability of agriculture."[28] Environmentalists wondered how much Ave Maria would take of what the rural lands program was supposed to save?[29]

Second Rural Lands Program

The legislature amended statutes governing rural lands a number of times over the next few years, but Collier County's program was exempted from statutory modification until mandatory review scheduled for 2007.[30] In November county commissioners appointed a thirteen-person team heavily loaded with mining, agricultural, financial, and development interests. It lacked the balance of the first group. Technical review of the existing program would precede any consideration of alterations, but the winds of change were calm. "Off the top of my head, I don't foresee any major changes," said Tom Jones, the Barron Collier Companies' representative.[31] In reference to Ave Maria, "so far, so good" was the quote from Brad Cornell of Audubon, the lone environmental member of the review committee.[32] But one change had occurred on the environmental side that would eventually affect the process. The Conservancy had hired Andrew McElwaine as its new chief executive to replace Kathy Prosser-Bovard. Coming from the major statewide land trust group in Pennsylvania, he was a learned student of history with an encyclopedic mind and a singular gift: the ability to explain complicated issues in brief, understandable language, which would stand him in good stead when RLSA revisions came before county commissioners. Prosser-Bovard was a natural conciliator who preferred to work matters out in private when possible, but McElwaine was a different breed of cat.

During the leadership change, discussions were being held outside of the public process between environmental groups and property owners to deal with one of the nation's most endangered species: Florida's iconic panther. ECPO's efforts, begun prior to creation of the RLSA review committee, were led by Paul Marinelli of Barron Collier Companies, a large man and incurable optimist with abundant and well-deserved faith in his ability to iron out differences of opinion. He had great credibility; his word was good as gold. He was concerned about the intergenerational transfer of property among large landowning families, fearing that ownership dilution would create pressure to monetize illiquid assets, resulting in the sale of agricultural land and a disastrous fragmentation of wildlife habitat. He approached all environmental organizations, including the Conservancy, to propose a countywide habitat preservation plan for all endangered species that would ease the regulatory burden on developments proposed for the eastern lands, with special emphasis on the panther.

The plan would be funded by landowners who would accept higher levels of mitigation requirements as the price for developing primary panther habitat and would contribute up to $150 million to purchase critical buffer zones and build roadway underpasses to allow animals to access their normal travel corridors. Marinelli met with Conservancy officials three times asking them to support the plan. He reiterated his overriding fear of a hodgepodge of unsustainable developments in the eastern county, with little unified planning for transportation corridors and infrastructure. Marinelli was supportive of population clustering and community planning similar to the large Babcock Ranch, which had recently been proposed in Hendry and Charlotte Counties, and he hoped the RLSA revision could accomplish a similar outcome in Collier County. The Conservancy was interested but asked Marinelli for more detail as to specific locations proposed for development in the eastern rural lands, a request he was unable to satisfy for two reasons: Barron

Collier Companies didn't control all of the land, and not all landowners participated in the RLSA program.

At this point, ECPO executed a successful divide-and-conquer strategy. It began with a notice of "intent to sue" from Laurie MacDonald at Florida Defenders of Wildlife as a result of a biological opinion from the U.S. Fish and Wildlife Service on the effect of Ave Maria on Florida panther habitat. Marinelli cast about for a way to satisfy the desires of both sides, which led to a meeting at which Marinelli asked environmental groups to join in a "bigger and broader plan."[33] Florida Audubon was quickly brought into the process because Marinelli was on the board. A series of private discussions were held with all environmental groups, including the Conservancy. Laurie MacDonald was optimistic: "I was taken by the idea. It was the willingness to be collaborative, to solve problems cooperatively. That was important."[34]

While the Conservancy continued to participate sporadically in meetings on the panther plan, it was debating internally its most important objection, the proposed location for a new development in the rural lands, a Collier Enterprises project called the Town of Big Cypress. Its location, according to the Conservancy, flew in the face of the only peer-reviewed study of suitable Florida panther habitat, authored by eleven scientists from Florida and the southeastern United States. Known as the Kautz study, named after the primary author who was an employee of the Florida Fish and Wildlife Conservation Commission, it divided southwest Florida into primary and secondary habitat zones.[35] The primary zone was the minimum area necessary to ensure survival of the Florida panther on a self-sustaining basis. The secondary zone was sufficient in size and prey base to allow expansion of the population, desirable because the gene pool of the animals was limited. The population was estimated then at a little more than 100 big cats, and the Town of Big Cypress, a big-box shopping center in its initial phase, was smack-dab in primary habitat.

Marinelli persevered by putting his proposal in writing to McElwaine. He believed deeply in the protection program and wanted the Conservancy in, not out, but the executive committee finally decided the organization could not sign on. The first bugaboo in the document was dropping the single word "avoid." The organization had concluded that the concept of avoidance was being replaced by mitigation, and mitigation wasn't always adjacent to the locus of environmental destruction. At one site, the animals would be "buffered" from civilization by an aquatic moat built adjacent to the Camp Keais Slough to protect inhabitants of the Town of Big Cypress and their pets from predation by hungry panthers. Development would be allowed in the ACSC near the Okaloacoochee Slough panther corridor, where the cats would be forced into a small transition zone to allow them to move from the Florida Panther National Wildlife Refuge under Oil Well Road and up into the slough.[36] Florida Audubon, Collier County Audubon, Defenders of Wildlife, and the Florida Wildlife Federation did eventually sign the panther plan, but unfortunately Paul Marinelli was not present. He had passed away in early April, and southwest Florida lost the one person who could bridge the divide between recalcitrant environmental groups and responsible landowners in eastern Collier County.

ECPO continued to press forward, dispersing a team of lobbyists who could handle the situation in Tallahassee. Local attorney John Passidomo, who had been brought into the Sabal Bay case, was assigned to handle the county. With a virtually unparalleled record of turning his clients' dreams into reality, he attended nearly every meeting of the review committee so he could fully respond to any questions or criticisms from county staff and commissioners when the time came.

The major political obstacle in Tallahassee remained DCA. It had issued a report to the state legislature highly critical of the Collier program, pointing out that the stewardship credit system was "extremely complex" because 20 attributes were involved in the evaluation of every single acre. In addition, there were seven layers of land use that could be stripped, some more than once, leading DCA to the startling conclusion that "credit values assigned are over five times the density value of the underlying land use." To compound the problem, DCA's report continued, "the maximum number of stewardship credits in the RLSA is not known and thus the maximum potential development footprint cannot be determined."[37] This was a departure from assurances made to the county commission in 2002 that development would amount to only 16,800 acres, or 9% of the rural lands. Stewardship credits had inexplicably multiplied like Everglades marsh rabbits, with the mama bunny being additional high-value restoration credits. According to Wilson-Miller, the credit calculation in the first iteration actually translated into 43,312 developable acres.[38] But even this estimate was at the low end.

The review committee became concerned when it turned out that credits potentially available, absent any modifications, could be translated into as much as 57,000 acres of new development. "I don't know how palatable that is in a lot of quarters,"[39] commented committee member Tom Jones of Barron Collier Companies. The number also alarmed many of the environmental groups supporting the program. Finally WilsonMiller, in a presentation to county officials, settled on 404,000 credits as the available maximum. By recalibrating some SSA credits and counting open space within SRAs (including John Norris's golf courses), the total at build-out was reduced to 47,120 acres. In the same presentation, the consultants confirmed that estimated recalculated SRA entitlements under the existing program was 43,300 acres, not the 16,800 originally presented in 2002.[40] After a great deal of back-and-forth, ECPO and WilsonMiller agreed to place a cap on development at 45,000 acres. The complexity of the credit system was too arcane and difficult to explain to the public and to county commissioners; acreage was a simpler denominator.[41] But there was still the matter of those excess credits.

Much of the difficulty in arriving at hard numbers in the estimates related to the introduction of credits into the system to encourage environmental restoration of compromised land. But some of the confusion was a result of having professional planners and lawyers produce a complex document couched in ambiguous language beyond the comprehension of both the public and their elected officials. The outcome favored their clients—which is what the clients paid for.

DCA's report also criticized the program's apparent lack of protection for agricultural lands. "It is questionable whether this very large amount of development is consistent with rural sustainability including maintaining the viability of agriculture."[42] Under the existing program, the county had lost a little more than 5,000 acres of row crop, citrus, and open range land between 2002 and 2007. According to the RLSA technical review, there were roughly 64,000 acres under cultivation in 2007. A subsequent report prepared for review committee member Tom Jones asserted "using assumptions provided by the Barron Collier Companies . . . (there will be) approximately 28,000 acres of agricultural land under cultivation (at build-out)."[43] If in fact the rural lands program's original intent was to maintain agriculture in rural Collier County, it apparently failed to do so. But Alan Reynolds, president of WilsonMiller, disputed that conclusion: "The data show the program is doing precisely what it is intended to do."[44] To get around this rather delicate point, the review committee then decided to abandon the state's objective of preventing "premature conversions of agricultural land" and replaced it with a restated goal of "preserving agriculture." Words changed; problem solved.

The committee moved ahead with revisions to the original plan during the summer of 2008, using cooperating environmental groups and lobbyists to assuage skeptics in the state capital. But the process hit a bump in the road in July. Since the new RLSA would be a large-scale comprehensive plan amendment, DCA exercised its statutory power to raise questions in what was known as the Objections, Recommendations and Comments (ORC) review. The department was concerned about four things, but the overriding issue was that data submitted to the department did not adequately "demonstrate a need for the amount of development possible in the RLSA."[45] The comments also expressed the department's strong feeling that the Big Cypress, an "area of critical state concern," would suffer adversely from multiple impacts and thereby violate the Florida Administrative Code. In addition, mitigation credits, which in the original plan were restricted to use in sensitive areas, would apply throughout the county.

The review committee was working on adjustments to defuse DCA's objections when a map titled "Conceptual Build-out Roadway Network" emerged. The map had 23 little red dots identified as "Town Nodes," as well as widened arterials throughout the county. Twenty-three towns were simply too many if the scale was anything like Ave Maria or the Town of Big Cypress. The gazetteer was WilsonMiller, which quickly backtracked, arguing that the map was simply conceptual and that the little red dots were Transportation Activity Zones (TAZs), which had nothing to do with population centers and everything to do with transportation intersections. The Conservancy seized upon this point, arguing that once again roads, not sound growth management policies, would be the driver of development, with the inevitable results including urban sprawl, strip malls, and a fragmented landscape.

Finally, Paul Marinelli made it clear in his conversations with the Conservancy that his group intended to work with the U.S. Fish and Wildlife office in Vero Beach to create a multispecies habitat conservation program (HCP). But the Conservancy's Natural Resources Policy Director, Jennifer Hecker, had hands-on experience as cochair of an appointed Collier County committee that spent more than two years working on a multispecies plan. She was convinced there was insufficient evidence to prove its value over a series of single-species plans. USFWS, on the other hand, wanted to see only multispecies plans even though the few in effect throughout the country had resulted in a decline, rather than recovery, of endangered populations.[46] In all fairness, the service's view was also colored by a lack of staff time to work through the intricacies of multiple single-species HCPs in the State of Florida with nine birds and animals on the "endangered" list.

With opposition building, the review committee decided to fast-track its plan. Supported by WilsonMiller, members discussed the possibility of circumventing two citizen's advisory boards, the Environmental Advisory Committee, and the planning commission to bring the amended plan directly to the county commission as a comprehensive plan amendment.[47] Resistance was fierce. The two advisory bodies had already been through the technical review phase as a first step and were preparing to hear the amendments. Expertise abounded on both panels. The EAC had two PhD members including Judy Hushon, a woman with an incisive mind and a doctorate in biochemistry who chaired EAC hearings on the proposed revisions. The Collier County Planning Commission was led by Mark Strain, an able and experienced man who had worked as a consultant to builders for years. The idea behind bypassing advisory boards was to move as quickly as possible into a special cycle amendment process. By presenting its second-phase report in language that could be directly inserted into the county comprehensive plan, the review committee felt it could avoid passing through the process twice— once for conceptual review and a second time for technical amendment approval. It made the argument that since "county staff intends to rely upon WilsonMiller to help complete the data and analysis to support a GMP [Growth Management Plan] amendment, on behalf of our clients we need assurance that the County intends to initiate the amendment process."[48] Plus, the change minimized the opportunity for public input. The Conservancy jumped on this as a complete breach of process. It argued that allowing WilsonMiller to prepare growth plan amendments was transparently ceding authority to developers with a direct financial interest in the outcome.[49] Review committee chair Ron Hamel backed off fast-tracking, and commissioners decided to stick with the protocol of using their appointed advisory boards instead of going directly to a special cycle amendment, despite protests by WilsonMiller.

The revised RLSA wound its way through split votes at the EAC and CCPC. Those recommendations, generally considered helpful, were summarily brushed aside at a tumultuous meeting, but the county commission needed a supermajority of four votes to move the RLSA into a special cycle, and two of the five commissioners were opposed. After hours of back-and-forth, Fred Coyle, the former city councilman who had helped Collier Enterprises with Hamilton Harbor, called a recess to negotiate a compromise between the Conservancy's Andrew McElwaine and attorney George Varnadoe (representing the landowners). Coyle's compromise was to cap both credits and acreage, which was agreeable to the opposing parties. Upon reconvening, Commissioner Frank Halas looked at the landowners' attorney and asked who would pay for a special cycle amendment process. The reply was a negative shake of the head, at which point the commission tabled the entire issue.

Florida Panther Habitat Designation

Even before the meeting, McElwaine was irritated that the review committee sought commission approval prior to receiving a report from seven scientists hired by ECPO to review the effect of amendments on the Florida panther population. Known as the Florida Panther Protection Program Review Team, the group had, under some duress, agreed to try to settle some of the political differences in a study that, when issued, was generally supportive of the program based primarily on the fact that 141,000 acres, or 70% of the RLSA, was likely to be saved under the program (leaving about 45,000 acres for development). But the devil, as always, was in the details. There were a number of substantive changes to the design and width of large animal transit corridors and the location of new roads; a provision allowing mining to be deducted from development acreage when "mining constitutes a loss of habitat that is not compatible with conservation of panther habitats"[50]; and most importantly a recommendation that development take place *first* in the "secondary" habitat zone before moving into "primary" lands. This last irritated Hushon, who chaired the review of RLSA revisions. She was adamantly opposed to any invasion of primary panther habitat under any circumstances, and when asked for her bottom line replied, "The first RLSA was a much better deal for citizens than the revised plan."[51]

Final approval was put on hold for more than two years, but the review committee never pressed for adoption. Southwest Florida's economy had slowed dramatically, and some landowners were not happy with the cap on credits. They had openly discussed using excess credits outside the RLSA, perhaps in the rural fringe, and the Conservancy was prepared to wrestle that idea to the ground. In addition, landowners believed they could get a fast deal with USFWS for a multi-species habitat program and bring the matter back as a complete package. The multi-species plan would allow landowners' incidental destruction of some endangered creatures as long as the overall impact offered a reasonable chance of survival. But the deal never materialized because the service realized that the sheer number of endangered and threatened species in southwest Florida demanded full investigation, and the multi-species concept was running into trouble.[52] But the most important point of all, in the Conservancy's view, was that the concept of avoidance, as the best way to protect the Florida panther, was being replaced by the idea of minimizing impacts, and broad discretion available under a multi-species plan would do just that.

Conservancy policy staff trusted staff biologists working for the US-FWS but were leery of upper level supervisors' susceptibility to political pressure. Since 1993 the service had not issued a single "jeopardy opinion" to preserve Florida panther habitat. Environmental groups were also still stinging from a decision by Paul Souza, of the USFWS office in Vero Beach, to reduce the panther "consultation area" by 900,000 acres. Souza, in a letter, claimed his decision was based strictly on scientific analysis.[53] Not so, said Kevin Dugan of the Collier County Transportation Department: "The reason they changed it is because we asked them to. . . ."[54]

Sierra Club, supported by the Conservancy and other groups fed up with the approach in Vero Beach, filed suit in federal district court against the service for its "failure to designate" habitat for the Florida panther. Bad blood became even worse when the Conservancy filed a public records discovery request in January 2010 to produce documents and minutes from discussions between ECPO and the RLSA Review Committee. The service ignored the request for fifteen months.

By August 2010, ECPO tried another tack. This time around it offered to support public acquisition of a 50,000-acre addition to the Florida Panther National Wildlife Refuge. The refuge, consisting of more than 26,000 acres in the heart of the Big Cypress Swamp, was believed to be home range for five to ten of the big cats, and the additional lands were estimated to have a value of more than $200 million.[55] But some of the land involved had already been placed into conservation easements, which, if subsequently sold to the state, would amount to double-dipping. The idea never got traction because the recession that began in 2008 had taken its toll, and Florida Forever funding was drying up.

In April 2012, federal court tossed out Sierra Club's "failure to designate" suit on a technicality, leaving the environmental plaintiffs to swallow hard and accept the fact that the service would continue on its own path, unencumbered by a judicial mandate to better define what it would take to ensure recovery of the panther population. That left the landowners' panther protection program, which, while suffering from a number of imperfections in its final form, may yet be the only way the species can survive a future onslaught of bulldozers, particularly if the state is able to open a corridor allowing the animals access north of the Caloosahatchee River.[56]

To add insult to injury, in May 2012 the U.S. Fish and Wildlife Service, under terms set forth in Section 6 of the Endangered Species Act, entered into a conservation agreement with the Florida Fish and Wildlife Conservation Commission, granting the state broad powers in managing threatened and endangered species. The controversial agreement gave the FWC authority, without federal review, to issue incidental take permits for the destruction of species and habitat for development, construction, and mining purposes. There would be no appeal to FWC and no right of review of each permit at the federal level (as there is now), preempting a chance for a second opinion. The move was interpreted as an attempt by USFWS to reduce manpower levels for permitting reviews, but the state agency was no better off because, as part of Governor Scott's austerity program, its budget and personnel has been cut back as well. The Center for Biological Diversity, Everglades Law Center, and the Conservancy sued in U.S. District Court in March 2013, alleging the agreement was made without proper notice. No public hearings were advertised or held, and there was no chance for public comment. The suit has a good chance of success on the technicality of improper notice but less chance on the substance of the complaint: that the federal government is washing its hands of the ESA as it relates to incidental take permits.

RLSA in Retrospect

In January 2013, county commissioners voted to put the revised RLSA program on hold. First, population estimates made at the millennium were turning out to be highly inflated as more retirees were choosing to live in

Georgia and the Carolinas rather than southwest Florida. As a result, pressure to develop the rural lands had diminished. Second, Commissioner Jim Coletta was defeated by Tim Nance in November 2012, shifting the balance of power on the county commission from full-speed ahead to a more reflective posture. The first iteration of the cooperative venture between large landowners and the environmental community remains in effect as a constructive way to approach land-use planning. A long-term partnership would eliminate the uncertainty surrounding permitting agencies and the courts, and it has the ability to engender public support if the planning process is carried out in full transparency. The most unfortunate outcome of the protracted RLSA review was a temporary splintering of southwest Florida's environmental coalition, once so fiercely united in the Cocohatchee Slough case. There were other moments, notably in the case of TwinEagles and Fiddler's Creek, when groups came down on different sides of an issue but the rift over the rural lands program was serious and long lasting. In Laurie MacDonald's words, "It was one of the most painful experiences in my career. We believed in the program; we believed we could get the science right."[57] During the process, large landowners confirmed what they already suspected: When environmental groups circle the wagons, the guns usually point inward.

At the most obvious level, the RLSA emerged as a way to accomplish land preservation without running headlong into the property rights issue. It was a cooperative undertaking among private landholders, local government, and citizens. In its first iteration, the program was a model of participation and collaboration, overseen by a committee broadly representative of diverse community interests and large property owners willing and able to direct incompatible uses away from critical watersheds and sensitive habitat. In return, landowners received increases in density allotments for clustered housing and a degree of certainty as to the rules under which development could take place. They felt their private property rights had been given recognition, and in the process a viable roadmap had been created to minimize future conflict.

The RLSA program also served another purpose: to integrate water planning with land use on a landscape level. Each clustered development would require permitting since Collier County defers major decisions regarding water to the state and water management district. But for the first time a coherent plan was created by landowners who understood the need to maintain an adequate water table for multiple uses, no longer treating it as an inexhaustible resource. During RLSA hearings, it was concluded that the availability of water in eastern lands converted from agriculture to residential and commercial use was not a restricting factor when all sources were considered (including aquifer storage and recovery wells and brackish water reclaimed for agricultural use). The numbers were challenged during the amendment process, but the review committee was wedded to its conclusion. Whether there is adequate water in the eastern lands is a critically important question; planning for 45,000 acres of development in the broadest sense was painstakingly done within the context of large watersheds, avoiding the pitfall of permitting reverting to approving one subdivision at a time with little regard for cumulative impacts on nature's thousands of years of work. By both fiat and necessity, supply will also depend upon maintaining flow ways and recharge areas intact as development takes place. The RLSA identifies those areas. Whether or not the bulldozers respect their critical functionality remains to be seen.

WATER

CHAPTER 13

REVIEW OF FEDERAL AND STATE WATER LAWS

*H*ow could the bottom third of a peninsular state with more than 50 inches of rainfall each year have a care in the world about water? The answer begins before the Civil War and extends to the present day. In 1850 Congress passed the Swamp and Overflowed Lands Act, giving states the right to claim land unfit for agriculture and allowing the young State of Florida to gain domain over nearly 21 million acres. By 1855 the Florida legislature passed a law creating the Internal Improvement Fund, overseen by the governor and four Cabinet members, to control how the newly minted asset could best be put to use. The fund figured prominently in battles between environmentalists and developers covered earlier in this book, but during Reconstruction it was the conduit to legally deed land in exchange for running rails throughout the state. These efforts sputtered, with the east coast developing slowly, but in 1881 Governor William Bloxham sold four million acres to a Philadelphia businessman named Hamilton Disston. As part of the deal, Disston agreed to drain 12 million acres in the Everglades, provided he could lay claim to half the affected acreage. Disston's scheme never worked, but his sweeping approach was the first of a series of Brobdingnagian schemes to drain land and sell it to gullible buyers—often sight unseen—leaving behind a series of floundering developments like southern Golden Gate Estates and giving southwest Florida the reputation as a place where charlatans thrived on a glib tongue to make a fast buck.

Washington's Intercession

The earliest federal efforts were aimed at distribution: controlling the timing and quantity of surface water flows. Beginning in 1907, the Everglades Drainage District created a network of canals to serve a vast area spread over miles of flatlands south of Lake Okeechobee, where the Southern Sugar Company used migrant laborers to plant and harvest cane sugar, the region's preferred and most profitable crop. Two powerful hurricanes in 1926 and 1928 overwhelmed the lake and killed more than 2,000 working people in towns like Clewiston, Belle Glade, and Moore Haven. The devastation brought President Herbert Hoover to the scene. He left promising it would never happen again, calling upon the U.S. Army Corps of Engineers to build an 85-mile-long dike. Hoover personally supervised the plans, which led to the structure being dedicated in his name, but as time passed the project went well beyond its original purpose of protection by expanding into a water control system for the benefit of agricultural interests south of the lake.

Severe droughts in 1944 and 1945 in south Florida were followed by the inundation of Miami, with 102 inches of rain during the summer of 1947. This brought Congress to authorize the Central and South Florida Project for Flood Control and Other Purposes in 1948 (C&SF Project), where the state and Corps combined to create a water control and management plan that took more than 20 years to complete. The project covered 18 counties and more than 15,000 square miles. It was supplemented the following year by the Florida legislature's creation of a flood control district to manage the federal undertaking. Water conservation to the west of the area south of Lake Okeechobee and north of Everglades National Park became a primary objective to be managed by a series of levees, canals, and pumps designed to direct excess water into a series of outlets, including the Caloosahatchee River. As part of the project, the Hoover dike was expanded again to cover 147 miles; it now surrounds most of Lake Okeechobee, which was originally designed to hold water at a level at least 16 feet deep. The Corps now attempts to keep the lake at no more than 14 feet by periodically releasing water into the St. Lucie and Caloosahatchee Rivers due to deterioration. As an intended consequence, areas previously at risk for flooding and inundation became safer for occupation. As an unintended consequence, a line of related ecosystems, beginning north of Lake Okeechobee and extending to the Big Cypress Swamp, were severely compromised.

The most important federal initiative was passage and amendment of the Clean Water Act of 1972, an expansion of the Federal Water Pollution Control Act of 1948. Targeted at water quality throughout the country, it was motivated partly by a rising environmental conscience in the nation and partly by awareness that water quality data varied greatly from state to state. After passing in Congress, it became law after an override of President Richard Nixon's veto and was it designed primarily to prevent the release of toxic substances into the "waters of the United States." The act dealt with both point and non-point sources of pollution, and its enforcement was vested in the Environmental Protection Agency (created by executive order by Nixon in 1972). Enforcement of the CWA has been a struggle since the beginning. Most pollution is regulated by permit, a license to flush agreed-upon levels of toxins into the waters of each state. Most important, the act required states to adopt standards for water quality appropriate to use of the water, subject to review by the EPA. This would become the basis for a prolonged and bitter battle in Florida, to be covered in a later chapter titled By the Numbers.

At the federal level, the U.S. Army Corps of Engineers is responsible for looking after some aspects of surface water management, including the power to issue Section 404 permits. There are two frontline agencies reviewing Corps permits: the U.S. Fish and Wildlife Service and the U.S. Environmental Protection Agency. The first is required to issue a "jeopardy opinion" on the permit and to consult with the Corps if it finds peril to listed animals. In this process, called elevation, the USFWS does not have veto power. But the EPA does. The agency does not routinely approve Corps projects; it intervenes only when asked to do so by formal notification. The EPA prefers to play watchdog at both the regional and national levels; it contested only 11 Section 404 permits between 1972 and 2007.[1] In the rare case where either one or both of the reviewing bodies object and the matter cannot be worked out, then the foreseeable consequences are dire, with emphasis on the word "foreseeable."

Florida

Under Governor Claude Kirk, who had little patience for environmental issues but had Nathaniel Reed there to prompt him, the state made its first real attempt to deal with pollutants with the Florida Air and Water Pollution Control Act of 1967. The act established a process by which toxic levels of discharges could be both permitted and regulated through a state control commission. Later, under Governor Reubin Askew, there was another approach to water quality and distribution, beginning with the governor's Conference on Water Management in South Florida, convened to deal with integrating land use and water management planning into a cohesive whole. The result was the Environmental Land and Water Act of 1972. As covered earlier in the chapter on growth management, the legislation was sweeping in its creation of "areas of critical state concern." The Florida Water Resources Act of 1972 (covered in earlier chapters) was also passed, creating five water management districts along hydrologic (basin) boundaries. For the next 25 years, the districts issued thousands of "consumptive use" permits to allow people to take water from surface sources and undergrounds aquifers and return it (sometimes to a different source). Few permits were denied, and those held up generally had conditions attached that allowed the permit to go through after design modifications. Ad valorem taxing powers were granted to the districts by a referendum in 1976. Board members were appointed by the governor, giving the executive branch indirect control of water policy in the state and allowing special interests with access to the governor a chance to influence appointments. This was followed by the Florida Environmental Reorganization Act of 1975, which created the Environmental Regulatory Commission to review actions taken by and to set standards for the DEP. Later, under Bob Graham's leadership, the legislature passed the Water Quality Assurance Act of 1983, which dealt with a series of specific problems and, most significantly, reasserted the need for water quality data by each of the five water management districts. Finally, swamps, bogs, and low-lying areas throughout the state were recognized in the Wetlands Protection Act of 1984, designed to protect Florida's abundance of "nature's kidneys."

While each of the aforementioned acts was directed at a specific problem, the rapid-fire frequency with which these laws were passed carried with it two deeper implications. First, implementation of the early legislation was sporadic at best, requiring further clarification, refinement, and (in some cases) sanctions in order to put the laws into practice. Second, as data became available, it was obvious to observers that the safeguards put in place were simply not working. It is to the progressive deterioration of water quality in southwest Florida that we now turn our attention.

CHAPTER 14

WATER WARS

As covered in this book's introduction, the interior of Florida has always been a place of schemes to drain the land for human occupation and use. While the quantity and timing of Lake Okeechobee water releases for multiple users, mainly agriculture, was carefully overseen by government agencies since the 1948 C&SF project, water quality was largely taken for granted until a major shift in public attitudes—beginning with Rachel Carson's publication of *Silent Spring* in 1962 and *Time* magazine's photos of the Cuyahoga River on fire in 1969—forced state and federal officials to begin accumulating information on untreated water in lakes, rivers, streams, bays, and estuaries. Once that data was available and the public had some idea of the dimensions of compromised water quality, the issue could no longer be ignored. In southwest Florida, the most unlikely candidate to address water quality problems was the federal agency most favored when it came to managing quantity and releases, the Corps of Engineers. But in the late 1990s, the agency was dragged into creating an environmental impact statement conflating quality and quantity into a single, controversial document. Before looking into the substance of that document, we need to understand how the mighty Corps became trapped in a corner from which it could not escape.

An important federal check and balance, not covered up to this point, is the Council on Environmental Quality (CEQ), an independent advisory agency reporting directly to the president of the United States. It is responsible for implementing the National Environmental Policy Act (NEPA) of 1969, the first piece of federal legislation passed by Congress to directly address problems created by suburban sprawl throughout America, but it is only as effective as the occupant of the White House wants it to be.[1] In January 1997, the CEQ issued a non-binding guidance revision on "cumulative impacts," which expressed concern that permitting for large construction projects throughout the country was occurring without regard for either context or direct and indirect aftereffects.[2] This had an impact on water issues because, as part of the guidance, the Corps was required to produce an Environmental Impact Statement (EIS) for publication in the Federal Register as part of statutory procedures for implementing NEPA.[3]

The council's directive coincided with formation of a working group in southwest Florida to spur the Corps into rethinking its approach to issuing Section 404 permits.[4] The Corps, to its credit, had already recognized that permitting was fragmented and cumbersome. Sensitive lands were being chipped away piece by piece with no overarching vision as to how natural elements, mainly water, functioned systemically. Procedurally, there was little coordination among various agencies. The SFWMD had done a workshop on the subject in 1996 in an attempt to emphasize the necessity of looking at projects from the watershed perspective, but it had little effect and the mill continued to grind out permits. Only three permits were denied by the Jacksonville office of the Corps during the 1990s.

By 1996 Collier County had more than 620,000 acres of land in public ownership and had identified another 207,000 acres for protection of wildlife habitat, ecosystem preservation, and public use.[5] The Conservancy saw this as an opportunity to return to its roots of advocating for land purchase. With funding from the J.C. Penney Foundation, it organized a working group to examine the future of lands identified for preservation.[6] While the report was ready to go in 1997, the Conservancy knew that the Corps, reacting to CEQ's guidance, had to produce an EIS for southwest Florida and decided to withhold its own report, hoping the two would supplement one another.

Corps of Engineers Environmental Impact Statement

David Guggenheim, hosting a session at the Everglades Coalition[7] meeting in January 1998, did his best to broaden the geographic scope of the Corps study: "This is a most significant discussion, one of the most in-depth examinations of a Florida west coast issue," he said. "It emphasizes growing concern for the western edge of the Greater Everglades Ecosystem."[8] He complained that permits had been issued serially, the last phase inevitably leading to the greatest destruction of natural resources. TwinEagles was an example of this, and it was standard procedure by some developers. Once a project was in the works, a series of variances was sought that inevitably increased the size of a development footprint based on the argument that changes were absolutely necessary to the economic feasibility of the project.

Opposition ripened at once. Developers and large landowners, along with a covey of consultants, formed an organization called Partners for Environmental and Economic Progress (PEEP). Progress, of course, meant more dollars in their pockets. The initial thrust of PEEP was to limit the scope of the study, but Guggenheim and the coalition won the day: Study boundaries would run from the Caloosahatchee River south through the Ten Thousand Islands and east to highway SR 29 in the rural lands of Lee and Collier Counties, covering more than 1,500 square miles. Reluctant from the beginning, the Corps had slowed the process to a crawl, so Guggenheim decided to release the local study funded by J.C. Penney. The report had a strong bias for outright purchase of environmentally sensitive lands and identified three factors that could further compromise the environmental value of lands on the county's priority list: (1) further disruption of natural water flows beyond damage already done by canals to the southern half of Collier County below I-75; (2) fragmentation of habitat, breaking up symbiotic plant and animal communities; (3) increasing concentrations of nutrients from both point and non-point sources, compromising Lee and Collier's coastal estuaries. The report mapped out a series of goals for future protection of sensitive lands, ending with the admonition "managing land for 'ecosystem health' remains in the expert domain."[9] And expert domain meant the Corps and water management district.

The Corps, in cooperation with the district, finally opened its study by inviting elected officials, civic associations, agricultural interests, developers, and sportsmen's groups to offer advice. As the number of participants grew, so did the cacophony. The man in charge of the project was John Hall, a gruff supervisor at the Corps office in Jacksonville who had been overseeing wetlands destruction in Florida since 1990. He had a doctorate in biology and, after a brief encounter with university life, worked for various federal agencies for the balance of his career.[10] As he analyzed the lack of progress, Hall admitted "(w)e have engendered unreasonable and unrealistic expectations amongst a variety of special interests including: the environmental community, the regulated community, private property rights advocates, landowners and the County Commissions."[11] Then he zeroed in:

> Now to southwest Florida. The Corps has had regulatory concerns in this area for over ten years. We were aware of the enormous growth pressures from first simply noticing the number of Development of Regional Impact reviews. . . . This was followed by an increasing number of Section 404 permit applications for residential, golf course and retirement community developments. We watched as developments slowly moved eastward. Issues of appropriate wetlands mitigation, endangered species and surface water management became increasingly common. With each tendered application, our concern grew.[12]

Hall and the Corps suggested addressing upcoming county growth plan reviews through an interagency partnership, but commissioners balked. They resented meddling in local land-use planning. In response,

Hall and the Corps cited Florida Gulf Coast University in southern Lee County as an example of cooperation in a project beyond the urban boundary, where a permit was granted after a judicially mandated agreement set up an advisory body to create a unified plan for the Estero River drainage system. Finally, pressure got to the point that the Corps decided to release a preliminary white paper accompanied by Hall's postulate that recent history was owned by the "tyranny of small decisions."[13]

When the white paper was made public, a furor arose over the data. The draft contained an overall analysis of water quality in southwest Florida, with practically no documentation as to the source and reliability. It overlooked the essential point that systemic management of a watershed was the most critical element of all; no mention of it was made anywhere in the study. The Conservancy favored establishing minimum flow levels as well as numeric quality standards for each watershed or basin within SFWMD jurisdiction, arguing that once these were clearly set forth, an applicant for a Section 404 permit would have an objective standard to achieve and maintain and would not degrade water quality or flows on adjacent lands outside the basin boundaries. The Corps responded by proposing to use historical data for creation of standards but admitted such information was unavailable for the majority of southwest Florida drainage basins. Concern grew that the Corps might arbitrarily choose its historical data, but Tampa Bay had recently gone through a similar exercise to set nutrient and dissolved oxygen goals, and the Conservancy saw no reason southwest Florida could not do the same.

The Corps, whose main mission was protecting navigation on America's waterways, was in over its head on the subject of water quality, and Guggenheim would not let up. In a conversation with John Hall in October 1999, his notes show this comment: "We want responsible growth within urban boundaries and more caution outside boundaries. John spending too much time on legal arguments."[14] In the conversation, Hall had brought up the Bert Harris Act cited by developers and landowners and asked for an additional six months to work things out. But the Conservancy, along with the Florida Wildlife Federation and National Wildlife Federation, was adamantly opposed to any extension.

"If the Corps decides to extend the comment period, the Conservancy requests the Corps immediately begin enforcing the permitting criteria now in place with the use of currently available data through the EIS process to determine cumulative impacts to wetlands."[15]

Guggenheim's notes from this period bring to light another nagging problem that would plague southwest Florida for the next 15 years: "DEP (Florida Department of Environmental Protection) is the chief water quality agency here. EPA thinks it must get together with DEP on EIS water quality but state doesn't want to get involved. Bruce Boler says non-point source pollution is the problem."[16] Boler was a blunt and outspoken EPA employee. He would become embroiled in a controversy over wetlands a few years later but was the first person to sound the alarm in 1999: The EPA had better take control of the situation in southwest Florida because the state was going to sit on its hands. He pressed for more data, knowing the state's record on granting permits within impaired watersheds was overly accommodating and that once the data was made public it would pressure DEP to acknowledge that many of Florida's waters were being dangerously compromised. Hall disagreed. He felt water quality standards should be the exclusive purview of the state. With a deadline approaching for closing public comment, he decided to test the waters by issuing a first draft of the EIS. The preliminary version caused an eruption of displeasure from nearly all concerned parties. On one map, the massive Fiddler's Creek development on the east side of highway CR 951 was shown as preservation land. Environmentalists looked at proposed destruction of an additional 23,000 acres of wetlands as unacceptable. Developers felt that too much land had been placed into conservation and argued that any future permit denials under the Clean Water Act and Endangered Species Act would be considered a government "taking" of private property.

On the subject of water quality and quantity, southwest Florida politicians were up in arms. "Collier County concurs with Lee County in requesting that water quality models be made available for public review. . . . (T)he process of delineating flow ways, identifying significant hydrological natural resources and ranking water quality issues by group consensus is subjective and lacks scientific objectivity."[17] But the problem was and would remain that the counties had little staff expertise in water management. Decisions had to be handled by the state through the water district and through the Corps (with 404 permits). The Conservancy remained adamant on the need for precise numeric criteria but added a condition: "Minimum flows and levels and minimum acceptable water quality standards for each drainage area in the system should be established over a five-year period, during which no dredge-and-fill permits would be issued. Only after acceptable levels are attained should the Corps grant a permit to any applicant."[18] The recommendation went on to suggest that once standards were scientifically and quantitatively established, responsible agencies, namely the SFWMD, should be required to create a plan to meet or exceed those standards and further require any applicant to commit unequivocally to participating in that effort as a condition of approval. Finally, the recommendations placed great emphasis on monitoring and enforcement for compliance because constructed water control systems had a tendency over time to atrophy and needed periodic refreshment to maintain functionality at intended (permitted) levels. This was a major concern with wet and dry detention ponds built in lieu of naturally functioning wetlands. Pond bottoms, as a result of the life cycle of aquatic weed infestation supercharged with nutrient runoff, had a tendency to harden and diminish percolation for aquifer recharge.[19]

In August 2000, the Corps released a final draft of the EIS for comment. Two inches thick, it was the last act of Colonel Joe Miller, the district engineer in charge of the Jacksonville office at the time. It represented thousands of hours of work and comments distilled by long-serving civil servants like John Hall and Bob Barron, who made the point when releasing the document that it was not intended to stop development but rather to identify elements involved in permitting decisions. PEEP was circumspect when questioning how the Corps arrived at its basin boundaries but bluntly asserted that the Corps had not fully complied with public process, saying it violated "fundamental principles of fair notice and due process and is arbitrary and capricious."[20] An economist friendly to developers, Hank Fishkind inflamed Lee Building Industry

Association members by reporting that the Corps study, if implemented, would cut potential development by 100,000 rooftops. However, he noted, "They've pulled back from the most egregious of their policies."[21] Susan Asmus, of the National Association of Home Builders, was not so kind. "(Regional regulators) are 23-year-olds who live with mommy and daddy. . . not people who have any clue about economics."[22] Taken together, most of the comments from developers were critical of the process but not of outcomes. As beneficiaries of the status quo, they had no desire to earn the enmity of the agency that dispensed 404 permits like hard candy at a Mardi Gras parade.

Not so with environmentalists, who couldn't wait to pile on. "The Army is in full retreat," said Kris Thoemke of the National Wildlife Federation. "I'd say it's full steam ahead for east coasting the west coast."[23] Wildlife organizations put out a white paper entitled "Road to Ruin," pointing out that during the study period the Corps had issued permits for the destruction of nearly 4,000 acres of wetlands in Lee and Collier Counties. The Corps responded by saying it had also worked toward restoration of 8,000 acres by removing exotic plants but the fact remained: the Corps did not turn down a single Section 404 permit during the time the EIS was under way. In its final form, the study was covered with the fingerprints of developer lobbyists from Washington to Tallahassee; it never became meaningful. But in all fairness, the Corps was not the best organization to conduct a regional EIS. Corps personnel were trained for a singular purpose: to subordinate nature for man's benefit. Besides, being a military organization, the Corps preferred to make its decisions in secret, which defied the norms of an increasingly open society and the public process. Its expertise lay primarily in engineering management of inshore waterways like canals and rivers, not in the broad-brush approach needed in ecosystem analysis, which included water quality analysis, adjacent land uses, and habitat preservation for plants and animals.

Conservancy Leadership Changes

About the time of the Corps' final draft, one of the most engaged personalities from the environmental side had left. David Guggenheim, after four years as president of the Conservancy, had moved on to the Center for Marine Conservation in Washington, D.C., in June 2000. He left behind an invigorated organization of more than 700 volunteers and nearly 6,000 members. His tenure had been marked by missteps in the case of Fiddler's Creek and TwinEagles, but he had increased the organization's visibility by making himself accessible to the media. Publications were brighter and more colorful. A comfortable public speaker, he was at ease with almost any audience and highly capable as a fund-raiser. During his term, more women were brought onto the Conservancy's board and Ellin Goetz was elected to a term as chair. The science component of the organization was given greater prominence, but there was concern about how government regulatory bodies were reacting to the sometimes combative approach taken by Guggenheim toward challenging development. In a memo, the head of the science division wrote, "The reputation of the Conservancy is perceived as adversarial to many of the agencies [to which] we would normally make application. This issue will become more important as agencies seek cooperative partnerships to solve problems as opposed to the current, although changing, system, where proposals are solicited from the scientific community."[24]

When Guggenheim left, Ellie Krier was asked to serve as interim chief executive. Her steady hand and facilitation of the search committee made the board comfortable with a woman running things and helped pave the way for Kathy Prosser to be hired as the first woman president of the organization. Prosser was a superb fund-raiser and moved well in the community. Deeply committed to land preservation, her easy manner was able to overcome some of the development community's suspicions about the Conservancy, and she played a large part in convincing county commissioners to approve ballot-specific language for a vote on Conservation Collier in November 2002. The election effort, well funded and guided by a Washington public relations firm, passed with more than 60% voter approval, enabling the county to sell up to $75 million in general obligation bonds to purchase critical natural resources. Prosser helped spearhead the effort and was named chair of the Land Acquisition Advisory Committee.[25]

She also believed environmental groups needed to rethink how they approached the most serious problem: urban sprawl. She soon discovered that Guggenheim, with his ability to gather headlines, had alienated other environmental groups by taking exclusive credit for successes and deflecting criticism. She sought with some success to mend fences to create a more powerful coalition among environmental groups operating in southwest Florida, but lingering doubts about the Conservancy's commitment to collaboration always remained. During her tenure at the Conservancy, from 2000 to 2006, she set the wheels in motion for a capital campaign that would eventually raise more than $38 million to build a new campus and endow major positions in science, policy, and administration. She was able to recapture the interest of major donors disaffected over the years by various missteps made by the organization, and through her work on Conservation Collier she helped establish a $100-million fund to purchase environmentally important lands.

Prosser built a strong legacy in land acquisition, but during her tenure a frontal assault on the functionality of natural wetlands began and proceeded largely unchecked. Booming construction was stressing the capacity of regulators and permitting agencies. One of the bottlenecks was that many subdivisions presented hydrological engineers with the problem of how to deal with post-development storm water discharges where sites contained combinations of uplands and wetlands. Calculating the interaction of the two was complex and arcane. It was slowing the permitting process, powerful builders were complaining, and something needed to be done quickly. Prosser believed environmental groups were in a "reactive mode" when it came to water issues. Nowhere was that more evident than when, in the middle of her term as president, the bureaucratic view of wetlands changed suddenly from being nature's kidneys to a source of pollution. We now turn to how that happened.

Florida's Polluting Wetlands

The State of Florida defines wetlands as "those areas which are inundated or saturated by surface water or ground water at a frequency and duration sufficient to support . . . a prevalence of vegetation typically adapted for life in saturated soils."[26] They do not stay fully submerged or saturated year-round but are subject to periodic influxes of water, leading to a sufficiently high level of soil moisture to prohibit the growth of upland plant species. Additionally, wetlands are populated by plant communities uniquely adapted to intermittent saturation. In technical terms, wetlands can be swamps, marshes, or bogs. In south Florida, many wetlands are transitional features, or zones, between aquatic systems and uplands.

Many developments were allowed to destroy wetlands in exchange for mitigation, both on-site and off-site. But once the permit was in hand, the vast majority of mitigation projects were either never attempted or completely non-compliant. One study showed that between 1985 and 1990, of more than 1,000 permits issued by the Florida Department of Environmental Regulation, only 6% were in compliance for mitigation required as a condition of the permit.[27] The main reason was that developers were becoming more expert in shading environmental impact statements, and some counties simply lacked the right people to ask the right questions. This was not the case, however, in southwest Florida, where local government planning staff and citizen's advisory boards had sufficient expertise to ferret out inconsistencies and deficiencies in development proposals. What both counties did lack, however, was adequate staff to follow up on compliance regarding the creation and ongoing functionality of areas set aside for mitigation offsets.

Beginning in 2002, 50% of wetlands destroyed in Florida came from development permits in Lee and Collier Counties, but the story actually began in November 2001, when the EPA, after 25 years of research, reported that Florida's storm water regulations resulted in removal of between only 15% and 40% of nutrients (primarily phosphorous and nitrogen) from farm fields, parking lots, and sprawling developments. In rough numbers, urban runoff accounted for 75% of polluting nutrients; agricultural activities, about 22%; and golf courses, the balance. The

EPA-imposed restrictions loomed large, but the federal agency agreed to back off if the state would require projects to reduce nutrient outflow.[28] The following year, a small group of state and county agencies began working with the EPA on a Water Quality Initiative (WQI) to meet the condition of no increase in nutrient loading after development occurs, avoiding the subject of reduction entirely. The first agreement, which would become a model statewide, was reached with Lee County Airport Authority, but the powerful southwest Florida development community hung back. It had plans of its own.

Harper Methodology

In the fall of 2002, a group called Water Enhancement and Restoration Coalition (WERC) was formed by Bonita Bay Group, a developer in Collier and Lee Counties with a burnished reputation for environmental respectability. The Conservancy was familiar with Bonita Bay Group from the days of its timid opposition to TwinEagles in the rural fringe of Collier County and with the work of one board member, Rick Barber, a development consultant on the Mirasol project and principal of an engineering firm. Barber would be appointed by Governor Rick Scott in 2013 to be a member of the governing board of the SFWMD, the agency that issues permits for wetlands destruction. The group's first project in 2002 was to develop a plan for a filter marsh to rehydrate Ten Mile Slough in Lee County, running alongside Ten Mile Canal between Daniels Parkway and Six Mile Cypress Parkway. The plan was touted as an exemplary collaborative public/private partnership solution to a water quality issue and got the group off to a good start in both the media and the public eye. Then it introduced the work product of a newly hired consultant.

Harvey Harper was owner and principal of Environmental Research & Design of Orlando. He was hired by WERC to create an easily understandable mathematical formula for use in the permitting process to assess the impacts on functioning wetlands. In its first iteration, the model estimated predicted runoff from a new development and quantified pre-development and post-development loading of pollutants based

upon the rate of runoff and retention time.[29] His model led to the conclusion that water exiting natural wetlands contributes to downstream
pollution and that a predictable level of pollutants could be removed by
man-made wet and dry detention ponds built for the single purpose of
storm water treatment. But according to the environmental community,
Harper had used data collected from questionable sources by factoring
in average annual runoff without taking into account seasonal variability.[30] This resulted in a single mathematical factor applied to all wetlands
in south Florida. In other words, all wetlands polluted at a single uniform rate adjusted for detention time whether they were located adjacent to a highway or in the middle of a swamp. In the first Harper model,
there was no difference. It also assumed that a wetland's "water quality
capture volume" is emptied after each storm event, but the efficacy of
a wetland is highly dependent upon the time between events and the
loading level of each, because once a natural wetland becomes saturated
it can no longer absorb nutrients. The model suggested that man-made
wet detention ponds were a suitable substitute for nature's kidneys, capable of removing up to 90% of phosphorous and 70% of total nitrogen
with extended residence times. The methodology also measured output
values as a single metric but failed to give adequate consideration to the
condition of waters flowing into the wetland. By measuring only outflow, if a wetland received heavily polluted runoff, it could easily appear
that the wetland was actually creating or enhancing pollution levels. Finally, variations in soil types and multiple land uses were not taken into
consideration in creating the first iteration.

Both WERC and Harper were recognized for their work by the Estero
Bay Agency on Watershed Management in July 2003. The SFWMD, DEP,
and Corps all quickly adopted the Harper methodology despite the fact
that they were exercising regulatory authority based upon a model that
had not been subjected to scientific peer review. The model was quickly
embraced, and agencies were reluctant to consider objections to it because
its mathematical simplicity allowed faster permitting. In the superheated
boom of the era, both developers and overworked government staffers desired speedy approvals. The three agencies approved more than 99% of the

permit requests that came before them from 2003 until 2008, when the building boom in southwest Florida came to a screeching halt.

With the logjam blown apart by the Harper model, development permits flowed. Winding Cypress in Collier County, with 2,300 homes and destruction of 200 acres of wetlands, was quickly approved by SFWMD and the Corps. The Mirasol project, for which the EPA had recommended denial, was quickly approved to destroy 1,500 acres of natural wetlands on the southern fringe of Corkscrew Regional Ecosystem. In the face of a torrent of permits, reaction reached a fever pitch. John Cassani, Southwest Florida Watershed Council, said, "Harper's report was sold as a step forward in addressing the concerns of impaired waters in this region. . . . It's exactly the opposite."[31] EPA employee Bruce Boler objected to adoption of the Harper methodology by resigning. He joined Public Employees for Environmental Responsibility, which blasted his former employer. "EPA's new position that wetlands pollute stands the Clean Water Act on its head and sends the all-clear signal to developers that no project is out of bounds."[32] The Conservancy and its local partners immediately challenged the Mirasol development.

Politics played heavily into the mix. The EPA still wanted to defer decisions to Florida, so when the DEP and the SFWMD adopted the Harper methodology, it went along. The Atlanta regional office was controlled by a political appointee of President George W. Bush named Jimmy Palmer. He may have had reservations about the Harper method but was reluctant to overturn state agencies.[33] What reservations he did have were manifest in early 2005 when he requested from Versar, Inc., of Springfield, Virginia, a peer review of Harper's work.[34] The generally critical report was submitted in draft form that April but never saw the light of day in final form. Harper never responded publicly to the Versar report. He vigorously denied that his model assumed that all wetlands pollute, but he did make revisions in 2007, taking into account some, but not all, of the criticism leveled during the prior four years. For example, he reduced the efficacy of man-made wet detention ponds. In his 2003 version, 90% phosphorous removal was predicted; in 2007 this was reduced to 80% to 85% with 200 days' retention. Total nitrogen removal in

2003 had been estimated at 70%; in the 2007 version that was reduced to 40% to 45%. However, he never backed away from the underlying assumption that wetlands have a positive annualized loading rate.

The other problem environmental groups had with the Harper methodology was its embrace of constructed systems for nutrient removal. In southwest Florida, dry and wet detention ponds had been used for years as a surrogate for natural wetlands. These engineered impoundments, designed to capture and retain overflow during wet season, worked superficially in the short term, but over time pond bottoms tended to harden and become unable to filter or absorb nutrients. The result was that outflow was just as contaminated as inflow. Permits issued in southwest Florida required developers to monitor the functionality of these constructed systems, but the condition usually expired when the property was turned over to homeowners' associations. This neglected aspect of long-term consequences was brought to the attention of the Collier County Commission but blissfully ignored and, combined with proliferating strip malls with impervious parking surfaces, contributed to a gradual decline of water quality in the final repository for runoff: coastal estuaries of southwest Florida.

Adding to the Conservancy's concern, the DEP was willing to allow developments that could achieve a condition of no net increase in loadings. In other words, if the pre-development level of pollution exceeded existing standards, it would continue to be permissible after development occurred. There would be no effort to rectify past mistakes, no attempt to clean up the mess. DEP secretary Mike Sole defended his agency's position at the time. "Harper was about streamlining the process. We had a lot of conversations about it. At the time we needed to find a regulatory mechanism, and Harper was the best available source at that time. We felt it would improve the storm water situation—that's where we really needed to do better."[35]

Despite objections raised about the Harper methodology, there was a move afoot by the DEP and the SFWMD to expand its application to storm water management.[36] Conservancy staff was completely unaware of this until late August. This was particularly galling because the Conservancy had been working with the SFWMD and other organizations to create a protocol called the Southwest Florida Basin Rule (SFBR) to provide a system of incentives that would reward low-impact development with a goal of removing 80% to 95% of post-development pollutants, a rule already in effect but not being enforced. The basin rule had been in the works for more than two years. The Conservancy had filed an administrative challenge in 2003 against the district's issuing Environmental Resource Permits, which allowed developers to treat only the first inch of storm water runoff, usually with wet detention ponds. Settlement discussions among environmentalists, developers, and district staff led to the SFBR's becoming a means of incorporating a menu of flexible best practices based upon the size and impact of each development. It would not apply a positive loading value to natural wetlands and meet anticipated standards for Total Maximum Daily Loads (TMDL)[37] of south Florida's inland and coastal waters designated as "impaired." The development community, a reluctant party to the discussions, adopted a wait-and-see attitude toward the new rule despite the incorporation of incentives. Then, when the Harper methodology was introduced, the SFWMD, despite being deeply involved in creating the basin rule, began to backtrack in favor of the mathematically simpler formula, with its positive loading value in natural wetlands.

The DEP then decided to abandon the SFBR as applicable to storm water and replace it with something called "policy guidance," without the power of regulation behind it. The first memo, from district engineer Terri Bates, established a standard of status quo or no worse than existing conditions to storm water treatment. It was replaced by a second advisory memo from Robert Brown requiring a standard of net improvement to existing conditions. However, both failed to question the underlying assumption of a positive loading value of natural wetlands. Andrew McElwaine, the Conservancy's president, believed the Harper methodology had some legitimacy as an underlying tool but was fatally flawed. "It was the assignment of positive loading rates to natural wetlands. With proper calibration the model could have been much better."[38]

Jennifer Hecker, Natural Resources Policy Manager at the Conservancy, wrote "we've repeatedly voiced that the application of the Harper methodology in permitting is resulting in decreased storm water regulatory stringency and efficacy, as well as incentivizing the destruction of wetlands for development."[39] The EPA in Washington was also skeptical, saying it "cannot verify the conclusions of the new statewide model. For this reason, we would recommend that Florida DEP conduct an independent peer review of the new model. . . ."[40] But the state agency was not about to upset the development applecart in Florida and warned the Conservancy that any attempt to offer a scientific study to invalidate the revised Harper model would be looked upon as biased.

Conservancy Challenges Harper Methodology

Undaunted by this threat and based upon its belief that Harper had not incorporated sufficient source variables in building his model, the Conservancy engaged the Center for Watershed Protection, an independent organization located in Ellicott City, Maryland, with deep knowledge of wetland ecology, to oversee a peer-reviewed study analyzing wetland nutrient loading from a variety of sources: highly developed, urban storm water runoff; commercial developments; lower density residential developments; golf courses; and agricultural fields. Once collected, the variety of natural wetland discharges would be measured over various time periods for post-loading concentrations of phosphorous, nitrogen, and other pollutants. Data collection and interpretation would be managed entirely by the Center. The Conservancy was relying on the study to support its opposition to the 2007 Harper methodology, but the outcome was uncertain, as the study was an independently conducted scientific endeavor. It contained the normal ambiguities and contradictions common among scientists but was generally unfavorable to Harper. After the study was presented to the EPA's Atlanta and Washington offices, the Conservancy's Hecker described the reaction: "We have been as high as the deputy administrator's office in Washington to ask them to put their foot down to prevent DEP from using the Harper methodology in Florida. After all, it's their duty to make sure the state is in compliance with the Clean Water Act but we haven't made much progress."[41] She believed the DEP would pay little attention to the study, but Mike Sole denied that. "We always looked carefully at the Conservancy's opinions. We knew their science was good, and our staff respected their work."[42]

Impaired Waters

The Harper methodology came into play again in 2009, when the DEP issued a draft nutrient TMDL for the Caloosahatchee River as required by law for "impaired waters." In its modeling, the state assumed that natural wetlands possessed a positive loading rate based upon Harper's 2003 methodology. Although Harper had revised the model in 2007, DEP bureaucrats were inexplicably sticking to the earlier version. The agency defended its actions by stating that a zero or negative load factor "was not an approach that could be used with the models selected or for the modeling process adopted for setting the Caloosahatchee TMDL" but immediately skewered itself by arguing that "upland land uses" contributed to the positive load assigned to wetlands.[43] This was one of the Conservancy's arguments from the beginning: a failure to take into account the range of inputs from adjacent land where the nutrients originated.

The draft TMDL went a step further. It failed to include a limit for dissolved oxygen because, according to the state, model runs showed negligible differences between dissolved oxygen levels under existing conditions and under "baseline" conditions. However, the DEP chose to take its "baseline" data from two monitoring stations, one in the Tamiami Canal and the other in Rookery Bay estuary, neither of which came close to duplicating conditions in the Caloosahatchee River. When questioned, the department responded that the Tamiami Canal was a completely unaltered *natural* system. The argument was specious. The canal was a constructed conveyance used to drain storm water from row crops and pastureland with high levels of nutrient runoff, contributing to high dissolved oxygen levels. It was unfair to compare a canal to a river, even a river with flows manipulated by the Corps. Finally, by using Rookery Bay as a reference site, the department was violating its own protocols, which stated that when making comparisons it had to "identify waters in the same bioregion." Rookery Bay was in the DEP's Everglades bioregion; the Caloosahatchee was entirely within its peninsula bioregion.[44] This contradiction, pointed out to the department in a memo from Jessica Stubbs, a natural resources department staffer at the Conservancy, was met with stony silence.[45]

By 2013 the state had not assessed one third of its water bodies for impairment. According to McElwaine, that meant that no TMDLs could be issued and, in his opinion, the state was operating under the adage that "unassessed is unimpaired."[46] For example, according to Jennifer Hecker, Marco Island, with its aging septic systems, is not impaired because it doesn't take samples. "There is simply not enough data for it to be declared. Everything around Marco is impaired, and if the island did sampling it would amount to self-incrimination and would have to be cleaned up. But there is no penalty for not sampling. This is going on all over the state; insufficient data is increasing exponentially. And DEP is doing nothing about it."[47]

But the DEP was about to have its proverbial feet put to the fire, and we now turn to one of the burning controversies of the twenty-first century, pitting entrenched and powerful inland interests against the coastal communities of southwest Florida: the issue of creating and implementing maximum numeric nutrient pollution limits for all of the state's waters, not just those adjudged "impaired." We'll also look at the controversial corollary of applying the highest standards (usually downstream ones) throughout an entire watershed. These are the subjects of the next chapter.

CHAPTER 15

BY THE NUMBERS

*I*n 1998 the U.S. EPA ruled that Florida was violating the Clean Water Act by failing to set quantitative standards for nutrient pollution of water bodies within the state and gave Florida a deadline of 2004 to put clearly defined limits into effect. The prevailing state rule at the time: "In no case shall nutrient concentrations of a body of water be altered so as to cause an imbalance in natural populations of aquatic flora and fauna."[1] Known as "narrative criteria," the definition of "imbalance" was left dangling. President George W. Bush, with his brother sitting in the governor's chair, torched the 2004 deadline but continued to insist mildly on promulgation of numeric standards at some unspecified future date. Florida, which by then had elevated procrastination to high art, breathed a sigh of relief and did little for the next six years.

As the Florida DEP looked out over the state in 2010, here is what it saw: 1,918 miles of rivers and 378,000 acres of inland lakes "impaired" by nutrient pollution, compared to 1,000 miles and 350,000 acres in 2005.[2] More than half of the state's lakes and rivers were compromised. Part of the reason, in the opinion of former DEP secretary Michael Sole, was "more aggressive analysis over the years. If you look at concentrations and how they are measured, it is easy to see how the 'impaired' list went up. I don't think we are creating significant new levels today; we are just better able to quantify the problem with the amount of data we have available in Florida."[3] Sole was a career employee at the DEP, having held positions in every major department within the agency. He knew that pressure was building and sought to find a path that didn't lead to court.

The main culprit was non–point-source pollution, ranging from animal waste flowing off farms during summer rainstorms to bags of fertilizer being spread on suburban lawns to make them green in the winter. In southwest Florida, the Caloosahatchee River and Charlotte Harbor estuaries were the largest and most problem ridden, being periodically flooded by the Corps of Engineers' tsunami-like releases of nutrient-laden water from Lake Okeechobee. While the Corps' primary mission was to maintain the navigable waters of the United States, its management of south Florida's big lake was driven by another imperative: to protect the towns of Clewiston, Moore Haven, and Belle Glade from inundation by lowering lake water levels to maintain the integrity of the gradually deteriorating Hoover dike.

Historically, water oozed slowly south but once the dike was built and the C & SF canals were completed, the lake's peripheral water management system became ideal for artificially creating wet and dry cycles needed to grow and harvest cane sugar. Nitrates, such as phosphorous and nitrogen, were using for fertilization and back-pumped into the lake for years, creating a stew of nutrients released down the St. Lucie and Caloosahatchee rivers when rising water levels threatened the Hoover dike. Below the Caloosahatchee lay Naples Bay, Camp Keais Strand, Pine Island Sound, Faka Union Canal, and Estero Bay, all listed as 303(d) waters but with no plan in place to reduce existing pollution levels.[4]

Another factor at work in compromising southwest Florida's coastal waters was a vast hydrologic phenomenon called the Gulf of Mexico's "forbidden zone." The area stretches from Bradenton down to Key West, out about 80 miles, and was discovered by researchers who dropped nearly 200 floating "drifters" into the northeast Gulf of Mexico and measured their movement over 12 consecutive months by satellite. The Florida Loop Current moved the drifters, depending upon the amount of heat energy, in a large circle running close to the west coast of Florida to Tampa,[5] where they began to move offshore, with some drifting haphazardly into the central Gulf and others running down along the Keys. The study clearly demonstrated that little flushing occurs within the forbidden zone eddy. What is dumped there stays there, a factor contributing to the high incidence of red tide and isolated "black water" events off the southwest Florida coast.[6] The forbidden zone is more than the canary in the coalmine; it is a scientific reality that contributes to the stagnation of nutrient-laden water entering Greater Charlotte Harbor, Estero Bay, and Naples Bay estuarine systems in massive doses from Lake Okeechobee, urban runoff and the Golden Gate Canal.

The Games Begin

Governor Charlie Crist's four years were marked with little change in the status quo on the land acquisition and growth management fronts. Despite rumblings in the legislature about rolling back environmental initiatives, Crist fully funded Preservation 2000 during his time in office. He supported purchase of the Babcock Ranch near Lake Trafford, a project advocated by the Conservancy as part of a large group of conservation organizations. He kept his door open to environmental advocates while confronting a deep recession that hit Florida's number one growth industry, construction, hard. His administration's Department of Community Affairs challenged a number of projects. It did a critical review of the first Rural Lands Stewardship program in Collier County. The Heartland Parkway was stopped dead in its tracks. A 152-mile toll road, the parkway would bisect the center of the state, providing access to some of Alico's land holdings. By going against plans proposed by the head of the state senate's budget committee and a member of Alico's founding family, J.D. Alexander, the department earned the enmity of a powerful foe.

Though Crist had a generally good environmental record, one questionable initiative during his tenure was continuation of Governor Jeb Bush's bungled attempt to deal with the water quality situation in Florida. From the 1998 consent decree negotiated with the EPA, the state knew it would eventually have to wrestle with inland water quality before it could address problems on the coast. Convinced it was not politically feasible and earnestly seeking to avoid any federal sanctions mandating source control, the DEP came up with a novel approach. Florida's waters—lakes, springs, stream, canals, bays, and estuaries—have a "designated use," which ranges from "drinkable" to "industrial."[7] Existing Class III is the broadest classification for recreation and propagation and maintenance of a healthy, well-balanced population of fish and wildlife. It covers all surface waters of the state unless otherwise designated. It became the center of attention during Bush's second term when the DEP floated a trial balloon to add two new classifications: HU4 for recreation (fishing) and secondary human contact (splashable) and HU5 for limited human contact and no fishing due to unsafe conditions. HU3 (the old Class III) would remain the default classification for all other non-categorized waters.

The balloon was shot down upon release. The Conservancy's Jennifer Hecker was in constant communication with DEP personnel. Her position papers, thoroughly research, were largely ignored. The department was using a change in designated uses to kick the can down the road, knowing it would take at least another decade to determine which of the state's surface waters belonged in the new classifications. In the interim, the state avoided having to set hard, numeric standards. Residents of southwest Florida's coastal communities, having watched their bays and estuaries gradually lose functionality, were incensed. They believed that, despite the economic value of tourism, coastal waters were of secondary concern to the state. The department defended its proposal by arguing that "any reclassification must demonstrate that the downstream waters would be fully protected" and went on to assure the public it would "make sure the biological and recreational qualities of our water resources are not compromised."[8]

Despite their assurances, state officials knew that if they applied downstream standards to inland runoff, the agricultural community would raise the roof. The likely outcome would be pressure on non–point-source polluters to clean up effluent before it left private property and entered the watershed. Farming was the least-regulated activity affecting the state's watersheds. This would bring industrial agriculture to arraignment in the court of public opinion, and in Florida agriculture was always the big dog in the fight. To be able to hold to existing designated uses and apply scientifically calculated maximum numeric criteria, another thing would have to happen. Municipalities, sewer districts, and counties would be required to treat pollution before discharging it, bearing the expense of cleaning up someone else's mess. The whole idea sank of its own weight but would return with a vengeance two years later.

Stung by defeat and with opponents referring to it as the "Department of Environmental Degradation" and "Don't Expect Protection," the agency under Governor Crist enlisted support from groups most affected by enforceable numeric standards. The Florida Stormwater Association, with its membership consisting primarily of public and private water treatment facility operators, would lead the charge. Florida League of Cities, Inc., the lobbying group for municipalities, joined in, along with an influential business group, Associated Industries. They were backed by the heavyweight Florida Farm Bureau Federation, whose members knew they would be criticized for non–point-source pollution running untreated off their land. They formed a group called Don't Tax Florida. Supported by a massive public relations effort, the organization raised the specter of increased ad valorem levies to pay for cleanup, which could be avoided by simply changing "designated use" categories. The state then ditched discredited HU4 and HU5 reclassifications and substituted something called Class III Limited, which would apply to any artificial or altered waterway. It would allow consumption of fish caught in those waters but no full-body human contact. This covered mainly drainage ditches, roadside canals, and storm water conveyances used to funnel nutrients from agricultural operations, lawns, and golf courses into canals and ultimately to coastal bays and estuaries. Downgrading would be done on a case-by-case basis.

The lobbying effort, underwritten by 67 national organizations, met with furious resistance from the environmental side based upon three points. First, by introducing a new category, "not safe for human immersion," the state was failing to address the pollution situation head-on. Second, if the new designated use category applied upstream, it would make it more difficult to promulgate different standards downstream. Third, the whole discussion completely avoided the subject of source control. The nut of the matter was simple: No corporate farm wanted to pay one penny for source control. It was better to throw the cost onto the back of the public, and Florida taxpayers didn't want more taxes. That was the coded message from Don't Tax Florida.

The DEP's recalcitrance was now out in the open. Fed up with years of inaction in enforcing the 1998 ruling, environmental law firm Earthjustice filed suit against the U.S. EPA in June 2008 in the Northern District of Florida, with the Sierra Club, St. Johns Riverkeepers, the Conservancy of Southwest Florida, Florida Wildlife Federation, and the Environmental Confederation of Southwest Florida as plaintiffs. An accompanying letter to EPA cited nutrient pollution as the cause of toxic cyanobacteria found throughout the state, including blue-green algae blooms that shut down all boat traffic on the St. Johns River in 2005 and forced temporary closure of a water treatment plant on the Caloosahatchee six years later.

Michael Sole, secretary of DEP at the time, decried the lawsuit. "I knew it would delay things. The challenge we saw ahead in implementing was that every watershed was not the same. For instance, there were artificial conveyances that would fall into the Class III Limited use category because they were not restorable . . . not historical but part of the built environment. In retrospect, I wish we had been able to at least get things moving. We were within weeks of issuing standards when hit with the lawsuit. Had we done it, by 2013 we would have five years' data and be in a review cycle for public comment. We might have a better idea of what was working and what was not. It was very frustrating."[9]

As the DEP worked its way toward meeting EPA's timeline, it made clear that numeric standards would not apply to any water body within the state that had already developed a maximum load limit as required by the Clean Water Act for any water body classified as "impaired." Once in place, the act set very specific limits for nutrients causing the problems. The Caloosahatchee River was divided into downstream and upstream (east of Franklin Lock), but a TMDL was published for nitrogen in the tidal basin only. Michael Sole said nitrogen was the "limiting factor" below the lock. There was no phosphorous TMDL in effect for either part of the river. According to Sole, this was based upon the narrative standard in place at the time. The toxic blue-green algae bloom that afflicted the river for eight weeks in 2011 was the result of little or no flushing from Lake Okeechobee, which allowed nutrients to stagnate and reach noxious levels.[10]

It took the EPA six months to enter into a settlement, giving the state 18 months to issue numeric standards; otherwise they would be set by the federal agency. But to no one's surprise, the state skipped over the deadline and EPA issued its own set of numeric nutrient standards for Florida's lakes, streams, rivers and springs, with numerous site-specific exceptions; southwest Florida was temporarily exempted from the initial standards. Reaction to EPA's action was swift. The Florida League of Cities pulled out an old "whereas and now therefore" resolution, condemning the actions of the agency, demanding that standards be based upon "science, and not an arbitrary number,"[11] and raging at the cost, which the league estimated at between $4.2 and $6.7 billion, as opposed to the EPA's estimate of $130 to $200 million.[12] Then the lobbying group went over the top by projecting costs of 2012 numeric standards at between $25 and $50 billion. But there was one small problem with its numbers: 2012 standards hadn't even been issued when the estimate was released.

Politicians could not resist entering the fray. Southwest Florida state representative Trudi Williams, chair of the Florida House Select Committee on Water Quality, used her bully pulpit to say, "Florida has been a national leader in aggressively enforcing water quality standards to protect our streams, lakes, rivers and estuaries. EPA's mandates are unprecedented, unworkable and unscientific. . . ."[13] However, she failed to convince a retired professor from Hillsborough College, who gave her an F for her conveniently poor memory and emphasizing that the state "fought tooth and nail for over four decades to stop adequate nutrient removal from wastewater and storm water discharges in the name of an amorphous science surrounding 'narrative standards' for water quality."[14]

The EPA's action finally forced the state to issue standards close to federal numbers, with two critical differences: Federal numbers represented a "not to exceed" maximum with sanctions; state numbers represented only a threshold with zero non-compliance penalties. Under the state's plan, each water body, subject to annual average measurement, could exceed the threshold value once every three years and avoid being listed as impaired. Those water bodies out of compliance would then be placed on a list for further woolgathering, with the burden of proof of degradation set impossibly high.

Proposed federal rules started out insisting that downstream values, including all of southwest Florida's estuaries, should be the baseline for upstream standards. In other words, the highest standard should apply throughout any given watershed. The state continued to insist that all rivers and streams south of Lake Okeechobee be placed into the new Class III Limited designation, arguing that any differential in measurable criteria would have to be handled by regional treatment systems while failing to explain how this would work. Southwest Florida was looking at cleaning up already degraded and impaired estuaries, a nearly impossible task if upstream polluters were given a pass. The state was doing its best to avoid a public debate over source control by scheduling only one public hearing before issuing standards for some estuaries (excluding southwest Florida), arguing "that downstream protection values would be helpful, but neither DEP nor EPA has been able to derive scientifically defensible numbers for all water bodies to protect downstream waters."[15] The Conservancy's main problem was that the state's narrative standards, "policy guidance" coming out of the SFWMD and the "healthy existing conditions" as applied to Naples Bay (covered in the next section) all pointed to a tacit acceptance of the *status quo*. There would be no attempt to improve the sadly degraded status of southwest Florida's coastal waters.

In addition to Jennifer Hecker's advocacy, the Conservancy did its best to highlight the degraded status of southwest Florida's estuaries through what was known as the biennial Estuaries Report Card. Measuring water quality and wildlife habitat in ten estuaries from coastal Venice and Lemon Bay south to the Ten Thousand Islands, the report was in its sixth year and becoming useful as a baseline against which to measure efficacy of woeful cleanup efforts. The report used consistent indicators from DEP to allow comparability from year to year. By 2011 all ten estuaries failed in the category of existing water quality standards; many were worse off than in 2005. The highest water quality letter grade was a C in Charlotte Harbor. Naples Bay and Lemon Bay tied for last, both D–. Based upon wildlife habitat criteria, the Ten Thousand Islands and Pine Island Sound both received A+ grades, while Naples Bay and the Caloosahatchee River received another D–. Over the years, the report card showed continued decline of all of southwest Florida's aquatic nurseries.

Naples Bay Redux

Closer to home, while the debate raged over statewide standards, the DEP evaluated Naples Bay for impairment using a misguided application of something called the "maintain healthy existing conditions" approach.[16] This did little to allay the Conservancy's fear that the state would go to almost any lengths to justify doing as little as possible to clean up its jurisdictional estuaries.

Beginning with the Naples Bay Study of 1979, the bay's biological characteristics had been regularly measured and monitored ever since. In 2006 three Conservancy scientists teamed with two faculty members at the University of Florida to do a historical profile of the bay, with emphasis on the benthic habitat's potential for restoration. When it was a shallow, mangrove-fringed estuary, the bay had been lined with oyster beds nearly up to the highway US 41 bridge, with four large sea grass beds along the shoreline, the largest at the mouth of Haldeman Creek. Nature's two highly efficient filtering mechanisms were able to keep the ecosystem in balance despite freshwater flows from Haldeman Creek and the Gordon River. But once the Golden Gate Canal added anywhere from 20 to 40 times the load (depending upon rainfall), oysters and sea grasses were unable to adapt quickly enough to the changes in salinity and nutrient loads, suffering catastrophic mortality. The second factor affecting the bay was massive, unregulated dredging in the 1950s and

1960s, which opened up the bottom to channelization and sedimentation. The study team was intent upon finding substrate in the bay coarse enough for transplanted oysters to build bars and reefs without being washed away in the early phases of the life cycle. The study made no conclusion as to whether the bay's benthic habitat was suitable for supporting natural filtering systems such as sea grasses and oyster beds, suggesting that further analysis of the chemistry would be necessary to a final determination of likely success.

When it came to Naples Bay, DEP took a different tack. It issued standards based on sampling done by a team from Florida International University at points near the Gulf of Mexico, locations that reaped the benefits of tidal flushing. The state set a nitrogen standard at 0.3 parts per million (ppm) for the bay, compared to 0.57 ppm for other regional estuaries. The City of Naples complained bitterly, arguing that its own measurements showed variations between 0.7 and 1.2 ppm, as much as four times higher than the state's, due mainly to urban runoff from city streets and parking lots as well as the nutrient load from inland Collier County via the Golden Gate Canal.[17]

A much larger problem was evident with the DEP's approach to Naples Bay. The bay was "impaired," which required specific numeric nutrient limits be established, but the "healthy conditions" designation was reserved for pristine estuaries unaffected by anthropogenic sources of pollution. The Conservancy's Hecker objected to using this protocol because it would condone the status quo and make no effort to restore biological health to the bay. The response from DEP was that narrative standards in place at the time governed its decision and that there was no discernible deterioration leading to an "imbalance of flora and fauna" within the bay.

The Court Intervenes

By November 2011, the EPA admitted Florida had at least made an attempt at writing draft rules, which it acknowledged "appear to comport with the CWA . . . but could change should modifications be made before and/or during the State ERC or legislative process or our review of the technical information and public comments identifies reasons why the final rule does not meet the requirements of the CWA."[18] However, the proposed numeric criteria were only a marginal improvement over narrative criteria, with a threshold of proof set so high that the standards promulgated had little chance of improving the quality of Florida's waters. Omitted were any criteria for hundreds of miles of canals in south Florida. The absence of meaningful recommendations for implementing regional treatment systems made the proposal useless in the eyes of the Conservancy. Finally, the DEP's draft rules had not been peer reviewed, the same bugaboo haunting the agency after its rush to embrace the Harper methodology.

Legislation was introduced in the United States Congress in early 2012 by Florida's Republican delegation to prevent the EPA from enforcing federal standards, an action quickly mimicked by lawmakers in Tallahassee obeisant to utility and agriculture industry lobbyists. There was virtually no time for public comment, but that mattered little to legislators anxious to get the issue behind them while pleasing their powerful supporters.

A major breakthrough occurred in February 2012, when U.S. District Judge Robert Hinkle, presiding over the Northern District of Florida, issued a ruling on the combined cases, filed from one side of the issue by the Florida Wildlife Federation and other parties and on the other side by the Fertilizer Institute, Inc., and the Florida Cattlemen's Association. In his decision, the judge noted that narrative criteria used by DEP over the years had failed to prevent higher levels of pollution in Florida's waters, despite the fact that the standards prohibited "harmful" changes to aquatic flora and fauna. He ruled that TMDLs were not a proper surrogate for numeric criteria. Finally, and most importantly for southwest Florida, he ruled that the EPA's insistence on applying downstream values throughout a given watershed was defensible and logical, although unprecedented. The effect of this last point was that if upstream waters contributed measurable pollution downstream, the entire system should be assigned numeric standards based upon the designated use of the receiving water bodies, i.e., Florida's estuaries. The decision was a major victory for southwest Florida's environmental community and marked a turning point in the debate. It also brought into focus a much larger issue: state's rights weighed against federal powers. It changed the dynamics by placing hard deadlines on the EPA and thus the DEP to promulgate numeric criteria. And the judge, who retained jurisdiction, clearly understood the issues and intended to oversee the implementation and enforcement of new standards.

The case remained at a slow boil until 5:00 P.M. on November 30, 2012, when Judge Hinkle refused to grant a hearing on a 120-day extension requested by the EPA for further negotiations with the state. He was fed up with inaction. The plaintiffs, led by David Guest, issued a celebratory press release: "After years of court battles and foot-dragging, the federal agency has agreed to establish numeric pollution limits for some 100,000 miles of Florida waterways and 4,000 square miles of estuaries." Not really "agreed to." More like "forced to." Hours later, in a classic case of rope-a-dope, a revised release came from the plaintiffs: "In a last-minute decision Friday, the EPA also approved a set of state pollution limits developed by the Florida Department of Environmental Protection which will cover a fraction of waters in the state—about 15 percent. The other 85 percent of the state's waters will be subject to the numeric federal standards."[19] Later in the evening, the number was refined down to 82,000 miles but Jim Giattina, the EPA's Region 4 water protection director, said: "We're approving Florida's rules and we're proposing numbers that will fill the gap that may exist in Florida's rules." He added that further changes were possible after holding discussions with state officials. The EPA's press release, issued at 10:00 P.M. with the headline "EPA Approves Florida's Rules to Protect Waterways from Nutrient Pollution," confirmed that the agency had, in fact, approved the DEP's criteria. And, in a stunning reversal for south Florida, the feds came off their position that downstream criteria should apply upstream by allowing graduated standards within a watershed.

As further details of the judge's ruling became clear, the environmental community had reason to become disheartened. There was a good possibility that the state's standards would prevail because the federal agency had accepted virtually everything submitted to it by the DEP and abandoned its position of upstream and downstream compatibility. Five days later, the Florida League of Cities and its allies were in a celebratory mood. The EPA was in an orderly retreat, and they had another nine months to pressure Washington. Agriculture and local utilities praised the outcome as "a more cost-effective way to promote water quality in our state."[20] But "cost-effective" had not solved the problem since 1998, and environmental groups knew exactly what those code words meant: Florida was attempting to establish standards at the least possible cost while at the same time protecting special interests that caused the problem in the first place. The state's rule would apply to all lakes, rivers, streams, and freshwater springs except for flowing inland waters and a number of estuaries in central and northern Florida. The EPA's rule would cover only those rivers and coastal waters south of Lake Okeechobee, including the Caloosahatchee and St. Lucie temporarily.

An important reality emerged here, the same one learned in 2005 with adoption of the Harper methodology: First and foremost, the EPA is an agency subject to politics, which doesn't affect its science as much as its level of enforcement. Looking toward the 2012 presidential election, the Obama administration was dealing with the swing state of Florida with kid gloves. It preferred to have the state promulgate its own standards, believing those would have a better chance of being fully implemented than compulsory criteria imposed by Washington, D.C., partly because the federal agency lacked enforcement powers under the CWA. In other words, any violation of federally imposed standards would have to be prosecuted by DEP, which would more than likely look the other way. A large part of the state agency's job is to decide how much developers, mines, industry, agriculture, and municipal treatment plants can alter the chemical composition of the state's waters. Compliance is enforced only to the extent the agency investigates violations.[21] It does not exercise direct control over water management districts. That is left to boards with members appointed by the same governor who selects the person to head the DEP.

Quantity and Distribution

The second and third components of water issues in southwest Florida, quantity and distribution, are closely interrelated. Nature delivers more than 50 inches of rain every year, but who gets how much is becoming a more contentious issue. The subterranean aquifer system in Lee and Collier Counties consists of four layers: the surficial, or water table, aquifer; the Lower Tamiami for Collier; a sandstone aquifer for both counties; and the Upper mid-Hawthorn for Lee County (the most accessible, separated by a confining layer from the other three). The U.S. Geological Survey has nearly 100 monitoring wells at varying depths to measure the availability of water and chloride concentrations. Annual rainfall had maintained surficial aquifer levels in both counties, but the sandstone level and mid-Hawthorn have been seriously compromised by drawdowns since 1960, due to increased usage and inadequate recharge. Since the better quality water is found in the lower confined aquifers, agricultural withdrawals generally take place at the surficial level, away from recharge areas. Saltwater intrusion beneath both counties, occurring closest to the coast and mainly in the Lower mid-Hawthorn aquifer, has resulted in the abandonment of some deeper wells, but, according to one study, the problem is localized and not a matter of concern at present. However, the same study stated that "the rate of growth of withdrawals may not be sustainable" in the long term.[22] The good news is there are numerous monitoring wells throughout Lee and Collier Counties. Run by the U.S. Geological Survey, the network produces extraordinarily detailed data to assist in making real-time judgments about the cumulative effect of development on groundwater supplies.

There are two types of water use: consumption and withdrawal. Consumption, more properly termed "consumptive use," is water that is withdrawn and not returned to the source. Withdrawal is a right to extract water, some of which may be returned. Agriculture—including sugarcane, row crops, citrus, and golf courses—accounts for more than half of the withdrawals historically, but population growth since the 1950s has led to hundreds of thousands of small wells that suck from surficial aquifers and do not require individual permits. Industrial and commercial usage has not increased as a percentage of total withdraw-als during the past 50 years. There is a statutory/regulatory allocation available for environmental purposes, but it is hardly ever used because of the requirements for human needs. As a result of increased demand, water restrictions, once in place only during periodic drought, are now permanent in southwest Florida.

Agriculture

Sugarcane production takes up nearly 100,000 acres in the Caloosa-hatchee watershed and two-thirds of the Everglades Agricultural Area south of Lake Okeechobee. Along with livestock operations, it is a heavy water user, creating more than 86% of the nutrient pollution in SFWMD jurisdiction but paying only 13% of the costs of cleanup.[23] The district is loath to distribute allocations and usage of water by type of user. If the facts were known, the powerful agricultural lobby would be hard-pressed to explain its overt opposition to measures designed to minimize downstream effects on coastal communities and industries that depend upon Florida's estuaries for their livelihood. One of the most effective instruments to control this damage, the Clean Water Act, is deficient in its failure to address depletion. The act is limited to the regulation of the chemical and biological characteristics of water supplies, not to their replenishment, because when the CWA was enacted in 1972, it was in-conceivable that the nation would ever run out of water.

Part of the problem is historic. For years Floridians had ample water for their needs. Rapidly growing population centers on the east coast were eating into supplies, but farming had established usage patterns and entitlements. While human consumption has increased dramati-cally, agricultural consumption has stabilized over the past 40 years in south Florida, due in part to precision irrigation technology that delivers water directly to root systems rather than widely broadcasting for indis-criminate soaking of the soil. The SWFWMD based in Tampa has been successful in offering financial incentives to farmers for using recovery ponds, soil moisture indicators, and other simple technologies to use water more efficiently. This emphasis on the demand side of the equation is both helpful and hopeful, as best practices in agriculture have been encouraged by organizations like the Florida Farm Bureau with gradual acceptance.

Residential

The rapid growth of population offered another opportunity, largely unfulfilled, for simple conservation measures. As new homes were built, some building codes suggested, but did not mandate, measures like low-flow faucet and showerheads in bathrooms. Moisture level sensors to shut off lawn irrigation systems during wet times are mandated in Collier County. Use of native plants in landscaping is encouraged as a way to save water and reduce fertilizer use. The SFWMD and home builders' groups encourage conservation, but in the end the market dictates and progress has been negligible.

The Future

The DEP's version of numeric criteria amounts to little more than aspirations. One important factor going forward, according to former secretary Sole, is that Florida has more data on water quality from water management district sampling than any other state. Jennifer Hecker disputes this: "District data is mostly SFWMD data which is largely restricted to phosphorous and is mostly from pumping stations . . . where it is required by the Lake Okeechobee permit or in place due to the federal consent decree. It isn't helpful in the broader sense. In fact, Florida has few streams that are monitored . . . to establish baselines, much less compliance."[24] Having that data cuts two ways. First, it lowers the threshold for designating "impaired" waters, and there is simply no escaping reality. Second, it forms the baseline from which to measure alternative mitigation strategies. Monitoring systems are in place, and well-established protocols have been around long enough to minimize arguments about the underlying science, eliminating one of the main obstacles to evaluating the success or failure of future efforts.

The state's numeric standards issued as of publication of this book have conformed, in the EPA's opinion, to the Clean Water Act. Approximately 85% of the state's waters have standards, but "flowing waters," many of which are conveyance systems and not rivers, are mostly exempt. The federal agency has indicated it will withdraw and not impose its criteria on those waters. The unspoken aspects of the process are enforceability and penalties, which are set forth in federal code but not by the state. If the state's standards are accepted by the EPA, sanctions will be the next battle. "Agreed to" criteria must have viable enforcement provisions to back them up, with the burden borne by those parties responsible for releasing pollutants into the system.

Oversight by the court is the best hope for cleaning up Florida's waters, but that hope is slipping away. Whether the EPA and the state follow up by establishing and enforcing appropriate standards remains to be seen. According to the Conservancy's Jennifer Hecker, the response so far had been less than hopeful. The EPA decided to hold a two-day hearing in January 2013 to receive public comment on DEP standards. Comments were received by a bank of computer terminals to eliminate the opportunity for inflammatory speeches and disruptive harangues from the disgruntled assembly. Andrew McElwaine of the Conservancy waggishly suggested that Florida's state song be retitled "Way Down Upon the Slimy River," to little effect.

The issue of consistent values throughout a watershed is off the table. It was set forth in a determination letter that the EPA amended and, since it never appeared in the consent decree itself, is not binding or enforceable. The EPA is slow-walking a retreat on downstream values, and it is likely the state will prevail on all fronts. Florida's $67-billion tourist business is based upon attracting visitors and vacationers to constantly renourished white-sand beaches bordering sparkling Gulf waters. A phenomenon such as red tide, a naturally occurring eruption of dinoflagellates, goes into overdrive when boosted by nutrient releases, whether from Lake Okeechobee or urban and agricultural runoff. The result is human respiratory stress and dead fish covering the beaches. Commercial fishing and sportfishing industries, which rely upon productive estuaries to reproduce exploitable species, have "skin in the game" as well. Damage to coastal waters—caused partially by destruction of natural wetlands, partially by excess upland discharge of dissolved nutrients, and partially by interruption of natural flushing systems—could create an economic calamity for the southwest part of the state.

CONCLUSION

Studying history informs the present by allowing thoughtful people to consider mistakes and offers an opportunity to avoid going down the same path again. Failure to extract lessons from the past is at times a conscious choice, other times willful neglect. There is a leitmotif running through the past 50 years of environmental history that may only repeat itself in the future: a willingness to ignore accumulating consequences in favor of the expedient solution of the moment and the easy way out. This reaches well beyond the ambit of a single organization; it applies broadly to how we develop, manage, and preserve southwest Florida and what we leave for future generations. It is a matter of intergenerational equity that we not transfer the cost of current resource exploitation into the future.

The story of the Conservancy has flowed from the rivulet of buying land in the early years to the alluvium of collaborative environmental policy and practice. In the process, Conservancy leaders recognized that public education played a critical role in the organization's development, hence, the merger with the Big Cypress Nature Center. But it is fair to ask the question, Has it worked? Has the emergence of a strong regional voice and more enlightened citizenry affected the larger picture of federal and state protection and of natural resources? To these questions comes a qualified answer.

First, land acquisition programs throughout the state have worked magnificently. Second, it is obvious from the last two chapters of this book that the paths of guidance and regulation have been largely ineffective. Strong suggestions, such as the Corps' 2003 environmental impact statement for southwest Florida, have been ignored. The visible hand of regulation can be bent or replaced by advisory memos, as in the case of the Southwest Florida Basin Rule. Procrastination has worked for Florida since the 1998 consent decree with the EPA on creating water quality standards, with dismal results.

The debate over public policy during the 50 years covered in this book has been increasingly conducted in the language of economics suited to short-term productivity rather than long-term sustainability. Initiatives are now all eventually reduced to a budget, a calculation of the dollars-and-cents impact to help us decide how and where to allocate resources. Most people understand this because they live within a closed system of constrained finances themselves. While the numbers may be incomprehensibly large, most people believe that governments should live generally within their means over an extended period of time. But the questions become these: Should a project be analyzed from both an environmental and a monetary perspective? Are the short-term financial consequences of a project calculated absent any quantification of the longer-term costs of replacing resources? Are too many real costs externalized?

This country is unlikely to abandon the principal mechanism that has elevated America to world preeminence over the past century: consumption of goods and services through a free-market system. In the lexicon of business, markets and price are two mechanisms for allocating resources; depreciation accounts for renewal or replacement. A realignment of assumptions will require that we look at markets not simply as a mechanism for resource exploitation but also as a means of avoiding resource depletion. The real problem is that markets are most efficient in allocating scarce resources over the short term, using immediate feedback to make adjustments in both quantity and price. Fair enough, but if the Fakahatchee Strand and the Everglades happen to be scarce resources—and they are—how does the price component work into the metrics? There is a way: life cycle costing. For example, when an automobile battery is sold today in Germany, the buyer pays not only for the battery but for its disposal as well. The lifetime cost of managing a device with acid harmful to Germany's groundwater supplies is not borne by the taxpayer; it is priced into the product and paid for by the user. The underlying weakness of this system is the difficulty in accurately predicting environmental and social costs over the life of an asset.

To do so requires being brutally honest about the future environmental impact of battery acid leeching into groundwater, and to do that requires broad agreement on indirect costs. This is a simple and straightforward calculation in the case of an automobile battery. Not so in the case of nutrient outflows, the Harper methodology being on point here.

As we draw down the capacity of our natural systems, we also reduce their ability to replicate. We are, in essence, throwing away thousands, sometimes millions, of years of experimentation and natural selection because it does not happen to fit into a short-term paradigm of consumption and material well-being. At some point, we need to find a new way to relate biological imperatives to economic outcomes, but perhaps there is so much raw land in southwest Florida that we can continue to assume it is either inexhaustible or resilient enough to tolerate any amount of abuse, allowing us to look away from the harder reality.

If the system favors short-term exploitation, as it has for years in Florida, do we even need to think about long-term consequences when technology is there to save us? Reduced hydrologic pressure in the aquifers created by canals in failed developments, modifications to natural sloughs and flow ways, excessive drawdown, and storm water control structures have all contributed to increased salinity below the surficial aquifer. But why should we be concerned about salinity creeping into our drinking water, this putatively inexhaustible resource, when a large reverse-osmosis plant can be installed to solve the problem? It worked in Tampa, which has the largest seawater desalination plant in the United States. It can work anywhere. But that assertion begs to be challenged on the basis of comparative economic values. Is the true cost of cleaning up natural ecosystems to allow surficial recharge in south Florida less expensive, in the long run, than building and operating treatment facilities to make water potable? This is the argument of restorative economics, which says that it is generally better to look first to natural processes and systems for a simple reason. Natural systems are, by the very fact that they exist, self-sustaining. In southwest Florida, aquifer recharge requires no intervention and little exogenous energy except sunlight and rainfall to function. A reverse-osmosis plant requires electrical power and constant maintenance. In the long run, wouldn't it be better to rely upon naturally replicating processes than on a constructed system that may not even scale properly as demand increases (or decreases)?

Either way—desalination or restoration—involves taking the long view and depends upon building consensus, beginning with individual citizens and going all the way up to governing bodies agreeing that planning should start at the ecosystem level, with geopolitical fences temporarily lowered when it comes to evaluating natural systems. But how can that occur when we can't even solve issues within a single jurisdiction? Fertilizers and pesticides not sucked up by tomato plants in Immokalee end up affecting Naples Bay because water flows downhill. The entire system is within the limits of Collier County. Has it been possible to get a consensus between inland agricultural interests and downstream users of Naples Bay? Is it fair to assume that landowners, whose boundaries are clearly marked and recorded at the county courthouse, would be willing to make sacrifices disproportionally benefiting other property owners or people downstream? No, not when almost every party involved is fiercely protective of its turf, its jurisdiction, and thus the status quo. Parties at interest have become combatants in a game of winners and losers to see who gets to pay the cost of cleanup rather than participants in discussing how to address the problem. The success of this approach depends upon that scarce commodity called political will, a desire and ability to introduce a combination of incentives and penalties to encourage fully costed outcomes.

One reason this has not happened is that people feel distant and disconnected from the inscrutable processes by which we make decisions in our society. How does it fit into the mediation of daily existence when the cost of cleaning up other people's messes is buried in an ad valorem tax bill? Therein lies the nut of the matter. Our greatest problem may not be water quantity or water quality. It may be us. We tend to focus on things we know and see, on our immediate surroundings. We want the detritus of our daily lives removed as far as possible from the places we care about. Take the raw sewage somewhere else, do something with it, and bring back clean water to my faucet. Take my trash and bury it somewhere where I can't see it or, my goodness, smell it. These things happen every day and as long as they do, the subtropical paradise of blooming flora, butterflies, wading birds (albeit diminished in population), blue skies, clean air, and puffy white clouds that surrounds us will make it hard to worry about anything as discomforting as the unyielding reality lying just beneath the surface. After all, it is only when the status quo suffers significant modification that people react, and even then only when the threat is real and immediate and affects their homes, schools, neighborhoods, and churches. There is a water shortage in southwest Florida, but reducing lawn sprinkling to twice a week and asking people to refrain from washing their cars have very little impact on the mindset of most Floridians. These are little more than inconveniences.

A realignment of the assumptions set forth here will require that we, as body politic, view growth not simply as resource exploitation but as an opportunity for restoration within our own shores, creating both jobs and environmental sustainability. That concept seems simple enough until we arrive at the point where the presumptive rights of vested interests are challenged, where the desire to monetize every available asset drives decisions, and where something is worth doing only if it can be turned into a profit.

We are currently on another "road to nowhere." It doesn't lead to Isles of Capri, and we cannot return to that simpler time when a few men and women gathered on a porch on Keewaydin Island to determine that progress is not always measured by miles of road and acres of rooftops but by preservation of essential resources. Those values are important, but the State of Florida has outgrown the front porch and the likelihood that a very few committed private citizens can enact paradigmatic change.

What we can do is build a road to the future. It will require overcoming the pluralistic politics of division with a straightforward view of present reality based upon sound and agreed-upon science. We need to look first to the future rather than discounting it in favor of the present; look toward ecosystem analysis overriding geopolitical demarcations as a central propaedeutic of planning; introduce life cycle costing in choices involving resource exploitation; and find a way to equitably balance property rights with the common good. If we can do all of that, we will improve the sustainability of southwest Florida's natural systems for those of us living here now and those generations to follow.

EPILOGUE

*E*liminating state-mandated concurrency, using small-scale amendments to local plans more broadly, and eliminating "financial feasibility" justification had been sought by developers for years. Legislation was introduced in the 2009 session to downsize and redistribute the responsibilities of the Department of Community Affairs in order to stimulate the moribund construction industry in Florida. Led by State Senator Mike Bennett from Sarasota/Bradenton, a contractor with ties to the building industry, the effort was notably unsuccessful in its piecemeal approach until the whole pie was delivered on a silver platter.

Election of Rick Scott

Two generations of commitment to growth management and planning in the State of Florida came to a screeching halt with the election of Governor Rick Scott in 2010. Scott had no environmental agenda at all. A former for-profit hospital executive and Northern transplant, Scott reportedly spent more than $70 million of his family's money to be elected to Florida's highest office.[1] His platform was simple and straightforward: Cut government and create jobs. One way to take care of both was to do away with land-use regulations and review agencies at the state level, the most prominent being the Department of Community Affairs. As soon as Scott took office in January 2011, the development lobby went to work. Bills rolled through the state legislature like Everglades thunderheads with little debate, few amendments, and absolutely no concessions to environmental protection. The most significant bill, Florida's Community Planning Act of 2011, virtually eliminated the state's role in growth management planning and placed all of the responsibility at the lowest possible level of local government. State review would occur only when "important state facilities and resources" were involved.

State-mandated concurrency, part of the Local Government Comprehensive Planning and Land Use Act of 1985, was revoked for parks and recreation facilities, schools, and transportation. Counties and municipalities were given the option to continue with impact fees to support concurrency; a prior requirement that local comprehensive plans be "financially feasible" was repealed as well. The last provision meant that a local government's capital project budget was no longer required to coordinate with other objectives of the corresponding comprehensive plan. Transportation concurrency, designed to provide adequate roads as development took place, became a local option. A heavy dose of conditions applied, including detailed procedures as to how proportional cost sharing among landowners should be calculated.

The DRI process, carefully codified in the State and Regional Planning Act of 1984, was curtailed by limiting it to extremely large projects. Scott cut the Department of Community Affairs budget from $780 million in 2011 to $70 million in 2013 and merged it into something called the Department of Economic Opportunity. In doing so, he virtually gutted the one agency designed to monitor growth, paving the way for development to once again run roughshod throughout the state. To use building as a way out of the brutal recession, small-scale private amendments to local comprehensive plans were encouraged on an as-needed basis, avoiding review at the regional and state levels. Local governments were no longer required to show a "need" for new land for development. Construction was the name of the game, whether the need for additional housing and strip malls existed or not.

The rationale offered by Scott was similar to the ELMS III committee's conclusion: Local governments had the capacity to develop and oversee their own comprehensive plans with less need for state oversight. The changes were cheered by many of the same groups fighting federally imposed numeric nutrient criteria to clean up Florida's waters. Associated Industries of Florida expressed delight with the results of the legislative session. The DEP saw an opportunity to loosen permitting requirements. Water management districts saw a number of new appointments. In the south Florida district, Scott filled one seat in June 2011 with a former Miami incinerator company executive who, according to local newspapers, ran a company that had been fined $640,000 in 1991 for environmental and safety violations. Scott's appointee listed his employment with a company that had gone out of business the prior year.[2]

A second tectonic shift after Scott's election was the capping of revenue for the five water management districts while giving the governor line-item veto over district budgets, a refinement of 1996 legislation. The following year, the governor, realizing district operations had been cut too deeply by the cap, worked in the 2012 session to partially restore ad valorem revenues. However, the political price was more legislative control over district budgets and operations. Lawmakers, always careful to maintain their power over the governor and anything having to do with jobs or money in the state, decided to require each district to submit its budget to the legislature prior to any review by the governor, effectively giving each state senator and representative the opportunity to plump a favored project or two. By December 2012, DEP Secretary Herschel Vinyard, a former shipyard executive, moved vigorously and bluntly by laying off 58 longtime employees in his department. He had been installing engineers and consultants working for regulated companies in high-level positions on a regular basis, but he was unable to manipulate compliance and enforcement sufficiently. The best way to deal with that was to simply eliminate those jobs, most in regulatory positions.

Reaching beyond statutes and going deeply into regulations, state agencies led by Scott appointees started to rewrite the rules. The DEP hastily rewrote the 1995 Environmental Regulation Permit (ERP) program in two separate manifestos. Designed to review any alterations to surface flows of water in the state, including water running off uplands and dredge-and-fill activities, ERP had been under the aegis of water management districts created in 1972 in recognition of the differences within each of Florida's five major watersheds. But the "first volume" of new ERP rules would apply uniformly to all districts. Standards would be at the least common denominator based upon a proposed land use. As a result, the lowest baseline in any district would become the statewide canon. The DEP allowed each district to set its own rules for regulation of certain activities in a "second volume" but lowered thresholds to make for a more lenient permitting process. Whether it would do a better job of protecting Florida's surface waters was open to question.

A second practice previously handled by each water district since 1975 was subsumed into a larger statewide permit process: consumptive use permitting. These permits allowed withdrawal of water, from either surficial or subsurface aquifers, for "reasonable and beneficial" purposes such as drinking water, irrigation, and agriculture.[3] In this case, control was being taken back at the state level, while in growth management planning it was being pushed down to local governments.

McElwaine Departs

Andrew McElwaine left the Conservancy in July 2013 to become chief executive of the American Farmland Trust based in Washington, where he spent his early working years on the staff of Senator John Heinz. He completed the fund-raising drive started by Kathy Prosser and left a legacy of elevating policy issues to a high level of awareness within the organization. Before departing, he described two issues as dominating the future environmental debate in southwest Florida: development of rural lands and storm water management.

> There are large blocks of undeveloped lands out there. In my opinion, how they are built out will determine the future of southwest Florida. Someday we might end up being 'Broward on the Gulf' instead of 'Naples on the Gulf.' I don't think anyone wants that. Rock mining is another issue. The Hogan Island Mine just south of Lake Trafford could compromise the Camp Keais Slough. It sits just at the bottom of CREW land adjacent to Corkscrew Marsh. Mining in the DR/GR in

Lee County presents many of the same problems. Farms are flooding the system with mining permits to get the highest and best use out of their land so they can file Bert Harris claims. And I don't think the Collier RLSA program is going to be able to do much about that because mining is outside the forty-five thousand acre cap.[4]

His second concern was with waste and storm water management.

Septic systems in southwest Florida are aging. Many are twenty to thirty years old. We have large quantities of non-point source pollution coming off agricultural lands in Collier and Lee County. For example, take tomato farms. When you think about it, those farms basically kill the soil before each growing cycle—soil which isn't really suited to growing tomatoes in the first place—and then load it up with nutrients. Some of the runoff after heavy downpours ends up in Naples Bay and Rookery Bay and Charlotte Harbor. We have to find ways of controlling those two problems, and I don't see any easy path.[5]

As of the publication of this book, rule-making is proceeding at a breakneck pace in Tallahassee in an attempt to satisfy the governor's jobs agenda. People and processes responsible for McElwaine's two major concerns, land-use planning and water management, are being pitched out the window in a deliberate attempt to reduce personnel in compliance and review jobs. Since environmental regulation without sanction is meaningless, these changes constitute an attack on the state's long-term growth management planning structure harking back to 1972, just as the failure to set hard numeric criteria for water quality since 1998 is an attack on outcomes, a classic pincer movement. The process is less meaningful when the outcome alternatives are not clearly defined. Certainty of purpose demands clarity of process, and the State of Florida is moving rapidly toward having neither. McElwaine's concerns were hauntingly echoed six months later—with a different emphasis—when his successor was hired.

Rob Moher Named President

On October 17, 2013, Rob Moher took over as president and CEO of the Conservancy. Educated in Canada, he came to the Conservancy in 1999 from the Bahamas National Trust, where he had managed three coastal and marine parks. He had been with the Conservancy for 14 years, most recently as chief operating officer.

Taking advantage of his environmental background, he became an effective fund-raiser for the Conservancy, the primary person overseeing the successful $38.8-million capital campaign. The campaign, begun under Kathy Prosser, took seven long years, overlapping one of the worst recessions in Florida's history. The proceeds funded several strategic programs and construction of an environmentally friendly campus. Much of the money was raised from families involved in the Conservancy for multiple generations. Many of those families were winter residents of Naples in the 1960s, most from the Midwest. Conservative and cautious by nature, they managed to survive the economic setback beginning in 2008. Seven pledges were for $1 million or more. Prosser had built a board of directors for the purpose of raising money, and as the capital campaign wound down, a progressively larger portion of the board was populated by people who lived and worked year-round in southwest Florida. Some of those directors had children in the Conservancy's summer education programs. The logic was simple: to gain broader support within the growing body of full-time residents. The Conservancy knew it could not depend forever on part-time residents, even those with a high net worth, to carry the burden of political advocacy on issues so critical to Florida's future. Moher agreed with this approach as part of a broader strategy, which he set forth in an interview.[6]

"I have thought a lot about the future of the Conservancy, and there are some opportunities that stand out. The first is a chance to mend fences with other environmental organizations, fences that need not be there. Second, we need to have a conversation with landowners in eastern Collier County." Moher feels he is in a unique position. "I don't have lot of baggage. I'm the new guy. That allows me the opportunity to listen to what people have to say without compromising the Conservancy's deeply held policy positions. In doing that, we should seek areas where we can agree. That won't include everything, but it would be a start. We built relationships in the past with people like Dennis Gilkey from Bonita Bay Group that helped us with the Mirasol settlement. That served us well. Maybe we can do that in the future."

"Second, the State of Florida is not headed in a sustainable direction. Thirty years of growth management policies are being thrown out the window. State employees responsible for regulation are being replaced with others aggressively seeking growth at all costs. The state's rules are gone; federal rules are weak. Things probably have to get worse before they get better." Moher believes the cost of deregulation, abruptly applied, is far too high. "Historically, a bipartisan sense of regulatory balance emerged in the form of sensible legislation. They didn't always get it right the first time, but the ultimate result was fair. That's gone."

In order to counteract the effects of these changes on southwest Florida, Moher believes the Conservancy needs to broaden its geographic reach with greater emphasis on Hendry, Charlotte, and Glades Counties and dramatically increase membership over the next five years. "I see growing tension between coastal and inland communities. We have to ask ourselves, 'What is a sustainable level of development in the rural lands?' Coastal communities, with nearly 60% of the population, are funding massive infrastructure to the east. Look at Oil Well Road; it is now six lanes. Very few people use it. I know landowners take a long view, but the question is who should be paying for development. Right now, with rules of concurrency a local option, it's the coastal folks."

Moher admits that the issue of property rights will arise in any conversation. "The question of how you reconcile an owner's right to develop land with the common good is a tough one to answer. However, we have a great example just to the north at Babcock Ranch. There, environmental organizations cooperating, as they did in the Cocohatchee Coalition, worked with the owner to maintain the rural character of the land while preserving 80% in its natural state. Our staff worked on a financial package, and their analysis was correct. It made sense for all the parties at interest. That was a great model."

On the issue of water quantity, Moher said the Conservancy will press for Comprehensive Everglades Restoration funding at the federal and state levels, but he is concerned that the focus—and the money—is less on the western Everglades and more on moving water south from Lake Okeechobee. "We are part of a larger effort, but the western counties need a strong advocate, and our job will be to educate decision-makers on the economic effect of restoration on our coastal communities." He is less sanguine about efforts to establish clear standards for water quality. "The Conservancy is one of the few forces in the state that has the scientific background to counter the amount of misinformation being spread when it comes to water quality. Jennifer Hecker has deep knowledge of the situation; we need to use that effectively."

Moher believes the Conservancy's successful capital campaign was a watershed, a moment of institutional transformation. Major gifts came from families and individuals devoted to the Conservancy and its mission. "Our members want us to be independent. We can stay the course; we are not going to weaken. Everyone knows that now. We're here for the long run."

ENDNOTES

Introduction

1. Every now and then nature has its way, as it did in New Orleans when Hurricane Katrina wiped out the now-infamous lower Ninth Ward in 2005.

2. James A. Farr and O. Greg Brock, "Florida's Landmark Programs for Conservation and Recreation Land Acquisition," *sustain'*, Volume 14 (Spring/Summer 2006).

3. One notable precursor occurred after Miami was inundated with 102 inches of rain during the summer of 1947. The state and U.S. Army Corps of Engineers combined to create a water control and management plan that took 20 years to complete, at which point it became painfully obvious that projections made for the heavily settled southeast corner of the state had grossly underestimated population growth. The problem was exacerbated by a series of interdependent construction projects. For instance, once a decision was made to dig a canal, there was no turning back and no feedback loop through which adjustments could be made while each component project was being built out. A feedback loop would have increased accountability and allowed revisions to adjust for inaccurate assumptions and unanticipated impacts, but this deficiency was, in part, a logical outcome of government, which was increasing in both size and complexity.

4. As a result, Florida took a first swipe at comprehensive statewide planning by ordering the Division of State Planning in the Department of Administration to "provide long-range guidance for the orderly social, economic, and physical growth of the state. . . ." The effort

took nearly eight years to complete, and the legislature turned it down flat during the 1980 session while unequivocally dictating that no component of the plan be adopted or enacted. The problem, as argued by Roy Carriker of the University of Florida, was that planners had no power of implementation, and affected agencies of government simply didn't want to implement a plan that diminished their power.

5. This was the Local Government Comprehensive Planning Act of 1975.

6. This came out of Governor Graham's study committee, ELMS II (referred to in detail in Chapter 10, Ebb Tide), which made revolutionary and far-reaching recommendations enacted into law as the Local Government Comprehensive Planning and Land Development Regulation Act of 1985.

7. For an interesting perspective on this matter, please see Mary Dawson, *The Best Laid Plans: The Rise and Fall of Growth Management in Florida* (Journal of Land Use and Environmental Law, 1996).

8. The author, as a member of the Collier County Environmental Advisory Committee, saw how this worked. When each project was reviewed for environmental impact, the subject of water was always deferred to the water district and the Corps of Engineers. The advisory committee could not recommend changes or conditions to plans submitted for review by either of those two agencies.

9. One example of this is the ongoing sea turtle nesting research project undertaken by the Conservancy on Collier County and City of Naples beaches for the past 30 years. It is one of the oldest and longest running surveys of its kind in the country and has among its graduates hundreds of respected scientists who were once summer interns in the program.

Saving Rookery Bay and the Ten Thousand Islands

1. This purchase may have been part of a larger business deal. See Te-beau, 84.

2. For an excellent history of this project, see Davis and Arsenault, 260–279.

3. The *Everglades News* was printed at the *Fort Myers News-Press* office, also owned by Barron Collier.

4. W.H. Turner to Fred Buffaloe (chief of technical service, Bureau of Land Management, U.S. Department of the Interior), June 5, 1962.

5. See Carter, 240.

6. George Vega to Collier County Board of Commissioners, March 4, 1964.

7. *Naples Daily News,* March 18, 1964.

8. John Walter, "Richard Pough, Conservation Pioneer," *Vineyard Gazette* (June 27, 2003), http://mvgazette.com/news/2003/06/27/richard-pough-conservation-pioneer?k=vg5249b0643854c.

9. Minutes, Organizational Meeting of the Collier County Conservancy, April 11, 1964

10. Ibid.

11. Ibid.

12. *Naples Daily News,* October 8, 1964.

13. Dr. Frank Craighead, a biologist from Homestead; John Burnham and Addison Wood of Naples; Jerome Anderson, regional director for outdoor recreation from the U.S. Department of the Interior; Joel Kuperberg; Ken Woodburn, who was by then with the Florida Department of Conservation; R.K. Robinson of the U.S. Bureau of Sport Fisheries and Wildlife; Joel Martz, a biologist with the Florida Fish and Game Commission; and Bernie Yokel of the Institute of Marine Science at the University of Miami.

14. Ibid.

15. *Naples Daily News,* April 26, 1967.

16. See Dasmann.

17. Roy Wood to Joel Kuperberg, dated April 1, 1968.

18. *Naples Star,* November 16, 1967.

19. Tom Richards to Joel Kuperberg, June 5, 1968.

20. *The Daily News,* September 5, 1968.

21. Terry Blunt (vice president, Nature Conservancy) to Joel Kuperberg, March 25, 1969.

22. Final legislature designation could occur only after public hearings.

23. Ney Landrum to Cynthia Medley, dated January 22, 1970.

24. Joel Kuperberg, personal notes, April 23, 1969.

25. A 1972 Norris Marine Research Laboratory map identifies this nomenclature.

26. Dr. Ted LaRoe to Thor Johnson, July 21, 1972.

27. *Fort Myers News-Press,* April 27, 1974.

28. The Internal Improvement Fund has a checkered past. When formed by the state legislature in 1885, its main purpose was to grant state-owned lands to railroads for right-of-way and development of the interior. The state went even further with the issuance of state-supported bonds to finance construction. The program ended up as a massive giveaway to the railroad companies. In order to salvage its tattered reputation and its bonding capacity, the fund began to sell land at ridiculously low prices—as low as seven cents an acre—and to beat the drums for draining the Everglades and any other wetland in sight. Overcome by swindles and mismanagement, the fund nearly went broke before the Depression, but by the time Reubin Askew took the oath of office on January 5, 1971, it had regained its footing and financial solvency.

29. Joel Kuperberg to Patrick Noonan (vice president, Nature Conservancy), December 11, 1973.

30. *Naples Daily News,* February 6, 1975.

31. The largest gift was from the Collier-Read Company: 400 acres bordering the south entrance to Rookery Bay. It was announced by George Huntoon, who would play a large role in further acquisitions. *Naples Daily News,* April 27, 1969.

32. State Senator Philip Lewis to Arthur McIntosh, February 1, 1977. McIntosh owned land along Henderson Creek and had been active in real estate development in Chicago. Merrihue had been after McIntosh's land since 1970.

Chapter 1. Land for Future Generations
1. This idea is more fully set forth in James A. Farr and O. Greg Brock, "Florida's Landmark Programs for Conservation and Recreation Land Acquisition," *sustain',* Volume 14 (Spring/Summer 2006).

2. RuBino and Starnes, 184.

3. Ibid., 5.

4. The Florida Communities Trust was established in 1989 to assist county and municipal governments in evaluating and acquiring natural and recreational resources in specified sections of their comprehensive plans. However, there were no state matching funds to encourage this until Preservation 2000 kicked in.

Chapter 2. Big Cypress Swamp and the Fakahatchee Strand
1. Myers and Ewell, 282–283.

2. For a well-documented history of Gulf American's activities in southwest Florida, see Carter, 233–245, 247–248.

3. For an interesting history of this episode, see Grunwald, 254–263.

4. Bernie Yokel, handwritten notes, undated.

5. *Naples Daily News,* November 14, 1973.

6. Some inholdings still remain in private hands.

7. It is divided into 582,000 acres of preserve and 147,000 acres known as the "addition lands," where a 2012 controversy exists as to acceptable levels of off-road vehicle use.

8. *Naples Daily News,* April 28, 2013.

Chapter 3. Southern Golden Gate Estates

1. McPherson and Halley, 48.

2. The upper layer aquifer is segregated by a confining unit from the next lower level, the intermediate aquifer system, which can be divided into two parts: the Lower Tamiami, used mainly by Collier County, and the Sandstone and Upper Mid-Hawthorn aquifer, runs from 100 to 300 feet below mean sea level and is the main source of potable water for Lee County water systems. Another confining layer beneath Collier County is the saline Lower Mid-Hawthorn, which is separated from the large and largely inaccessible Floridan aquifer.

3. The Conservancy paid $600 to bring Maloney to Naples. While this seems like a paltry amount for a credible expert, Maloney was interested in the case.

4. *Fort Myers News-Press,* March 25, 1975.

5. *Naples Daily News,* May 6, 1976.

6. *Miami Herald,* May 9, 1976.

7. *Naples Daily News,* June 6, 1976.

8. *Miami Herald,* May 23, 1976.

9. Minutes, Collier County Conservancy Board of Directors, March 1978.

10. These two earlier studies, referred to in the text, were conducted by the Conservation Foundation, with research done by the Conservancy's science staff.

11. Collier County Conservancy, "Naples Bay Study," Naples, 1979, A-14.

12. Appendices to the study approached 200 pages of statistical tables and charts and were the guts of the Naples Bay Study.

13. The measured density of salt water in Naples Bay was approximately 64 lbs/cubic foot versus 62 lbs/cubic foot for fresh water.

14. "Package" septic plants are ancillary (secondary) treatment systems installed to take pressure off larger, mainline plants. They generally use an aerobic process of agitation to break down wastes.

15. Collier County Conservancy, "Naples Bay Study," Naples, 1979, F-14.

16. Created by legislation introduced in 1976 by Rep. Mary Ellen Hawkins.

17. *Naples Daily News,* February 20, 1980.

18. *Quail County Crier,* Issue #2, undated.

19. *Miami Herald,* October 20, 1981.

20. Minutes, Collier County Audubon Society, February 11, 1980.

21. Bruce A. Simpson to Timothy A. O'Connor, dated February 12, 1981.

22. For complete coverage of this dustup, see *Miami Herald,* April 23, 1981; *Naples Daily News,* April 21, 1981; and *Fort Myers News-Press,* April 21, 1981.

23. Willard Merrihue to Honorable Lawton Chiles, April 2, 1981.

24. Honorable Lawton Chiles to Willard Merrihue, April 28, 1981.

25. *Miami Herald,* October 20, 1981.

26. Dan Crabb to Willard Merrihue, January 3, 1984.

27. *Miami Herald,* May 23, 1986.

28. The Save Our Rivers Act, heavily promoted by Governor Bob Graham, was funded in part by a documentary stamp tax.

29. *Naples Daily News,* September 23, 1986.

30. For a complete discussion of this, see an investigative report on the sale of distressed properties to the Latino population in Miami, *Miami Herald,* December 3, 1987.

Chapter 4. Keewaydin (Key) and Cannon Islands

1. The Australian pine (not actually a pine) may have been introduced from the Pacific Northwest by the U.S. Department of Agriculture in Homestead, Florida. For a discussion of foredune stabilization, see Myers and Ewell, 431–435.

2. Pulling had platted 100-foot strips running east to west, which he priced to sell at $1,000 each. A large chunk of the Pulling holdings—129 acres with a mile and a quarter of beachfront—was later sold to the Smith family of Atlanta.

3. *Fort Myers News-Press,* January 30, 1977.

4. Ibid.

5. Unsigned memo from the Conservancy's "Norris" file, February 16, 1979.

6. § 704.06, Florida Rev. Statutes.

7. Willard Merrihue to W.R. Timken, March 12, 1983.

8. Lavern Gaynor to Honorable Franklin B. Mann, May 19, 1983.

9. Lavern Gaynor, interview with the author, April 13, 2011.

10. The ownership situation on the island became even more complicated six months later with an announcement in the local paper that the southern mile and a quarter of the island, originally owned by John Pulling and later by the Smith family of Atlanta, was listed for sale at $2 million.

11. *Naples Daily News,* June 3, 1988.

12. Mary Dearholt to members of the Collier County Conservancy, July 25, 1988.

13. This same issue of developing city land adjacent to property owned in Collier County would become a critical element in Collier Enterprises' plan for the Villages of Sabal Bay.

14. The subject of annexation would come up again in 2008, when the City of Naples seriously considered annexation of all lands contigu-

ous to existing lands within the city limits.

15. The level had to be at seven feet or higher.

16. Rejection was based on Objective 10.3 of "Collier County's Growth Management Plan: Conservation and Coastal Management Element," which states in part: "Undeveloped coastal barriers shall be maintained predominantly in their natural state and their natural function shall be protected, maintained and enhanced."

17. Two boat clubs existed on the island at the time. They were both grandfathered when the more restrictive growth management plan was written.

18. Roger Reinke (assistant city manager, City of Naples) to William Moss (city manager), March 4, 2009.

19. Karl Haydn to Edwin J. Putzell, December 5, 1983.

20. *Naples Daily News,* June 26, 1984.

21. William Vines to Terry Virta (community development coordinator, Collier County), November 30, 1983.

22. The Director of Department of Natural Resources would designate land for purchase to be approved by the Internal Improvement Fund.

23. William Vines to Edwin Putzell, August 2, 1984.

24. *Naples Daily Star,* August 4, 1984.

25. Senator Franklin Mann to Edwin Putzell, August 1, 1984.

26. Edwin Putzell to William Vines, August 9, 1984.

27. *Miami Herald,* August 12, 1984.

28. Ibid., August 16, 1984.

29. The latest plan would cover no more than 50 acres with 86 dwelling units, a 200-seat dining complex with beachfront chickee hut, and an unspecified number of boat docks.

30. Karl Haydn to Edwin Putzell, March 1, 1985.

31. Karl Haydn to Edwin Putzell, January 17, 1985.

32. At the time, DeGrove was Secretary of the Department of Community Affairs for the State of Florida.

33. Transcript, Conservation and Recreation Lands Committee, January 29, 1985, as attached to Karl Haydn to Edwin Putzell, dated March 1, 1985.

34. Ibid.

35. Ibid.

36. The entire island had been appraised at $2.1 million.

37. Senator Franklin Mann to Art Harper, September 17, 1985.

38. Key, Little Marco, Johnson, and Coconut Islands were also high-priority targets because of their intrinsic ecological value.

39. Telegram from Finley, Kumble, and Wagner to Toivo Tammerk, October 2, 1985.

40. Victoria Tschinkel to Honorable Bob Graham, November 13, 1985.

41. *Miami Herald,* November 22, 1985.

42. *Naples Daily News,* November 15, 1985.

43. James McFarland (director, Division of State Lands in the Department of Natural Resources, State of Florida) to Karl Haydn, January 30, 1986.

44. George Vega to James Kessler, June 17, 1988.

45. Paul Darst to David Addison, October 15, 1985.

46. These seven points paraphrase contents of a letter from David Addison to Paul Darst, November 1, 1985.

Chapter 5. Florida's Growth Management Evolves

1. Carter, 125.

2. § 380, Florida Rev. Statutes.

3. For an excellent discussion of SB 629, see Carter, 125–137.

4. In Collier County, water management was overseen by a district set up by the county commission in 1961. Its jurisdiction was mainly swamp, wetlands, and the mangrove forests of Rookery Bay. It was also responsible for issuing permits to drain Golden Gate Estates—with disastrous results to the county's water supplies. In 1971 the Conservancy convinced the county to set up a second entity called Water Management District 6 to cover development in areas adjacent to Rookery Bay. Creation of the SFWMD preempted both districts.

Chapter 6. Deltona and Marco Island

1. B.P. is archaeological shorthand for Before Present era.

2. The argument goes that sea level rise from glacial melting, although sporadic, did not fill the estuaries until 2,700 B.P. Therefore, systematic harvesting of renewable marine food sources was not likely until that date. The work at Horr's Island also challenged the prevailing wisdom that shell tools were not used until later, when humans survived as nomadic hunters preying upon small animals and larger fauna during the Archaic Period.

3. *Naples Daily News,* March 12, 1964.

4. See http://www.themacklecompany.com/femjrstorypublic/00-index.htm for an excellent history written by the Mackle family.

5. Rookery Bay would be designated a NERR site in 1978.

6. Also presenting papers were scientists Tim Stuart and Gerald van Belle of Florida State University, Dr. Landon Ross, Dr. Paul Parks, Frank Phillips (employed by the department), and Robert Weinstein of the U.S. Naval Oceanographic Office in Washington, D.C.

7. Florida Department of Pollution Control, "Staff Presentation: Deltona Corporation—Collier Bay, Big Key Bay and Barfield/Blue Hill Bay Projects," February 1974.

8. For an excellent history of this long-standing battle between environmentalists, led by Marjorie Carr, and development-minded politicians in north and central Florida, see Noll and Tegeder.

9. Willard Merrihue to Colonel Charles C. Lee Jr. (district engineer, U.S. Army Corps of Engineers), June 3, 1975.

10. Willard Merrihue to Nathaniel Reed, August 11, 1975.

11. Bernie Yokel to Nathaniel Reed, August 15, 1975.

12. Bernie Yokel to Colonel Donald Wisdom, September 16, 1975.

13. *Naples Daily News*, April 17, 1976.

14. The agreement affirmed that 24,963 acres were slated for development at Marco Island, that 8,509 had been developed, that permit denial by the Corps affected 2,908 acres, and that an "inferred" denial would affect another 3,564 acres. It also noted that Deltona had purchased another 1,912 acres of uplands designated as Unit 30 after the Corps' denial in 1976. Unit 30, as it turned out, was a feeding area and rookery for flocks of wading birds and possessed high environmental value. Unit 24 adjoined Rookery Bay preserve.

15. Preliminarily, the swap had contemplated 15,000 wetlands acres, but after surveys and appraisals the amount of land was reduced to 12,400 acres.

16. Press Release, Office of the Governor, March 24, 1984.

17. *Naples Daily News*, March 21, 1984.

Chapter 7. Pelican Bay and Barefoot Beach

1. Osmotic pressure would move a fluid from one side of a filter to another in order to equalize concentrations of a solute. Reverse osmosis worked in the opposite manner by applying high pressure (in excess of the normal osmotic pressure) to one side of a semi-permeable membrane, from which water molecules, but not salt and other substances, could be passed from the higher to lower solute.

2. Ross Obley, interview with the author, March 23, 2011.

3. Resolution of Board of Directors, Collier County Conservancy, November 26, 1974.

4. This subject is covered later in Chapter 8, Changing of the Guard.

5. The footprint covered 285 acres, of which approximately 190 acres were submerged lands owned by the State of Florida. The northern 16 acres, including beachfront abutting the Lee County line, were excluded.

6. The Department of Natural Resources had a statewide setback line that would have moved the development border further inland than the county's line.

7. A historical study by the National Hurricane Center had found that substantial damage occurred to man-made structures within 300 feet of the mean high-tide line, which would have imperiled Lely's plans.

8. The plan would increase beachfront units at the narrow, filled-in former site of Little Hickory Pass from 209 to 492 and from 98 to 308 units in another location populated with native vegetation.

9. *The Conservancy News,* June 25, 1985.

10. The number was reduced from 272 to 97.

11. Settlement Agreement, Twentieth Judicial Circuit in Collier County Florida, filed January 16, 1986.

12. Lely Estates, Inc., to Honorable Fred Voss, September 26, 1986.

13. George Vega to Toivo Tammerk, December 2, 1986.

14. Conservancy of Southwest Florida to Paul Harvey, November 13, 2000.

Chapter 8. Changing of the Guard

1. Shomon's book on the subject was published by the National Audubon Society in 1962.

2. Joel Kuperberg to Tom Richards, March 7, 1968.

3. By 1977 SCCF had conserved 216 acres of land on Sanibel Island, although much of it was for the organization's benefit as the site of the nature center from which the staff ran tours and educational programs. By the 1980s, the foundation had installed an intern program and extended its land acquisition program into Cayo Costa and North Captiva Island. It later began to run docent-led cruises.

4. National Audubon Society, Nature Center Planning Division, "Big Cypress Nature Center: Interim Report," New York, 1973.

5. Willard Merrihue to Duane Julian, March 2, 1976.

6. Minutes, Collier County Conservancy Board of Directors, March 25, 1976.

7. Ross had extensive national contacts, particularly with the Kresge Foundation.

8. Stuart Douglas memo, December 9, 1977.

9. Willard Merrihue, Comments for Dedication, April 8, 1981.

10. He had convinced Provincetown-Boston Airlines, owned in part by Peter Van Arsdale, to expand in Naples by offering passenger service in coordination with Delta Airlines. He had also shepherded a new passenger terminal through the permitting process.

11. Edwin J. Putzell to board members, June 10, 1982.

12. Notes from Naples and Marco Board of Realtors luncheon, April 25, 1984.

13. Kushell, Merrihue, Quale, and Endler to Edwin J. Putzell, undated.

14. Bernie Yokel to Development Review Committee, May 12, 1980.

15. Minutes of Executive Committee, Collier County Conservancy, April 9, 1985.

16. Toivo Tammerk to Frank Jones, February 18, 1986.

17. Albert Hine and Christopher Jones, "Assessment of Dredging Activity at Gordon Pass and Adjacent Beach Replacement" (undated).

18. Mark Benedict to Toivo Tammerk, May 5, 1987.

Chapter 9. Villages of Sabal Bay and Hamilton Harbor

1. This is an inferential conclusion based upon Jeffrey Schmid, Kathy Worley, David Addison, Andrew Zimmerman, and Alex van Eaton, "Naples Bay Past and Present: A Chronology of Disturbance to an Estuary. Final Report to the City of Naples, February 2006." The data in the report compares 1950 to 2000, when 70% of the mangrove fringe was reported as having been destroyed, but little new development occurred on fringes of Naples Bay between 1985 and 2000 so this seems like a reasonable estimate.

2. Elton Gissendanner (executive director, Department of Natural Resources) to Roger Barry (community development director, City of Naples), January 30, 1987.

3. In many cases, conflicting testimony from expert witnesses on both sides caused confused rulings.

4. "Comprehensive Plan for the City of Naples," 1984 revised version, 161.

5. Dale Twachtmann (secretary, Department of Environmental Regulation) to Randy Armstrong (director, Division of Permitting), June 20, 1988.

6. Jon Steiger to Missy McKim (community development director, City of Naples), January 26, 1989.

7. Workshops are generally held by the Naples City Council to discuss important issues without the need to take action. The issues discussed almost always appear on the council's next meeting agenda.

8. Transcript, Naples City Council (March 1, 1989), 100.

9. John Radley to Randall Armstrong (director, Division of Water Management, Florida Department of Environmental Regulation), March 9, 1989.

10. Randall Armstrong to John Radley, March 13, 1989.

11. Gail Easley, Kevin Atkins, Jane Gray, Ron McCormick, Ernest D. Estevez, Greg Blanchard, and Judith Jones. "Boat Traffic Study Prepared for City of Naples, Phase I" (June 1989), 70.

12. This comment was quoted in The Conservancy, Inc., "Facts about Sabal Bay Marina," March 1989.

13. City of Naples, Resolution 89-586, 1.

14. CDC First Requests for Admission to Division of Administrative Hearings, State of Florida" (October 20, 1989), 6–7.

15. *Department of Community Affairs et al. v. Collier County et al.*, DOAH Case No. 98-0324GM (ACC 99-002).

16. The new facility would have 36 wet slips, 450 boats in dry storage, loading and fueling docks, additional public parking space for boat trailers launching at Bayview Park, a restaurant, and nautical supply store.

17. The principle of cumulative effects would become pivotal in later challenges by the Conservancy and other environmental groups to Section 404 permits issued by the Army Corps of Engineers for developments in the Cocohatchee Slough.

18. Conservancy of Southwest Florida, "Hamilton Harbor: A Summary," March 9, 1999.

19. *Naples Daily News*, May 13, 1999.

20. *Naples Daily News*, May 20, 1999.

21. The Conservancy had received information that Collier Enterprises had submitted to the federal government a detailed proposal for commercial and residential development of the base but had been unable to obtain specifics. This seems to be the basis for the suggestion in Guggenheim's letter.

22. David Guggenheim to Jeffrey Birr, August 13, 1999.

23. Ellin Goetz, interview with the author, March 8, 2013.

24. Ibid.

25. There is some controversy about this. The Conservancy executive committee minutes indicate the organization never officially withdrew from the joint lawsuit, which was dismissed on August 12, 1999. But in a memo dated September 30, 1999, Pfeiffer stated that he had filed a notice of voluntary dismissal, which removed the Conservancy. The judge had not issued a written order of dismissal by the date of the memo.

26. Dick Grant to Steven Pfeiffer, June 19, 1999.

27. Draft memorandum from Steven Pfeiffer to David Guggenheim, dated August 30, 1999.

28. § 163.3187 (1) Florida Rev. Statutes.

29. *Naples Daily News,* April 6, 2000.

30. The "II" was recognition of an earlier commission with the same name formed under Governor Askew in 1972.

31. § 70.001 (3)(b), Florida Rev. Statutes.

32. Of the three cases lost by government officials, one was tried in Collier County in 2005. After a judge supported the plaintiff's claim, the county commission settled for $2.75 million and had to cough up $175,000 (the balance was paid by insurance) in order to avoid a jury trial setting damages. That case made Collier County commissioners and Naples city officials much more cautious when examining future land use applications to come before them.

33. "Conservation vital" lands in state statutes are considered essential habitat for a functioning ecosystem; "conservation transitional" lands are in the zone between lands deemed as vital and those deemed as expendable.

34. Kathy Prosser-Bovard, correspondence with the author, November 2, 2012.

35. Kathy Prosser to Honorable Bonnie MacKenzie, January 2, 2001.

36. Kathy Prosser-Bovard, e-mail to the author, November 8, 2012.

37. See Response of the Conservancy of Southwest Florida, Inc., filed in Circuit Court of the Twentieth Judicial Circuit in re: Case No. 00-1562-Ca and Case No. 03-965-CA.

38. § 404 of the Clean Water Act authorizes the Corps to issue either general or individual permits including dredging, clearing and "discharging dredged materials" for construction projects affecting jurisdictional wetlands in the United States.

39. The side letter was not the Conservancy's first choice. Andrew McElwaine felt it did not carry the same power as it would if incorporated into the approved master plan.

40. *Naples Daily News,* July 24, 2012.

41. The five are Toivo Tammerk (1985–1991), John Fitch (1991–1996), David Guggenheim (1996–2000), Kathy Prosser (2000–2005) and Andrew McElwaine (2005–2013).

42. Tom Flood (president, Collier Enterprises) to Andrew McElwaine (president, Conservancy of Southwest Florida), October 7, 2008.

Chapter 10. Ebb Tide

1. This came out of Governor Graham's study committee, ELMS II (referred to in the introduction), which made revolutionary and far-reaching recommendations enacted into law as the Local Government Comprehensive Planning and Land Development Regulation Act of 1985.

2. Ellie Krier, interview with the author, January 16, 2011.

3. Gary Schmelz, interview with the author, April 14, 2010.

4. Norman A. Herren to Joel Kuperberg, dated September 20, 1967.

5. The Conservation Foundation, "Rookery Bay Area Project" (Washington, D.C., 1968).

6. Resolution re: Rookery Bay Area, Collier County Commission, July 13, 1969.

7. Ibid.

8. The study team was also able to convince Deltona Corporation to abandon plans for a vertical seawall at the north end of its Marco Island development in favor of maintaining the existing mangrove fringe in its natural state.

9. Funding from the second source was not surprising in that Marshall, as a special assistant in the department, had been instrumental in the decision to move the proposed Big Cypress Swamp Jetport from its recommended location adjacent to Everglades National Park.

10. *University of Miami News,* May 8, 1970.

11. Gary Schmelz, interview with the author, October 11, 2011.

12. The Conservancy, Inc., "Conservation Strategy 2001," February 19, 1991.

13. Deltona, as part of the 1982 agreement, had obtained the right to erect 300 homes on upland areas of the island but never exercised the right because it could not compete for buyers who preferred water access via the fingerlike canals throughout Marco Island proper.

14. Declaration of Protective Covenants, Restrictions and Easements for Key Marco, October 9, 1990.

15. Development of Horr's Island would take place sporadically over the ensuing decades, and the Conservancy would become periodically embroiled in controversies with homeowners and speculators on the island over proper maintenance of native vegetation and the remaining shell mounds. The state came close to buying the island from Ronto Corporation in 1998 but could not close the gap on price. It was a shame because the island was one of the few places in Florida where two entirely different ecosystems, uplands and mangrove fringe forests, existed in close proximity to one another due to the rapid change in elevation.

16. Briggs Nature Center was built with a $250,000 donation. Completed in 1982, its winding boardwalk through the saw palmettos and na-

tive vegetation was based on Audubon's Corkscrew Swamp pathways. It was closed in 2006 due to a lack of potable well water.

17. Gary Lytton to George Willson, June 12, 1990.

18. The Conservancy, Inc., "New Board Member Orientation," January 1994.

19. Krier left the staff in July 1994 but returned as a candidate to replace Fitch.

20. The urban growth boundary is shown on the Future Land Use (FLUE) maps for Florida's counties.

21. Conservancy of Southwest Florida, "Policy Statement," July 18, 1997.

22. This was not unusual in southwest Florida at the time. Once rezoning by commissioners was granted to a Planned Unit Development (the technical term for TwinEagles), the developer had great flexibility inside the perimeter.

23. *Naples Daily News,* July 21, 1997.

24. Anderson would later become chairman of the county's Development Services Advisory Committee.

25. This change increased density from 277 homes (based upon one per five acres) to more than 2,200 dwellings in the added acreage. Fiddler's Creek was already permitted for 2,379 acres, with nearly 6,000 units abutting the lush fairways of two 18-hole golf courses on agricultural land.

26. *Naples Daily News,* October 22, 1997.

27. George Varnadoe to David Guggenheim, February 23, 1998.

28. Kim Kobza (Treiser, Kobza and Volpe, Chartered) to Gary Lytton, June 2, 1998.

29. David Addison to David Guggenheim, June 15, 1999.

30. *Fort Lauderdale Sun-Sentinel,* February 20, 1994.

31. *Naples Daily News,* November 17, 2001

32. *Naples Daily News,* April 12, 1998.

Chapter 11. Watershed Under Siege

1. Florida Department of Community Affairs, Development of Regional Impact Report (1992), 13.

2. Estero Bay had been designated an Outstanding Florida Water (OFW), which carried broad implications, including heightened scrutiny and protection of the tributary's water by prohibiting discharge permits that could degrade water quality unless clearly in the "public interest." A series of threshold tests heightened restrictions to the point where wastewater discharges were all but prohibited. Most state and national parks in Florida contain OFWs. There were 41 designated outside the state parks system, among them four Estero Bay tributaries, most of which emanated in the DR/GR. The bay had enjoyed an additional level of protection since 1966, when the northern half was dedicated as the state's first aquatic preserve.

3. Density varied depending upon the environmental sensitivity of the land.

4. *Anchorage Daily News,* May 18, 2008.

5. The two cited here, Estero River and Estero Bay, were already compromised and failed to meet standards set by the Florida Department of Environmental Protection.

6. *Fort Myers News-Press,* May 15, 2008.

7. Dover, Kohl & Partners, "Prospects for Southeast Lee County: Planning for the Density Reduction Groundwater Resource Area (DR/GR)" (2009).

8. Geologically, the DR/GR had a substrate used as a base for road-building once the Calusa mounds had been shoveled out to exhaustion.

9. The companies involved were FFD Land Company, CEMEX Construction, Troyer Brothers Florida, and Old Corkscrew Plantation.

10. *Naples Daily News,* April 20, 2013.

11. *Fort Myers News-Press,* June 28, 1990.

12. Revenue in the first year would come from a tax on real estate transfers and investments. The legislature, wanting to retain control over funding, annually appropriated from documentary stamps and general revenue. Without bonding powers, the state would have been restricted to about $650 million over the next ten years.

13. Michele Hopkins, Mark Schwartz, and Nirjhar Shah, PhD, "Southern Corkscrew Regional Ecosystem Watershed Restoration Project," undated.

14. The power to designate is vested in the Department of Environmental Protection's adjunct body called the Environmental Regulatory Commission, a group of seven people appointed by the governor. Once designated (according to the DEP), permitted projects "must not lower existing ambient water quality."

15. The three developments have been through a series of name changes over the past 15 years in an attempt to rebrand and market each iteration. This is just one of the changes.

16. Laura Hartt to James Palmer, May 13, 2005.

17. *Naples Daily News,* November 10, 2006.

18. Sending lands were set aside for their high habitat value for endangered species and for wetlands functionality. Neutral lands could be designated as receiving, which would allow development subject to the normal zoning regulations and building codes.

19. Collier County issues Planned Unit Development permits for a period of five years. If all other required permits have not been obtained and construction has not commenced, the PUD authorization to build out a development becomes void.

20. "Significant modification to the design, size, or location of the flow way and/or significant changes to the Flow Way Agreement (Exhibit B of the Ordinance) as a result of, but not limited to, permitting or action taken by the parties to the Agreement shall constitute a sub-

stantial change to the PUD and shall require a re-hearing consistent with the provisions of Section 2.7.3.5.1 of the Land Development Code relative to substantial changes" is the relevant language, according to Mirasol PUD Section 2.2F.

21. Known as the Harvey Harper methodology, it was adopted by the state Department of Environmental Protection and the South Florida Water Management District and is covered in detail in Chapter 14 (Water Wars).

22. *National Wildlife Federation, Conservancy of Southwest Florida, Collier County Audubon Society, Florida Wildlife Federation, National Audubon Society, Inc. v. Paul Souza, Steve Sullivan, Pete Geren, Dirk Kempthorne,* Case No. 08-14115.

23. Ibid.

24. A three-judge panel in the D.C. District Court issued a June 2013 decision in the case of *Mingo Logan Coal v. Environmental Protection Agency,* holding that the EPA had the right to veto a 2007 Section 404 permit in September 2009, almost 18 months after the fact. See 33 U.S.C. § 1251 *et seq.*

25. From the author's notes.

26. *Sylvester v. US Army Corps of Engineers,* 884 F.2d. 394 (9th Cir. 1989).

Chapter 12. Rural Lands Stewardship

1. The CARL program and water management districts each received 35%, Florida Communities Trust was increased to 22%, and the remaining 8% was distributed among four land addition programs and a recreational facility fund.

2. Alico's corporate mission statement says in part: "To hold and operate rural lands, primarily in agricultural enterprises, in order to maximize income until these lands become available for development."

3. Florida's Growth Management Study Commission, "A Livable Florida

for Today and Tomorrow" (Tallahassee: February 2001), 43.

4. For an excellent discussion of this transition, see Rosenbaum, 140–170.

5. The underlying zoning in rural areas was one dwelling per five acres.

6. Belle Meade proper, south of I-75 and west of southern Golden Gate Estates, also known as the Picayune Strand, is being restored. North Belle Meade, north of I-75, was a small Natural Resource Preservation Area isolated from the larger ecosystem by the interstate.

7. In that agreement, any development larger than 40 acres was required to cluster housing and either to preserve 50% of land in a natural state with a conservation easement in perpetuity or to mitigate for natural areas lost to development at a two-to-one ratio.

8. *St. Petersburg Times,* June 14, 1999.

9. *Naples Daily News,* May 26, 1999.

10. Statement by David Guggenheim to Florida Cabinet, June 22, 1999.

11. In fact, more than 60% of respondents favored a moratorium on all new development in the two counties, with the most support from people aged 18 to 39, the youngest demographic.

12. TwinEagles is covered in detail in Chapter 11 (Watershed Under Siege) in the Lessons from the Cocohatchee section.

13. Based upon § 163.3177 (11), Florida Rev. Statute.

14. This March 19, 1999, workshop was a meeting of the commissioners to discuss, in informal public session, a topic of immediate relevance and import. Public comment was permitted but no decisions were made. The usual outcome of a workshop was to ask staff for further clarification and amplification on the relevant issue, which is what happened here.

15. *Naples Daily News,* March 21, 1999.

16. For a detailed summary of the scandal, see *Naples Daily News,* January 4, 2004.

17. *Naples Daily News,* December 10, 1998.

18. Russell Priddy was co-owner of 9,000 acres in the rural county; Ed Oates was development director for Collier Enterprises; and Michael Bruet's wife headed up development operations for Barron Collier Companies. Priddy had requested an opinion from the county attorney's office as to whether their role constituted a violation of the state's ethics laws, so the commission members were doing their best to avoid any potential problems.

19. Bauer remained active in environmental jobs. He is currently head of Natural Resources for the City of Naples.

20. WilsonMiller had an incentive to get the plan right, at least in the beginning. Many of Florida's 67 counties were highly dependent on agriculture, and the firm believed it could sell its assistance statewide.

21. Privately owned lands within the RLSA totaled approximately 182,000 acres.

22. Executive Summary, "Collier County Staff Recommendations: Draft of Collier Growth Management Plan (GMP) Amendments Addressing the Requirements of the Final Order (AC-99-02) Issued by the State of Florida Administration Commission on June 22, 1999, for the Eastern Lands Portion of the Rural and Agricultural Assessment (Transmittal Hearing)," 3.

23. Ibid., 5.

24. Kathy Prosser-Bovard, correspondence with the author, November 2, 2012.

25. The project was approved on March 23, 2004, when the county designated the new town as a 960-acre SRA within the rural lands, with a final determination the following year, when a DRI was filed, impacting 5,027 acres. The plan included 11,000 dwelling units, 950 acres devoted to Ave Maria University, medical facilities, office space, retail stores, and an array of civic facilities.

26. Florida Department of Community Affairs, "Rural Land Stewardship Program 2007 Annual Report to the Legislature" (December

31, 2007), 8.

27. The Collier County planning department did a restudy because earlier estimates had not taken into consideration an increase in a bewildering variety of credits to landowners. Additionally, the county's new number was 389,193 people.

28. Florida Department of Community Affairs, 8.

29. Later analysis showed that 87% of the Ave Maria's SRA (4,455 acres) was formerly row crops, pasture, sod, and fallow land. See Florida Department of Community Affairs, "2007 Rural Land Stewardship Program Annual Report and Rural Lands Stewardship Area Technical Review - Phase I," 11.

30. Many of the Tallahassee amendments were technical: There was increased emphasis on workforce housing, firmer population estimates for each 25-year horizon, and refinement of the system by which credits were awarded.

31. *Naples Daily News,* November 21, 2007.

32. Ibid.

33. Laurie MacDonald, interview with the author, January 11, 2013.

34. Ibid.

35. "How Much Is Enough? Landscape-scale Conservation for the Florida Panther," Biological Conservation, Number 130, 118–133.

36. The panther plan was to be proposed for implementation at the federal level through a Conservation Agreement, which was normally reserved for non-listed (not threatened or endangered) species on private lands. Eventually, the Conservancy got so fed up that it filed a lawsuit in federal district court to compel the USFWS to designate with exactitude the biological nature and spatial extent of habitat necessary for the survival and promulgation of the endangered Florida panther. The USFWS took great exception to the service, arguing that the panther had been listed before the Endangered Species Act was signed into law and was therefore exempt from the

requirement for critical habitat designation.

37. Florida Department of Community Affairs, 8.

38. WilsonMiller, Inc., "Collier County Rural Land Stewardship Five Year Review," 74–76.

39. *Naples Daily News,* September 24, 2008.

40. The original number of 16,800 did not include baseline sprawl of one housing unit per five acres, which accounted for some of the difference.

41. Landowners went on to point out that, according to RLSA policy, 35% of each SRA would be mandatory open space, leaving only 29,250 acres, with an average density of 2.5 to 3 units per acre.

42. Florida Department of Community Affairs, 8.

43. David Hoffman (Johnson Engineering) to Tom Jones (Barron Collier Companies), February 15, 2008.

44. *Naples Daily News,* February 1, 2008.

45. Florida Department of Community Affairs, "Objections, Recommendations and Comments Report," DCA No. 08-1 (July 14, 2008), 4.

46. Jennifer Hecker, interview with the author, December 6, 2012.

47. Alan Reynolds to Collier County RLSA Review Committee, October 22, 2008.

48. Ibid.

49. Andrew McElwaine and Nicole Ryan to Thomas Henning (chairman, Collier County Board of Commissioners), November 3, 2008.

50. Florida Panther Protection Review Team. "Technical Review for the Florida Panther Protection Program Proposed for the Rural Lands Stewardship Area of Collier County, Florida" (2009), 22.

51. Judith Hushon, interview with the author, January 24, 2012.

52. At last count, there were 44 species listed by the state and federal

government on the Endangered, Threatened and Species of Special Concern list.

53. Paul Souza (field supervisor, South Florida Ecological Services Office, U.S. Fish and Wildlife Service) to Margaret Gaffney-Smith (chief, Regulatory Division, U.S. Army Corps of Engineers), December 8, 2006.

54. *Marco News,* October 21, 2007.

55. Estimate by Eric Draper (president, Florida Audubon Society). *St. Petersburg Times,* August 23, 2010.

56. Both Russell Priddy and Tom Flood (president of Collier Enterprises) told the author in private conversations that they believe the population is closer to 200 in eastern Collier County.

57. Laurie MacDonald, interview with the author, January 11, 2013.

Chapter 13. Review of Federal and State Water Laws

1. Pittman and Waite, 167.

Chapter 14. Water Wars

1. Rosenbaum, 88–89.

2. "Cumulative impact" is defined as "the impact on the environment which results from the incremental impact of the action when added to other past, present, and reasonably foreseeable future actions regardless of what agency (Federal or non-Federal) or person undertakes such other actions. Cumulative impacts can result from individually minor but collectively significant actions taking place over a period of time." 40 CFR § 1508.7.

3. 33 CFR § 230.1.

4. Members included the Conservancy of Southwest Florida, the Environmental Confederation of Southwest Florida, the Florida Wildlife

Federation, the National Wildlife Federation, and the Sierra Club. Eventually the coalition would expand to include 30 organizations.

5. This was set forth in the county's comprehensive plan.

6. Funded by the J.C. Penney Foundation, it included the county's Rural Lands Committee, a citizen's study group called FOCUS, the Rural Fringe Committee, and the Select Committee on Community Character.

7. The Everglades Coalition is a group of more than 40 organizations, from the Corps to environmental groups, concerned with carrying out the Comprehensive Everglades Restoration Project (CERP).

8. Conservancy of Southwest Florida, *Eye on the Issues,* February 1998.

9. Conservancy of Southwest Florida, "State of Collier County's Environment: Risks and Solutions" (June 1998).

10. For a fuller picture of Hall, see Pittman and Waite, 61–65.

11. "The Southwest Florida EIS: Why it Is, What it Is, What Can it Do?" memorandum (undated), likely authored by Dr. John Hall.

12. Ibid.

13. Ibid.

14. David Guggenheim, personal notes, October 20, 1999.

15. David Guggenheim to Colonel Joe Miller (district engineer, U.S. Army Corps of Engineers), October 22, 1999.

16. David Guggenheim, personal notes, undated.

17. Chairman, Collier County Commission (unidentified) to Ken Dugger (Department of the Army Regulatory Division), January 11, 1999.

18. David Guggenheim to Ken Dugger, January 14, 2000.

19. This process was evident at Lake Trafford, a large, shallow, inland lake in northern Collier County that suffered a massive fish kill in 2007. A decision was made to drain the lake, scrape the bottom, and use the hardened muck as landfill. But once the front-end loaders started work, chemical sampling showed that the bottom soil was

laced with toxins and unsuitable for fill.

20. *Naples Daily News,* March 11, 2001.

21. *Fort Myers News-Press,* September 8, 2000.

22. *Naples Daily News,* September 8, 2000.

23. *Bonita Daily News,* August 3, 2000.

24. Steve Bortone, "State of the Environmental Science Division, 2000" (February 2, 2000).

25. In a 2006 advisory referendum, bonding capacity was expanded to $189 million, but the recession caused reduced tax revenues so the program was suspended in January 2011.

26. § 373.019 (17), Florida Rev. Statutes.

27. S.T. Bacchus, "Can Wetlands Be Successfully Created?" *The Palmetto* (Fall 1991).

28. This data was cited in "Resignation Statement of Bruce Boler, EPA, Leaving Southwest Florida" (undated). This may have been in reaction to interagency friction between the EPA and the Corps while Boler was working on the southwest Florida Environmental Impact Statement.

29. Harper, Harvey H., PhD, PE, "Evaluation of Alternative Stormwater Regulations for Southwest Florida" (2003).

30. Pittman and Waite, 245.

31. *Naples Daily News,* October 19, 2003.

32. Jeff Ruch (executive director, Public Employees for Environmental Responsibility), http//www.peer.org/news/news-releases/2003/10/22/.

33. The SFWMD issues permits separately from other agencies. The Corps of Engineers issues permits under Section 404 of the Federal Water Pollution Act of 1972, and the state usually ratifies Corps permits with a routine water quality permit.

34. Peer review is an essential element in the scientific process, stimulating critical thinking and strengthening scientific conclusions

through an iterative process of questioning both the assumptions and conclusions of a study. Reviewers are selected for their expertise on the subject reviewed and are expected to be rigorous, skeptical, and impartial.

35. Michael Sole, interview with the author, November 15, 2012.

36. Harper, Harvey H., PhD, PE, "Evaluation of Current Stormwater Design Criteria within the State of Florida" (2007).

37. A TMDL is required for waters unable to meet state pollution standards per § 303 (d) of the Clean Water Act. It is a calculation of the maximum level of pollutants that a surficial water body can absorb and meet quality standards appropriate to that water body. See http//water.epa.gov/lawsregs/lawsguidance/cwa/tmdl/.

38. Andrew McElwaine, interview with the author, December 3, 2012.

39. Jennifer Hecker (natural resources manager, Conservancy of Southwest Florida) to Eric Livingston (Bureau of Watershed Management, Department of Environmental Protection), July 22, 2008.

40. United States Environmental Protection Agency, "New Harper Statewide Model for Florida Technical Evaluation" (March 17, 2008).

41. Jennifer Hecker, interview with the author, December 6, 2012.

42. Michael Sole, interview with the author, November 15, 2012.

43. Jan Mandrup-Poulsen (administrator, Watershed and TMDL Section) to Jennifer Hecker, July 9, 2009.

44. The State of Florida is divided into four bioregions by the DEP: Peninsular (includes most of the center of the state); Panhandle; Northeast (includes the area around Jacksonville); and Everglades. Rookery Bay is in the Everglades bioregion, and the Caloosahatchee is in the Peninsular bioregion.

45. Jessica Stubbs (natural resources specialist, Conservancy of Southwest Florida) to EPA Region 4 Reviewers of the Caloosahatchee TMDL, September 8, 2009.

46. Andrew McElwaine, interview with the author, December 3, 2012.

47. Jennifer Hecker, interview with the author, December 6, 2012.

Chapter 15. By the Numbers

1. Fla. Admin. Code r. 62-302.530(47)(b).

2. According to the Florida Department of Environmental Protection, an "impaired" water body fails to meet established standards for particular pollutants, e.g., mercury, phosphorous, nitrogen, etc.

3. Michael Sole, interview with the author, November 15, 2012.

4. § 303 (d) is the section of the Clean Water Act requiring states to "identify those waters within its boundaries to which the effluent limitations . . . are not stringent enough to implement any water quality standard applicable to such waters."

5. Offshore near Tampa there is a smaller, secondary, circular current flowing counterclockwise, but the main Loop Current further out toward the central Gulf is seasonally clockwise.

6. H. Yang, R.H. Weisberga, P.P. Niilerb, W. Sturgesc, and W. Johnson, "Lagrangian Circulation and Forbidden Zone on the West Florida Shelf," *Continental Shelf Research,* Volume 19, Issue 9 (1999).

7. Classifications as of 2005 were as follows: Class I – Potable Water Supplies; Class II – Shellfish Propagation or Harvesting; Class III – Recreation, Propagation and Maintenance of a Healthy, Well-balanced Population of Fish and Wildlife; Class IV – Agriculture Water Supplies; and Class V – Navigation, Industrial and Utility Use.

8. Jerry Brooks (deputy director, Division of Water Resource Management, Department of Environmental Protection) to the author, August 6, 2007.

9. Michael Sole, interview with the author, November 15, 2012.

10. Ibid.

11. Florida League of Cities, Inc., resolution, January 18, 2010.

12. *Naples Daily News,* November 15, 2010.

13. *Ocala Star-Banner,* February 6, 2011.

14. Original letter to the editor, *Tampa Bay Tribune,* submitted by Roy R. Lewis III, former professor of biology, Hillsborough Community College, undated.

15. Florida Department of Environmental Protection, "Overview of State Nutrient Standards," November 2011.

16. These are the four ways in which the DEP develops numeric nutrient criteria: maintain healthy existing conditions, historical conditions approach, response-based approach using modeling, and reference site approach. The department has complete discretion as to which one to apply in a given situation.

17. The city won a reprieve when estuarine rule-making was pushed 18 months into the future.

18. Nancy Stoner (acting assistant administrator, U.S. Environmental Protection Agency) to Herschel Vinyard (secretary, Florida Department of Environmental Protection), November 2, 2011. The acronym CWA stands for Clean Water Act.

19. Earthjustice news release, November 30, 2012.

20. Associated Press wire service, 11:01 P.M., November 30, 2012.

21. This is not an original thought. It was expressed by Gary Colecchio, a former DEP supervisor in the Tampa office, in an interview printed in *Florida Weekly,* January 24–30, 2013.

22. Robert G. Maliva and Karl P. Hopfensperger, "Impacts of Residential Development on Humid Subtropical Freshwater Resources: Southwest Florida Experience." *Journal of the American Water Resources Association* (December 2007), 1540–1548.

23. RTI International, "Enterprise Assessment for the Reduction of Nutrient Pollution in South Florida Waters," January 2012.

24. Jennifer Hecker, correspondence with the author, October 16, 2013.

Epilogue

1. *Orlando Sentinel,* February 2, 2011.

2. *Broward New Times,* June 10, 2011.

3. See http://flwaterpermits.com/typesofpermits.html

4. Andrew McElwaine, interview with the author, December 3, 2012.

5. Ibid.

6. Rob Moher, interview with the author, October 22, 2013.

BIBLIOGRAPHY

Babbit, Bruce E. *Cities in the Wilderness: A New Vision of Land Use in America*. Washington, D.C.: Island Press, 2005.

Barnett, Cynthia. *Mirage: Florida and the Vanishing Water of the Eastern U.S.* Ann Arbor: University of Michigan Press, 2007.

Benton, J. Edwin, ed. *Government and Politics in Florida*. Gainesville: University Press of Florida, 2008.

Bortone, Steve, ed. *Estuarine Indicators,* Boca Raton, FL: CRC Press, 2005.

Carter, Luther J. *The Florida Experience: Land and Water Policy in a Growth State*. Baltimore: Johns Hopkins University Press, 1974.

Catlin, Robert. *Land Use Planning, Environmental Protection and Growth Management: The Florida Experience*. Chelsea, MD: Ann Arbor Press, 1997.

Clark, John. "Rookery Bay: Ecological Constraints on Coastal Development." Washington, D.C.: Conservation Foundation, 1974.

Colburn, David. *From Yellow Dog Democrats to Red State Republicans. Florida and Its Politics since 1940*. Gainesville: University Press of Florida, 2007.

Cushing, Frank Hamilton. "Exploration of Ancient Key Dwellers Remains on the Gulf Coast of Florida." *American Philosophical Society Proceedings* 35 (1897). Reprint, Gainesville: University Press of Florida, 2001.

Dasmann, Raymond. *No Further Retreat: The Fight to Save Florida*. New York: The MacMillan Company, 1971.

Davis, Jack E., and Raymond Arsenault. *Paradise Lost?* Gainesville: University Press of Florida, 2005.

Douglas, Marjory Stoneman. *The Everglades: River of Grass*. Sarasota, FL: Pineapple Press, 1997.

Dyckman, Martin A. *Reubin O'D. Askew and the Golden Age of Florida Politics*. Gainesville: University Press of Florida, 2011.

Gore, Robert H. *The Gulf of Mexico*. Sarasota, FL: Pineapple Press, 1997.

Grunwald, Michael. *The Swamp: The Everglades, Florida, and the Politics of Paradise*. New York: Simon and Schuster, 2006.

McPherson, Benjamin F., and Robert Halley. *The South Florida Environment: A Region Under Stress*. Washington, D.C.: U.S. Government Printing Office: Geological Survey Circular 1134, 1996.

Myers, Ronald, and John Ewell, eds. *Ecosystems of Florida*. Orlando: University of Central Florida Press, 1990.

Noll, Stephen, and David Tegeder, *Ditch of Dreams: The Cross-Florida Barge Canal and the Struggle for Florida's Future*. Gainesville: University Press of Florida, 2009.

Pittman, Craig, and Matthew Waite. *Paving Paradise: Florida's Vanishing Wetlands and the Failure of No Net Loss*. Gainesville: University Press of Florida, 2009.

Rosenbaum, Walter A. *Environmental Politics and Policy*. Washington, D.C.: Congressional Quarterly Press, 2005.

RuBino, Richard G., and Earl M. Starnes. *Lessons Learned: The History of Planning in Florida*. Tallahassee, FL: Century Press, Inc., 2008.

Tebeau, Charlton W., *Florida's Last Frontier: The History of Collier County*. Miami, FL: University of Miami Press, 1966.

Whitney, Ellie, D. Bruce Means, and Anne Rudloe. *Priceless Florida: Natural Ecosystems and Native Species*. Sarasota, FL: Pineapple Press, 2004.

LIST OF ILLUSTRATIONS

INDEX

Here are some other books from Pineapple Press on related topics. For a complete catalog, visit our website at www.pineapplepress.com. Or write to Pineapple Press, P.O. Box 3889, Sarasota, Florida 34230-3889, or call (800) 746-3275.

Florida Magnificent Wilderness by James Valentine and D. Bruce Means. A visual journey through some of the most precious wild areas in the state, presenting the breathtaking beauty preserved in state lands, parks, and natural areas. Valentine has used his camera to record environmental art images of the state's remote wilderness places. Dr. Means has written the detailed captions and main text, "Florida's Rich Biodiversity."

Priceless Florida by Ellie Whitney, D. Bruce Means, and Anne Rudloe. An extensive guide (432 pages, 800 color photos) to the incomparable ecological riches of this unique region, presented in a way that will appeal to young and old, laypersons and scientists. Complete with maps, charts, species lists.

The Everglades: River of Grass by Marjory Stoneman Douglas. Before 1947, when Marjory Stoneman Douglas named it a "river of glass," the Everglades was considered a vast, worthless swamp. She focused the world's attention on the need to preserve this unique ecosystem, the only Everglades on earth.

Marjory Stoneman Douglas: Voice of the River by Marjory Stoneman Douglas. This is the story of an influential life told in a unique and spirited voice. Marjory Stoneman Douglas, nationally known as the first lady of conservation and the woman who "saved" the Everglades, was the founder of Friends of the Everglades, a feminist, a fighter for racial justice, and always a writer.

Florida's Birds, Second Edition by David S. Maehr and Herbert W. Kale II. Now with color throughout, this new edition includes 30 new species accounts. Sections on bird study, feeding, and habitats; threatened and endangered species; exotic species; and bird conservation.

Exploring Wild South Florida, Fourth Edition by Susan Jewell. The new edition includes more than 40 new natural areas and covers Broward, Collier, Miami-Dade, Hendry, Lee, Monroe, and Palm Beach Counties.

Florida's Living Beaches by Blair and Dawn Witherington. Comprehensive accounts of more than 800 species found on 700 miles of Florida's sandy beaches. Fully illustrated in color and meticulously researched.

Snake in the Grass by Larry Perez. The nonnative Burmese python is now known to be reproducing freely in the Florida Everglades, wreaking havoc with the delicate balance of this unique ecosystem. An Everglades naturalist describes how the story unfolding in the famed "River of Grass" provides new opportunities to revisit our understanding of wilderness and man's place within it.

Florida's Rivers by Charles Boning. An overview of Florida's waterways and detailed information on 60 of Florida's rivers, covering each from source to end. From the Blackwater River in the western Panhandle to the Ichetucknee and Kissimmee Rivers in central Florida to the Miami River in south Florida.

The Springs of Florida, Second Edition by Doug Stamm. The deepest and best known springs in the world are in Florida. This new edition is completely updated to serve as a guide to the springs parks for canoeists, kayakers, divers, snorkelers, and visitors. Includes stunning underwater photos culled from hundreds of hours of diving.

Seasons of the Sea by Jay Humphreys. As the seasons change on land, so do they in the waters along the Florida peninsula—a world largely unknown but endlessly fascinating. Learn which creatures come and go in the waters of each of the state's six main regions. Charming illustrations accompany the text.

Myakka, Second Edition by P.J. Benshoff. Guide to one of the largest state parks in Florida. Discover its wild and scenic river, its shady oak hammocks and aerial gardens, its prairies, piney woods, and wetlands. Meet the gators, sandhill cranes, deer, and turtles that call Myakka home.

Paynes Prairie, Second Edition by Lars Andersen. Offers a sweeping history that spans millions of years of the unique shallow-bowl basin in the middle of Florida. It's also a guide to outdoor activities in the state preserve and includes maps of trails for biking, hiking, and canoeing.